OUR
GREAT
W·A·R

Memoirs of World War II from the
Wake Robin community, Shelburne, Vermont

Editors
Louise Ransom
Donald S. Robinson
Ruth W. Page
Sherry Worrall

Wake Robin Residents' Association

Cover photograph "Breaching the Siegfried Line, march into Germany" reproduced from the National Archives

All photographs are courtesy of authors and their families.

Published by Wake Robin Residents' Association in collaboration with Huntington Graphics, Shelburne, Vermont 05482

Wake Robin Residents' Association
Attn. Our Great War
200 Wake Robin Drive
Shelburne, VT 05482

Printed in Canada

ISBN 978-1-886064-34-8

First edition

Publisher's Cataloging-in-publication
     LCCN
     ISBN
     1.   World War II   2. Wake Robin Residents' Association   3. History — United States — 20th century

Contents

The Pacific Theater

The European Theater

Stateside Service

Medical Service

Wartime in Europe

Home Front

Post-War Service

Acknowledgments

The Editors wish to thank the many individuals who contributed to collecting and preserving the stories of those who lived through the greatest conflict the world has known — World War II. The fighting encompassed five continents, and surely affected nearly all lands. For our nation's oldest and now disappearing generation, the 1940s were their defining years.

The recollections of those connected to the Wake Robin community were destined never to be told and lost to posterity until founding member Louise Ransom had the idea of soliciting reminiscences from residents of our senior community. She suggested it to several other friends who thought it a great idea. The Wake Robin Residents' Association recognized the merit of the project and provided key support for publication of this volume. The Editors are grateful for the financial assistance of the Residents' Association and the efforts of Warren Francis, WRRA President, and the Executive committee, Lucy Blanton, Mary Hoffman, Larry Woolson, and Ken Severson, in helping bring this project to fruition.

The efforts of many people were vital in collecting these stories of the World War II war years. Most of all, the Editors wish to thank those who contributed their personal stories — servicemen whose lives were often in peril, those forced to flee oppression — yet were willing to recount painful as well as happy memories — some of the stories told for the first time.

Collecting these personal observations frequently required cooperation of family members, who tracked down letters, photographs, diaries, news articles, and other valuable documentation, for which the Editors are extremely grateful. Special thanks for the laborious tasks of processing manuscripts, recording oral histories, and archiving materials are due many residents and friends who freely volunteered their time and skills. Thank you to Joel Larsen, Patricia Haufler, Dick Walters, Ginny Walters, Jean Connor, MaryBeth Dudley, Josh Welch, Betty Miles, Mary Lou Robinson, Ellie Skolfield, Ruth Partridge, Betty Giddings, and Doug Hyde for valuable assistance in carrying out the varied tasks required to make this book of reminiscences a reality.

Finally, the Editors express appreciation to Jared Gange of Huntington Graphics and Andrea Gray for their helpful advice and guidance throughout the publishing process.

— The Editors

PREFACE

IT'S A HOT SUMMER AFTERNOON IN JULY 2008, but I've lived this afternoon in the summer of 1944 as I read this collection of World War II memories.

In Normandy, Dr. Ed Hyde performs surgery 15 hours a day, saving lives just behind the front line in hedgerow country. In Italy, Dr. Phil Giddings has treated lacerated organs in a newly formed Army surgical unit at the Anzio beachhead, a forerunner of M.A.S.H. Far away on the Pacific island of Saipan, Marine Sgt. John Carpenter is living in a foxhole while his unit hunts down the last Japanese defenders. Back home in Baltimore, Maryland, teenager Elizabeth Pasti takes her turn airplane spotting, while at a U.S. Navy air station — improbably located in Clinton, Oklahoma — Aerographer's Mate 3rd class Marianna Grimes collects weather observations.

Around the world, young people who will one day share retirement quarters at Wake Robin, train for infantry service in Europe, pilot fighter planes and bombers, intercept German radio traffic, fire naval guns and man destroyers that guard convoys in the Atlantic and Pacific. Others carry on at home. Some are Jewish refugees from Hitler's Germany. Many are young wives, raising children, planting victory gardens, guarding their gasoline rations. A goodly number are children who buy war stamps at school, track the Allies' progress on newspaper maps and complain about working in those vegetable gardens.

This book is a gift of that generation — to their children, to their grandchildren, to all the future generations who will wonder "how it really was."

"Our Great War" is not a comprehensive history of World War II. It is something more precious: the personal accounts of people who were there. Not the famous people who planned and won battles, but people who — like citizens around the globe — simply did their part. As a generation, they have a hugely important story to tell of sacrifice and bravery and at a time when those things were not considered a cause for self-congratulation.

In fact, you'll find no claims to bravery or sacrifice in this book. The writers are refreshingly candid — the soldiers and sailors about their fears and their focus on survival, the young people back home about what fun they frequently had during the war.

As a newspaper reporter, I've interviewed dozens of World War II veterans in the last decade. I'm always fascinated about what they want to talk about. It is almost never the battles, even for those who survived Omaha Beach or Tarawa or the Bulge. Instead, they talk about the lifelong friends they made in France or New Zealand or Belgium. They remember their own pratfalls, the comeuppance of uppity officers, the heaven of a hot meal or warm bed after weeks on the line: in other words, the small, the personal, the happy memories. You'll find such memories here in abundance, without any Pollyanna-ish overlay. Under every story lies the bedrock of serious purpose that drove soldiers on the front and the folks back home. Think of this book as a mosaic, shards of memories assembled into a powerful, impressionistic picture of the years between Sept. 1, 1939 and August 17, 1945.

Dr. Ralph Blocksma's diary gives us the searing picture of Buchenwald concentration camp just after its liberation. Dr. Richard Austin, a Navy pilot, tells the long, fascinating story of his service in the Pacific. Betty Corliss offers a tiny sliver — the memory of yellow food coloring being squeezed into colorless margarine. In assembling 65 such diverse pieces in a single volume, the residents of Wake Robin have created a time machine, transporting the reader to the world of their youth.

Death is winnowing the ranks of World War II storytellers. Often their children and grandchildren think too late, "I wish Grandpa (or Grandma) had told me about the war." We can only hope the example set by the editors and the Wake Robin community in capturing these stories will inspire other communities of elders to get out their pens or laptops and record similar tales for posterity.

— Candace Page

Candace Page is a reporter and former editor of the Burlington Free Press. *She is the daughter of Wake Robin resident Ruth Page, whose memoir appears in this volume, and the late Proctor Page Jr. (U.S. Army counter-intelligence service, China-Burma-India theater, 1944-45).*

The
Pacific
Theater

Sea Duty and Atomic Warfare

★

Richard Anderson
U.S. Navy

I WAS 15 YEARS OLD when the Japanese attacked Pearl Harbor and the United States got into World War II. We were living on a farm just north of Milaca, Minnesota. Because war jobs in Minneapolis were plentiful, we moved so that my father could work in a factory there. I attended Marshall High School, and in my senior year took what was called the "Eddie Test." This was named after a Navy captain (Captain Eddie) who thought that the Navy needed more people trained in electronics and devised a test that was given in high schools to assess one's aptitude for learning electronics.

Eddie Test Results

Four of us at Marshall HS passed this exam, and we all thought we might then join the Navy. My friend talked us into enlisting in the Navy on his 17th birthday, which was in March 1944. Since we were all 17 years old, we had to get the signatures of our parents so that we could enlist. He had problems at the induction center because he was missing one thumb. However, he talked the Navy people into accepting him because the missing thumb did not seriously hamper his dexterity. We also took the eye test, however, and he was essentially blind in his left eye. He first read the chart with his right eye, which was good, and memorized the chart. On testing his left eye, he just repeated it and joined the Navy with us three. We went to boot camp together at Great Lakes Naval Training Center, and there they gave him another exam. However, during this exam the eye chart differed when they tested each eye so he failed the vision test and was discharged from the Navy. Nevertheless, they let him keep his uniform. When he went back to Minneapolis, he wrote that it was great to wear a uniform and so be able to pick up girls more easily. This of course made us happy because he was the one who talked us into enlisting in the Navy in the first place.

After boot camp, I attended a five-week primary school in South Bend, Indiana where we learned the fundamentals of electronics. After that, we were given a choice of programs for additional training, depending on whether we wished to learn electronics for airplanes or for warships. I chose aviation electronics and went on to Corpus Christi, Texas for more training. There, we learned to repair aircraft radios and radar equipment.

Sea Duty

After I finished my schooling in Corpus Christi, I stayed on as an instructor. One day, the Navy was urgently seeking volunteers with knowledge of electronics for service on the ship *USS Avery Island*. Avery Island, which lies off the Louisiana coast, is where Tabasco sauce originated. I volunteered for this duty because it would give me a chance to go to sea. The *Avery Island* was a ship that was rigged with many antennas and all kinds of electronic detection gear. We were scheduled to fly to San Francisco to catch the ship. Instead we went by rail, which took several days. As a result we missed our ship and instead went to work at a Kaiser plant. This was not a manufacturing plant, but a place out in the country where they stored lumber for shipbuilding. We goofed off there for several days, when a jeep came along to pick us up. They hurried us out to the airport where we caught an airplane to Pearl Harbor. It was an overnight flight, and as we approached Pearl Harbor in the morning, we could see the half sunken *USS Arizona*, which became a national monument.

USS Shangri-La

In Pearl Harbor, we boarded the *USS Shangri-La*, an aircraft carrier (CV 38) and were given assignments to repair aircraft radios. When pilots complained about a malfunctioning radio, we would check it out. Usually, it turned out to be the pilot's malfunction — often, the pilots failed to turn on the radio. However, one piece of equipment that they always turned on religiously was what was referred to as IFF (meaning Identification Friend or Foe). When the plane was approaching for a landing, the carrier would transmit a signal to the plane so it would automatically respond with the signal for the day. If the signal was incorrect, the plane would be shot down before it could get too close to the carrier. The reason for this was to prevent an enemy plane from ramming the carrier. For security, the code for the IFF was changed periodically, usually once a day.

There was a Navy regulation that no one was allowed to drink aboard ship. (Of course this did not apply to the officers, just us enlisted men.) As a result, from time to time when we were anchored, a Navy boat would take us to a nearby island, accompanied by a supply of beer so we could drink the beer there. After the outing, a boat would return us to the carrier, and on the return journey some who had overindulged would attempt to dive off the boat. To prevent such behavior, each of us would receive three chits for beer; however, some of us did not drink beer so we would give (or sell) chits to our comrades, so this solution did not work so well.

I also spent time collecting seashells along the shore and exploring some of the caves that the Japanese had dug into the island. In one of the caves I found a Japanese 31 cal. rifle. It was pretty much scorched from napalm used by the Americans to eliminate the Japanese holed up in the caves. I brought this rifle home for a souvenir and planned to use it as a deer rifle. However, the only shells we could get for it were captured Japanese 31 cal. shells. The points of these military shells were made of copper, or maybe iron. For hunting use a lead tip was required, so the Japanese shells were not suitable.

In grammar school, I had a teacher who had a set of boxing gloves and taught us students to box. I continued boxing in the Navy and was classified as a junior welterweight. Over my entire Navy career, I weighed 147 pounds. I was reasonably good at boxing and won most of my fights. I was the junior welterweight champion of the Pacific Fleet composed of American and Australian ships in the area at the time. No Japanese ships were involved.

Bikini Atoll

After the war, the *Shangri-La* was directed to the Bikini Atoll to participate in three atomic bomb tests (Operation Crossroads). The tests were code-named Able, Baker, and Charlie. Unmanned fighter planes (drones) from our carrier, each controlled by a manned plane, were sent into the mushroom cloud and their flight path was monitored. We were some distance from the site where the bombs went off (but probably not distant enough). During the tests, we were assembled on the flight deck, where we could watch the mushroom clouds. We were instructed to look away from the site where the bombs went off until after the initial flash (the whole sky became pink), when we were then able to watch the mushroom cloud form. We saw the mushroom cloud rapidly rise and expand. It was very interesting. After the Able and Baker tests, the third test, Charlie, was canceled because the first two a-bombs produced much more radioactivity than anticipated. The military was not properly prepared to fully evaluate the after-effects of these atomic tests. I never knew why.

Following the two a-bomb blasts, little remained of Bikini atoll. This outcome inspired the apt terminology later conferred on skimpy women's bathing suits. Following the tests, our ship sailed to San Diego where I spent the next several months as a patient at a Naval Hospital for medical evaluation and treatment. I received excellent care at the Navy Hospital, and subsequently from the Veterans Administration hospital following my discharge from active duty. (This is in contrast to the scandals involving disabled military personnel returning from the current wars in Iraq and Afghanistan.) Since I was considered disabled and unable to operate a standard automobile, the VA issued me an Oldsmobile with an automatic transmission, which would not require use of both legs to operate the vehicle. The GI Bill allowed me to attend the University of Minnesota where I majored in electrical engineering, so I was able to make use of my Navy training and experience. In my subsequent career in both business and industry, the focus remained on the field of electronics.

Dick grew up on a farm in northern Minnesota. After the war, he attended the University of Minnesota and Syracuse University where he earned a PhD in Electrical Engineering. Professional experience included Research Engineer at IBM, Professorships of Electrical Engineering at Syracuse University and the University of Vermont, and Visiting Professorships (Fulbright) at the University of Madrid and Sao Paulo University. He also was a consultant to the United Nations, the Organization of American States, and the U.S. State Department.

ADVENTURES OF A CARRIER PILOT

★

Richard Austin
U.S. Navy

KANSAS IN WINTER CAN BE VERY COLD, especially in open-cockpit Primary Flight Trainers, as I was to learn after assignment to the Naval Air Station, Olathe, Kansas. This was to be my first flying experience in the Navy. The planes were bi-wing Stearmans, which had a windshield but no other protection from the elements. To shield us from the cold wind, prior to each flight aviation Cadets were issued a heavy sheepskin-lined jacket with trousers, helmet, face mask, gloves, and boots reaching almost to the knee; the leather and lining of the boots were so thick one felt like a mummy walking out to the plane.

We cadets learned acrobatic flying, including loops, rolls, wing-overs and other tricky maneuvers like the Immelmann turn. This turn consisted of half-a-loop with considerable positive "Gs" until the plane was inverted. At this point, pushing the "stick" forward stopped the loop at its top, exerting negative "Gs." If it were not for the seat belt, this action could promptly eject the pilot from the open cockpit. At the top of the loop with the plane upside down, we had to make a forceful side motion with the stick to return to right side up.

One particularly cold day, I was practicing Immelmann turns on a solo flight, one after another. Foolishly unnoticed by me, on one of the roll outs I disengaged my seat belt with my elbow. So, on the next Immelmann, at the top of the loop when the G's were reversed from positive to negative to bring the plane out of the loop, I found myself without an attached seat belt and suddenly leaving the bucket seat of the open cockpit. Instinctively I grabbed the control stick, and fortunately, the top of my special fur-lined boots caught on the front of the seat and prevented my ejection. However, my backside was hanging out in the breeze. After a few seconds, the gravity-feed for gas to the engine caused the engine to quit. When this happened, the plane gradually fluttered out of its inverted posture, and thankfully, I fell back into the bucket seat. The engine restarted itself, I refastened my seat belt, and forever after, became a committed seat belt checker.

We were required to wear parachutes at all times, and had I parted from the plane, that would have saved me (but not my aircraft!). The prospect of having to face the Commanding Officer and apologize for falling out and losing his airplane was indeed frightening. I quietly blessed the fur-lined boots and thanked my good fortune. I didn't advertise my close call to anyone, but quickly flew back to Base, landed and headed for my bunk. Thanks to those boots, my Navy flying career was still intact.

Emergency Landing

Torpedo Squadron Three was my first assignment after flight training. We assembled in Washington State, first in Seattle, then on Whidbey Island, and later at Pasco in the southeastern part of the state. One cloudy day, my section leader "Pop" Ensley and I flew from Pasco in our TBM Avenger torpedo bombers on a navigational flight over northeastern Washington, hoping to view Grand Coulee Dam. An hour into the flight, we hit a snowstorm that threatened to reduce visibility to zero. "Pop" decided we should land on a road that ran down the center of a narrow canyon that seemed straight enough for an adequate distance and free of traffic. He landed first, and as I came around to follow, a car was in my landing path, so I had to try again. By now, it was snowing pretty hard, but my second try succeeded. As I rolled along the road after landing, the driver in the car ahead of me looked in his rear-view mirror and saw this airplane rapidly closing on him. He promptly headed for the ditch though by then I was taxiing slower and under control. He waved from the ditch as I passed him! We taxied our planes into a farmyard, folded the wings, and cut the engines. The farmer proved to be most hospitable, pulled the car from the ditch with his tractor, and put me up for the night; the crewmen and "Pop" went to a motel.

The next day dawned cold and clear, but about 10 inches of snow had fallen. I had made frequent trips to the planes during the night to sweep off the snow and make sure they were secure. Morning brought a lot of curious onlookers since the snowplows had cleared the roads promptly. Cold temperatures caused us to burn out one plane's battery trying to start it. We warmed and started the second plane, and subsequently the first plane as well, by using a tarp the farmer loaned us to wrap around the engines. This held in the heat generated by a pot belly stove from his barn. We poked the stove chimney under the tarp and warmed the engines. The telephone company rigged a wire from the plane that was running to the one with the dead battery, enabling it to be started as well. The roadway was about 20 feet wide and lined with curious passersby. It seemed a safe runway, though the landing gear was 15 feet wide, leaving us little room for error on takeoff. We worried about the onlookers at the roadside but took off uneventfully and returned to our base in Pasco. Our CO was forgiving since the planes were undamaged. Our adventure was photographed by a visitor who had been at Grand Coulee Dam. He handed me the film pack, just before takeoff, capturing our planes in the farm yard and the efforts with the stove to start the engines. I still have these pictures.

Mid-Air Collision over Hawaii

Our next assignment was for further training in Hawaii. On a practice glide-bombing flight 50 miles off the coast of Hawaii we had a close call. Our target was a smoke bomb dropped on the water, and our bombs contained only water. Our formation consisted of two sections of six planes each. The lead six were to turn to the right of the target and dive to the left toward the target. The second six were to turn left and dive right. If timing was perfect, the second six would dive just after the first six. Unfortunately communications were faulty and the second six planes led by a great friend, Frank Frazier, did not turn left but stayed right below and behind us. I was the third plane to dive and as I turned and dove, Frank's section of six was immediately under me. I could see Frank looking up at me as I bore down on him. The others of his section saw what was happening and scattered. I banked sharply to the right to avoid flying into Frank's cockpit but the front of my left wing slapped the back quarter of Frank's right wing as I passed.

This only slightly dented my wing, but bent the back edge of Frank's downward. After being sure my plane was OK and flyable, we all radioed Frank, as he had disappeared. As we learned later, he experienced tremendous difficulty keeping his plane straight, with one wing bent down in back. He had to fly with both feet on the left rudder and was too busy to inform us where he was. After locating him, the Skipper assigned me to return to base with Frank while the others went on with the practice attack.

When Frank and I got back to Maui, we alerted the control tower to Frank's plight, and all the crash crews were out and waiting as he came in to land. Miraculously, he touched down OK but proceeded to ground loop on the roll out, though without injuries or further harm to his plane. I landed without incident. His right wing and my left wing were replaced and both planes and pilots lived to fly again, but it was a close call for Frank. His plane was disabled by anti-aircraft fire later in the war, and he crash-landed in the waters off the coast of Formosa (now Taiwan). He was captured and, as a prisoner of war, was murdered by the Japanese the day before the armistice was signed. He was a nice guy and a fine friend. What a waste!

In flight training, all Naval Aviation Cadets were required to learn Morse code and be able to read radio or blinker light messages at reasonable speed. This was a source of much anxiety among Cadets, but we managed to master it. Communications systems were pretty sophisticated by the time we finished our training so Morse code was rarely used. One day, while training off Hawaii, one of our planes ran out of gas and landed in water about 15 miles off the Island of Maui. Two of our pilots circled over the crew of the downed plane who were now in a life raft. I proceeded toward land where we spotted a destroyer on patrol duty. As I circled the destroyer, I pulled out my signal blinker light, and slowly, in Morse code, signaled the ship to follow me to a downed plane to pick up the crew. A blinker response from the destroyer was sent at incredible speed, much faster than I could read it. After the fourth or fifth plea from me to slow down, I was able to discern that they wanted to know the course and distance, which I signaled in return. The ship promptly proceeded to the downed crew floating in their raft and picked them up. Though learning the code was frustrating and hateful, it certainly came in handy that day.

Aircraft Carrier USS Yorktown

Our Air Group, flying torpedo bombers, practiced for months on what we called coordinated attacks where the fighters would first attack ships by strafing, followed by dive bombers that proceeded to dive while any enemy planes would then be occupied by our fighters. At the same moment our torpedo bombers would come in low over the water and drop our torpedoes as enemy gunners were peering upward at the dive bombers. By far the worst part of our training was night flights off aircraft carriers. Without question, the most difficult and frightening activities associated with flying from aircraft carriers during WWII were night flying and landing. We were required to make a minimum of eight night landings a year to stay qualified. Take-offs were not much of a problem, although assembling a formation of planes at night was difficult. With only an exhaust flare from the other planes as a guide, and lacking depth-perception at night, we crept in to a close formation. Then came the worst part of the operation — the landing.

The carrier *USS Yorktown* would guide us by radio and radar to a position exactly over the carrier and give us the carrier's compass course. We would break formation into a single line ahead of the carrier and individually make a left turn for 30 seconds and another left turn that would bring us back on the reverse course to the ship. We would use a radar altimeter which measures height above the water and descend to 125 feet. The carrier deck was 70 feet above the water. On the reverse course, by watching to the left as the plane passed the ship, a light was visible directed slightly above horizontal so as not to be visible to a submarine and shielded from above so as not to be visible to enemy aircraft overhead. After passing this light for a few seconds, we would begin a turn to the left towards the stern of the carrier. Lights on the deck became visible when the plane was 45 degrees off the stern. These lights also were projected in a narrow angle visible only to the approaching plane. As the plane approached the stern of the carrier, the landing-signal officer standing at the rear of the carrier and to the approaching pilot's left, came into view, waving his lighted wands. He guided the pilot the last few yards to a ramp (as the landing area was called) and gave either a "cut" or "wave-off" signal, depending on how things were lining up. At the time of the cut, many pilots experienced an exasperating mirage that the carrier had made a 30- or 40-degree turn to the left. Thus, every landing was a "turning" landing, as we were rarely perfectly lined up. So we dreaded night operations. Fortunately, we never had any tragedies on our ship. Subsequently, when jet aircraft entered service with their higher speed, I'm sure this all became even more frightening.

Invasion of the Philippines

In the fall of 1944 we went into Manila Bay, still held by the Japanese, to attack shipping there. We had been briefed that there had been a Jap carrier there a few days before. A ceiling of 1,000 feet negated a coordinated attack using an approach as described above. All squadrons of the Group thus attacked individually. Our nine torpedo bombers flew over the Bay from the West, past the island of Corregidor. We were flying at about 900 feet with the throttle wide open. Anti-aircraft fire from the shore tracked us all across the Bay. Ahead, close to the city, we saw something long and low that looked from a distance like a carrier. Six of the nine of us dropped torpedoes on this target. As we flew over it, we recognized it was not a carrier. Five of the six torpedoes were hits and the target sank immediately. Later, when the spotting pictures were developed, it turned out we had sunk the *USS Dewey*, a floating U.S. Navy dry-dock captured by the Japanese at the start of the war. Not wanting to boast to our friends that we had sunk the *USS Dewey*, we all claimed the "miss."

Out of Gas

On a "strike" to Formosa on January 3, 1945 I noted after take-off from the carrier that the gas cap on the right wing tank was loose and fuel was leaking out. The target was only a modest distance from the Task Force, so one had to consider whether to proceed or return to the ship. By using this tank first I thought there would be enough remaining fuel to make it back to the ship after the attack. On the return flight it soon became clear that it would be a close call.

The Japanese frequently followed our flights back to the Fleet, both to locate us and to hide behind the blip our returning planes would make on the ship's radar. To foil this trick, a destroyer, called a picket destroyer, was stationed 50 miles from the Force to search behind us for an enemy. At the 50-mile point, the gas gauge registered dry for the leaking tank, which we utilized initially, and about 1/8th on the remaining tank. I considered landing in the water near the picket, but decided to press on. I called the carrier on the radio reporting "Condition Queen," which meant low fuel. They ordered me to land with the fighters, which normally landed first. I lined up with the fighters and on my first "pass" to the carrier the fighter plane ahead of me blew out a tire on landing, and I was waved off, as he was still in the landing area.

Now the gas needle was resting on the empty peg. I had a cousin who was an officer on a destroyer in the screen of our force up ahead of the carrier. Should I land in the water next to his destroyer or try another pass? I elected to try again to land. This second landing was successful, but as I applied throttle to pull forward on the flight deck the engine quit — out of gas! That's cutting it close.

A Great Plane

The Navy Torpedo bomber, the Avenger, was a wonderful plane — sturdy, reliable, forgiving on carrier landings; but like all mechanical structures, it was subject to occasional "failures." On January 12, 1945 we were assigned a target of ships anchored off Saigon during an operation into the South China Seas. The Fifth Fleet was enormous and its Fast Carrier Task Force included a number of large aircraft carriers. We launched from our ship, the *USS Yorktown*, affectionately called the "Fighting Lady" by her crew. On the way to Saigon we spotted a Japanese convoy of ships protected by several destroyers. Our Air Group leader decided to make this convoy our day's target, but the plan changed; as we were organizing our attack, another Air Group from a different carrier beat us to it.

However, prior to attacks, pilots always shut off the safety switches that anchor our bombs to the bomb bay, thus arming the bombs for release. Bombs could only be dropped with these safety switches turned off. With the bomb bays open, the pilot would then push a button on the control stick to release the bombs. Though my switches were in the release mode, the attack was aborted before the bomb bay doors were opened. The bomb racks were designed not to drop the bombs with the doors closed. However, on the continuing flight to Saigon, my four 500-lb. bombs dropped out of the racks onto the bomb bay doors with a "thunk."

Dropped bombs required several hundred feet of air travel to arm them. However, there was no telling whether the air inevitably flowing through the bomb bay would arm the bombs. The dilemma was: should I drop the bombs by opening the doors now, before reaching the target, or take a chance they would not arm and prematurely explode in the bomb bay, and could later be dropped on targets by opening the doors. I elected the latter choice but pulled away from the other planes in the event they exploded in flight.

On arriving at the bay outside Saigon we saw four or five Japanese merchant ships anchored and proceeded to "glide bomb" them. I chose the smallest of the ships, which was separated from the others by perhaps a mile. I commenced the dive and dropped the bombs by opening the bomb bay doors at the release point. The ship must have been an ammunition ship, as it totally disintegrated in a giant explosion as the bombs apparently hit it. We returned to the carrier uneventfully. So a mechanical failure, though frightening, did not lead to a frustrating failure to complete the mission.

Pilots are Loyal Friends

On the same mission, one of our fighter planes was struck by anti-aircraft fire. The pilot was stunned temporarily but remained conscious and fully aware that he could not see. The plane was apparently flying itself, as best he could tell. His radio worked well and he called his section leader, informing him that he was injured, blind, and lost. The section leader broadcast to "all planes in the area" to look for a lone F6F fighter flying erratically. Fortunately, another Air Group flying to the Saigon area spotted the pilot and directed the Section Leader to his location. The two then started back for the *Yorktown*, which was 150 miles away, guiding the blind pilot using radioed directions. The wounded pilot kept telling his section leader he felt faint, but with persuasion and encouraging chatter, they both made it back to the Fast Carrier Task Force.

The Yorktown Signal Officer was alerted to the wounded pilot's plight. With extraordinary courage the Section Leader flew formation along with his wounded charge, told him when to lower wheels, flaps, hook, etc., and talked him down to low altitude required for carrier landing. It required two approaches, but the wounded bird landed safely. The Flight Surgeon then jumped up on the wing of the plane and removed the fuse of an antiaircraft shell from the back of the pilot's head with his fingers. The pilot recovered some vision but never enough to fly again. He was duly decorated with the Purple Heart and another award. The Section Leader's radio direction saved the pilot's life and earned him great accolades from his Squadron mates.

Bombing Runs over Tokyo and Iwo Jima

In February 1945 the Navy made a sortie to Japan. Several interesting, frightening, and in some cases, amusing things happened during this operation. The fleet traveled under radio silence and sent several destroyers ahead to sink any fishing boats from Japan that might warn of our approach. One such boat was sunk by the destroyers and its crew rescued. They were transferred to the Yorktown by breeches buoy, a set of ropes and pulleys. The entire ship watched this with interest from the flight deck because we had never seen any Japs up close.

We were perhaps cruel to cheer loudly when these frightened fishermen were inadvertently dunked in the water during the transfer. They were all teenagers and spoke no English. They had minor injuries and were put in sick bay under a Marine guard, who stood at the foot of the beds. After a few days, when the Docs were making their rounds, the fishermen sat up alertly when the team walked in and with big smiles proudly shouted, "Chicken-s... gold braid!" This was an unflattering title endowed on certain officers by enlisted men. The Marine guard stiffened but was expressionless as the doctors burst into laughter. The Marines, of course, denied having given them a crash course in English.

During an attack on an aircraft factory west of Tokyo, we encountered some Japanese Zeros that were not very aggressive. One of our fighter pilots had decided he was going to use the relief tube under the seat of our planes, which released urine into the air, and "pee on Japan." As he was occupied in this exercise, he suddenly was involved in combat with the Zeros. This led to dog-fighting tactics, which involved negative "Gs" and the urine in the relief tube ran backwards, all over the pilot. Such is the fate of the revenge-seeker!

We were all aware of the apparent brutal treatment of captured pilots by the Japs and were understandably nervous during the flight over mainland Japan. We were threatened by furious anti-aircraft fire but all returned safely. After the mission we were very respectful of the B-29 crews that flew over Japan daily.

Upon leaving Japan we proceeded to the Iwo Jima invasion on February 20, 1945 which made a deep impression on all of us. I was in the first flight of the day the morning of the initial landings, and watched the landing craft approach the beach, the only possible landing site on this miserable 3 x 5-mile island. We watched the battleship bombardment of the island, the rocket attack ahead of the boats, and the incredible napalm attack our planes made on Mt. Suribachi, which overlooked the landing site. The napalm literally set the mountain aflame. Unfortunately the enemy were well entrenched in caves and holes and largely avoided serious casualties. Their guns were all trained on the beachhead, and we watched helplessly as our Marines took murderous fire as they landed and took over the beach.

We later supported the Marines with low-level strikes with various weapons the torpedo bomber carried, such as 100-to 500-pound bombs, rockets, etc. These attacks were guided by air controllers in the Marine companies on the ground and used a grid map of the island that both we and they had, to locate targets. We often dropped strings of bombs 30 yards in front of our lines when mortars or other weapons had pinned down our ground troops. How much we helped I don't know. We came away with tremendous respect for the Marines and very glad we had our job rather than theirs. It was on one of these runs that my plane returned with holes in the fuselage and wings from fragments of one of our own bombs, which we dropped very low for greater accuracy.

Return to the States and Close Call

We returned to the U.S. in the spring of 1945 and re-formed our squadron on the East Coast. Several of us were privileged to be asked to visit the General Motors plant in Trenton, New Jersey where our TBM Avenger had been built. It was amazing to us to see how many women were involved in assembling our aircraft. The electric wire cable alone was mind-boggling. We were received as heroes, but came away feeling the women (and men) were equally heroic.

Another adventure involved the single-seat F4U Corsair that was thought by many to be the Navy's highest-performance fighter. We all wanted to fly one, so the day before I was released from the Navy, knowing it would be my last flight on active duty, I went to the CO of our squadron, which had just been issued new F4U-5 airplanes, and pleaded with him to let me fly one on my final Navy flight. He resisted, but finally consented and tossed me the pilot's handbook for the Corsair. This I read carefully, and he gave me a cockpit checkout himself. His parting words were, "You better not hurt this plane."

The take-off from Oceana Naval Air Station was uneventful, and I proceeded south over the Dismal Swamp area of Virginia. As I was enjoying acrobatics and the plane's superb performance, the engine suddenly sputtered, ran intermittently, and ultimately quit. Here I was in an airplane I had never landed, with the prospect of a "dead-stick" (no engine power) landing. Bailing out over the Dismal Swamps was an unappealing alternative. I decided to head back to Oceana, looking around the cockpit for a switch I might have forgotten or a gas tank switch I had turned the wrong way. Everything seemed OK. I arrived back at the Air Station with only 800 feet of altitude left, made an approach to the nearest runway, waited to put the wheels down until the last minute, and landed with the front wheels of the landing gear on the runway and the tail wheel in the grass. I had no power and therefore could not taxi. The tower, which had not been informed of my plight, called to ask if I needed assistance. When I picked up the hand-held microphone to answer, I found I could not talk, but finally stuttered, "Yes." A tractor came and pulled the plane back into the flight line. Mechanics opened the cowl and found a manifold had separated from the carburetor. They were surprised the plane didn't catch fire. I never doubted that some guardian angel was watching over me.

Richard Austin, U.S. Navy Air Corps, served several years in the Pacific Theater, flying off aircraft carriers. After the war, he went on to graduate from Cornell University Medical School and entered surgical practice in Concord, Massachusetts.

From Trinity College
to Guadalcanal

★

John Carpenter
U.S. Marines

O N GRADUATION FROM COLLEGE IN 1941, I became a master at a
private boarding school in Tucson, Arizona. With the outbreak of
war in Europe, our age group became subject to the draft for selective
service, and military duty overrode career commitments. On December
7, 1941 I listened to the radio message from President Roosevelt as had
most everyone in the nation: Japan had bombed Pearl Harbor, and the
U.S. was declaring war on Japan and Germany. A wave of enlistments
quickly ensued. I considered following the path of several of my friends
at home who signed up for Navy V-7 or V-12 programs and were on a
track to become Ensigns. When the school term ended May 11, 1942
I went to a nearby recruiting office in Phoenix to enlist in the Navy.
It was closed for lunch, so I walked across the hall and enlisted in the
Marine Corps instead.

Marine Corps Basic Training

I was sent by train to the San Diego training base along with some 20 other recruits, half of them from the Navaho Reservation. My first assignment was "Get them there"; I knew little about leading men then. I didn't know or appreciate, for instance, that some 450 of these Indians were to become essential communicators, encrypting messages in the Navaho language to transmit critical information during combat, especially from forward observation posts to Marine command posts in the rear, for directing artillery fire and relaying battle orders.

We were taught at boot camp and basic training to hate the enemy, to love our country, and to believe that there was no better service than being a Marine. We were really hyped up. During advanced training, we qualified as experts with the Springfield '03 rifle, the 45-caliber pistol, the carbine, and the Browning automatic rifle. We learned how to use a bayonet, gas masks, hand grenades, and other weapons. We had classes in chemical warfare, scouting and patrolling, mapping, Japanese and pidgin English phrases, and more. All of this actually paid off well during ensuing combat operations.

Shipping Out to the South Pacific

During World War II for the period from 1942 and 1944, I was involved in Marine Corps combat operations in the Pacific Theater. Unlike the European Theater, in the Pacific Navy and Marine forces, along with a few Army units, bore the brunt of the fighting and comprised the main forces opposing the Japanese in the South Pacific. The Marines were responsible for taking the islands of Guadalcanal, Tarawa, Saipan, and Tinian. These were important stepping stones in the advance of the U.S. towards the Japanese mainland.

I joined the Regimental Intelligence Section of the Sixth Regiment, 2nd Marine Division. We shipped out from San Diego in complete blackout aboard the Dutch ship *HMS Brastagi*, solo and without escort, bound for Wellington, New Zealand. Other elements of the 2nd Division had landed on Guadalcanal on August 7, 1942, which was to be the first Allied offensive in the Pacific against the Japanese. We were ready for combat physically and mentally. After further training in New Zealand, plus exercises and maneuvers en route, we joined the battle on Guadalcanal in early January 1943. Our unit helped capture, secure, and then along with the Navy Seabees, repair Henderson Field so our fighter planes could defend the island and transport and supply ships anchored off shore against attacking Japanese aircraft.

Our training for jungle warfare, in particular, paid off. Our unit encountered little initial resistance when our Higgins boats landed on Guadalcanal. The Japanese enemy was lurking in the jungle, hiding and harassing, or fleeing just in front of us as we advanced. We had to chase them down over many days and nights, often in rain, through dense jungle, barbed wire, up and down coral ridges and wet valleys, across rivers, among palm trees — all the time avoiding sniper fire and sneak attacks reminiscent of "Indian warfare." This was my first experience with hand-to-hand combat, foxhole living, mangled and stinking bodies, a diet of C and D rations, and shortage of potable water.

We encountered malaria, yellow jaundice, dysentery, and dengue fever. In late February 1943 our unit returned to New Zealand, a sick and sad lot. Many spent the next several weeks recuperating from tropical illnesses, but otherwise enjoying some R and R. Some required evacuation to the states or hospitals elsewhere for prolonged treatment. As replacement troops arrived, our unit resumed physical conditioning activities and began training for another island assault. I enjoyed a short respite, visiting Christchurch and the South Island, and I formed friendships with New Zealanders which continue to this day.

The Battle of Tarawa

In the fall of 1943 the 2nd Marine Division took off in hot, crowded troopships towards an undisclosed destination. All we knew was that it would be an entirely different kind of challenge from the campaign in the Solomon Islands. Our target proved to be the island of Tarawa. On November 20, 1943 our Marine Division — 18,000 men strong in a heavily-protected convoy — began landings on Tarawa in the Gilbert Islands. The attack was on Betio, a very flat coral island just two miles long and one-half mile wide, but the site of a large airfield that had been built by the Japanese. The island was heavily fortified, with underground concrete pillboxes, blockhouses, coconut sea walls, tank traps and underwater obstacles, and mines. More than 5,000 defending Japanese forces were prepared to repel the attack and were mostly underground.

The surrounding coral reefs made it impossible to transport troops all the way to the beach in the Higgins boat landing craft. Also, for the first time, the recently available amphibious crafts, known as Amtracs, were being used, but similarly with minimal success. The first waves of landing forces were wiped out before ever reaching the beaches. Our unit had to transfer in the surf at the coral reef to rubber boats, all the while being subjected to heavy enemy fire from mortars and machine guns. Capsizing boats inflicted more casualties. Although our group was not scheduled to be one of the early waves, we ended up being among the first Marines to reach the beach. We crawled along the side of a 700-yard long pier, which offered some protection from enemy fire, in water up to our shoulders and loaded down with heavy combat equipment. At the end of that first day, the outcome of the invasion still remained in doubt.

Once the Japanese communication system was knocked out, however, their units became isolated and more disorganized. By the second day, with aggressive use of flamethrowers and bulldozers sealing off openings to underground fortifications, the threat from the pillboxes was virtually snuffed out. Some 4,700 Japanese defenders were killed, leaving only 17 wounded remaining, who were taken prisoner. The sight and stench of the countless dead bodies were nauseating.

The whole operation lasted only 76 hours. Marine casualties totaled nearly 900 marines dead, 2300 wounded, and 88 missing. The stubborn resistance put up by the Japanese was unexpected. For several days leading right up to the landings, fierce naval gunfire and Navy torpedo bombers had bombarded nearly every inch of the island, so most observers could not believe anyone could still be left alive. Before we left the island I escorted several of the Navy pilots who had engaged in the bombing of Tarawa to view the coral terrain and the built-in defense pillboxes. They were flabbergasted, because these obstacles and fortifications had all blended into the topography and were never identified by aerial photography. The troopships that evacuated the surviving Marines were a sight for sore eyes. We buried many of our fellow marines at sea. Then we were treated to an old-fashioned Thanksgiving meal en route to safe haven in Hawaii.

The Battle of Saipan

Our next assignment was Hawaii for reinforcements, re-organizing, and re-building the 2nd Division, which took place on the King Ranch on the big island of Hawaii. Many of us felt it was time for our unit to be returned home to the states, but this was not the case. After five months of further training and maneuvers off the beaches of Maui, we found ourselves in one of the largest naval convoys of the South Pacific, carrying the 2nd Marine Division into what proved to be two more battles.

D-Day was June 15, 1944 on Saipan, a large, mountainous island in the Marianas. The campaign raged on for 40 days, even though the island was declared secure on July 9 after three weeks of fighting. Before it was over, 29,000 Japanese soldiers died in the battle, many by suicide. More than 3,000 marines and soldiers died, and over 13,000 were wounded or missing in action. A large number of native families were "captured" for their own protection, but many others fled to the northern cliffs and jumped to their deaths, as did hundreds of Japanese soldiers. Again, we encountered stiff resistance on the beaches from withering fire from Japanese artillery, mortars, and machine guns. The heaviest U.S. casualties occurred during the first couple of days on the beachheads.

Yet the battle raged on nearly six weeks before all resistance was overcome. Silencing the Japanese artillery and mortar barrage was frustrating because of their inaccessible gun positions in camouflaged cliffside caves on Mt. Tapochau, which towered 500 feet above sea level. Continued harassing enemy fire over many days required use of flamethrowers, bazookas, satchel charges, grenades, rifles, and many brave men to finally snuff out the tenacious resistance. Unlike the terrain of our previous campaigns, Saipan was hilly and rugged, providing many places for the enemy to hide. This was also the first time our Marines had encountered Japanese tanks.

Early in our advance across the island we kept our lines tied in with the 4th Marine Division, and also an Army division, which was their first experience in island combat. Because of the rapid advance of the Marines but slower progress of the Army soldiers, gaps in the lines started to create difficulties and cause problems. It turned out to be an unsuccessful arrangement. On June 24, Marine General Holland "Howlin' Mad" Smith relieved Army General Ralph Smith of his command; that action soon resulted in straightening out the problem. Apparently, this rift was heard around the world for years to come. To make matters worse, this army group suffered the heaviest surprise banzai counterattack of the Pacific war when 2000 enemy soldiers broke through their lines in a suicide mission.

Although Saipan had been declared secure in early July, it required several weeks to ferret Japanese soldiers out of their caves and other hideaways around the island. Most of the enemy fought to the death, or committed suicide at the final moment to avoid capture. This proved to be an extremely dangerous mop-up exercise. It was essential in order to secure the island so that B-29 flight operations could begin to attack the northward islands and the Japanese mainland itself. Our unit maintained combat readiness at all times, slept in foxholes every night, and continued to suffer casualties daily from well hidden snipers. The Japanese government headed by the infamous General Tojo fell as a result of their defeat on Saipan.

Battle of Tinian

Upon reorganizing and reinforcing our units, the 2nd Marine Division next made landings on the nearby island of Tinian on July 24, 1944. The Marine invaders bluffed landing on the southern beaches of Tinian, then went ashore without major opposition near the airstrip to the north. By the second day, all resistance ceased. In this engagement nearly 300 marines were killed and 1700 wounded. According to one report, "it cost the Japanese everything they had and it was the easiest conquest the marines had made to date." Compared with earlier assaults on Guadalcanal, Tarawa, and Saipan, where the heaviest casualties occurred on the beaches, we landed on Tinian in an area where there were no beach defenses, with an overwhelming force of two divisions. The first attempt by Marine units to use napalm fire bombs to burn out vegetation and camouflage proved to be a big success on Tinian. This island was rapidly converted to an airfield with runways for B-29 aircraft, the bombers that dropped atomic bombs on Hiroshima and Nagasaki. Tinian was declared secure August 1, 1944.

Return to U.S. Duty

After a week on Tinian, we returned to Saipan where I developed acute arthritis of the left knee. I was evacuated September 1944 to Hawaii, then Oak Knoll Hospital, Oakland, California and then the Navy Hospital, Astoria, Oregon. Finally, just before Christmas 1944, I was transferred to Portsmouth Naval Hospital in New Hampshire. There I had a reunion with my folks following a four year absence, beginning with my first teaching assignment across the country in Arizona, then serving three years as a Marine in the South Pacific.

After rehabilitation at the U.S. Navy facility at Springfield College and a brief home leave, I was given my choice of duty. I chose to "command" a detail of a dozen marines providing security at the U.S. Navy Blimp Base, South Weymouth, Massachusetts, followed by special duty at the USMC center in Boston, informing Marines about the GI Bill of Rights and other benefits.

I was discharged on November 20, 1945 at Great Lakes Naval Air Station in Chicago, Illinois, and arrived home Thanksgiving Day 1945.

John Carpenter, a Trinity College graduate and school teacher, was a beribboned Marine who survived four bloody Pacific battles. After the war, he held executive posts in Burlington, retiring as senior vice president of Chittenden Bank in 1988. He resided at Oakledge for over 50 years with his wife Connie and their five children.

Over the Hump

★

Beal Hyde
U.S. Army Air Force

I N JULY, 1945 MY SQUADRON OF P-38 FIGHTERS, together with several other units, was stationed in Dudkhundi, India, not far from
Calcutta. Our unit had been withdrawn from the Burma Campaign,
now winding down. By this time, the Philippines had been retaken
and plans for the invasion of Japan were well underway. War planning for the Pacific Theater called for transferring our P-38 squadron
from India to the Philippines. The planes were to be flown from our
base near Calcutta to an airfield in Burma, then "over the Hump" to
Kunming in Western China (as the flight path over the high Himalaya
Mountains to China was labeled during WWII). Our P-38s were then
to be ferried by other pilots to a base in the Philippines.

The flight to Kunming comprised eight P-38s, which were to follow
a lead B-25 bomber providing the navigation. There were four P-38s on
each wing of the lead B-25 bomber, forming a V-formation like so many
geese. I cannot remember to which wing position I was assigned, but

it was probably third from the B-25. The first leg from Dudkhundi to Myitkyina in eastern Burma went smoothly. We probably flew at 15,000 to 20,000 feet, using oxygen. Clouds and visibility were not a problem.

We landed to gas up for the last leg of our flight — Myitkyina to Kunming. A year previously, Myitkyina had been occupied by the Japanese, but now we were met by several American USO girls, who offered us food and drink. Because the Japanese by this time had been driven out of northern Burma, we were able to fly over the Hump farther south, a more desirable route because the mountains were somewhat lower although just as rugged.

A Game of Crack the Whip

We took off for Kunming in the early afternoon to fly a route of some 350 to 400 miles. But the distance as the crow flies was not weighing on our minds. We had allowed plenty of time to arrive in Kunming before dinner time, and the weather was said to be good at the lovely lake where Kunming is located. What ominously lay immediately ahead of us were lots of clouds. We flew up into them right away, climbing steadily on the wings of the B-25.

In the kids' game of "Crack the Whip" the group runs, all holding hands. Then the leader stops abruptly, and the rest of the chain swings around the leader, causing the individual at the end of the chain to run the furthest and fastest for as long as he can keep up, until finally he loses his grip and falls away. An analogous situation occurs when flying in formation. If owing to turbulence, the plane nearest the leader moves up or down, the next plane must try not to move too much or abruptly, but at the same time correct his course somewhat. Each plane in the flight chain has to make a similarly cautious change in course or altitude, but the planes farthest from the leader have, progressively, to make larger corrections.

Lost in the Clouds

In thick clouds, any plane in the formation that loses sight of the adjacent plane is in real trouble. And that's what happened. The last plane on one wing lost us. We were experienced pilots, but we lacked the navigational equipment and capabilities of a B-25 bomber. The B-25 calmly instructed us and our lost companion by radio to continue to climb at a constant rate and to hold the same bearing. For perhaps 10 or 15 minutes, we continued to climb to 20,000 feet or higher, when finally, the clouds began to thin. I cannot describe the intense anxiety we felt, and perhaps more importantly, our overwhelming sympathy for our lost companion. Would we find him when we came out into the open?

Yes! He was right there within our sight and quickly joined up with the squadron once again, just before we were to reenter the clouds to begin our descent from the high Himalayan peaks. It was not long before we broke through the clouds once more and could see the beautiful blue lake of Kunming, China. That was my sole but memorable experience flying "Over the Hump."

Born in Dallas, Texas, Beal grew up in Wellesley, Massachusetts and enrolled at Amherst College in 1941. Enlisting in the Army Air Corps, he became a fighter pilot serving with a P-38 squadron in India in 1945. Following the war, he went on to earn a PhD in Biology and served as chair of the Department of Botany, University of Vermont.

Medical Corps to Kobe PX

★

Charles Kellner
U.S. Army

I ATTENDED NEW YORK CITY PUBLIC SCHOOLS in Far Rockaway until high school when my father enrolled me in Woodmere Academy. My family placed a high priority on education and encouraged all five of their children to get college degrees. My brother, an M.I.T. graduate, attended an RAF school in Canada and then was assigned to Navy duty in Washington D.C. where he was responsible for installation of radar equipment on naval aircraft during WWII but never set foot aboard a Navy vessel. After the war, he worked for Raytheon Corporation as engineering manager of the plant that developed the Hawk, Sparrow, and Patriot missiles for the U.S. Army.

I attended Rutgers University, majoring in English literature. I played 150 lb. football and captained the fencing team. During my senior year, the Dean of the College of Arts and Sciences informed me that I had a good chance of winning a scholarship to Harvard Business School. I protested that my father still had my younger brother to send through college, and his furniture business was not too good. However with financial help, I was able to pursue an MBA before joining the working world.

Pearl Harbor Day

Nearly all Americans recall where they were on Pearl Harbor Day, December 7, 1941. I was at home in Far Rockaway, and like most people, my family and I were stunned. I also recall the day the Nazis invaded Poland on September 1, 1939, which was the official start of World War II. My date and I heard this news tuned to my car radio. A week later, I picked up the newspaper and learned that a Harvard classmate, Klaus von Bohlon un Halbach, who had returned to Germany, was shot down in a Stuka bomber over Poland. His brother headed the Krupp Works and was later convicted and executed as a war criminal.

Joining the Military

For my first two years of college, ROTC was compulsory because Rutgers was a land grant college. I declined to remain in the ROTC after the first two years, but in retrospect, probably should have stayed in. After the U.S. instituted the military draft in 1940, I failed the medical exam and was classified 4-H because of 5/200 vision in my left eye, an infirmity from birth that had not impaired my ability to play sports. I applied for a direct commission in the New York National Guard but was rejected because I did not read the top line of the eye chart correctly (I mistakenly believed I could memorize the eye chart). During this period I worked in the family furniture business in lower Manhattan.

Several months later the Army finally inducted me into a non-combat (4-H) service arm. I was initially sent to Governor's Island for special treatment of my eye condition, which did no good. I recall reporting to the Induction Center next to Grand Central Station on Lexington Avenue. We were sent to Camp Yaphank 100 miles away on Long Island where we were issued uniforms. The following day I recall having to unload turkeys coming in from the Midwest to feed the troops. While there, I was called out of the ranks along with another man, and sent to New York City for duty at the Lexington Induction Center. So as a buck private, I was responsible for helping put friends of mine into the Army. My buddies and I were out on the town every night (we were known as "the subway commandos").

After a month, I was transferred to Fort Totten, Long Island where I became permanently assigned to the medical detachment. This happened while I had weekend KP (kitchen police) duty. A colonel during his inspection tour recognized me standing at attention with a mop in my hand and said, "Kellner, what are you doing here in the company mess? Why is this man here? Get me the mess sergeant!" When informed that it was my turn on the KP roster, the colonel ordered the company commander, a young second lieutenant, to answer the question. Hearing a similar reply, the colonel said, "I have reviewed this man's record. Don't you know this man is a college graduate!" With that, I knew I was doomed — I was assigned to hoe the colonel's garden for the rest of the day, and then became a medic.

Soldiers passing through New York with a medical illness, especially venereal disease, would be sent to the Fort Totten station hospital for treatment before going overseas. My medic training consisted largely of learning how to carry a litter. When I was too unnerved to administer shots, I was assigned to the station supply officer, a career warrant officer, to whom I took an instant dislike. One of the first things he said was, "It's your ass if anything is lost or stolen!" Consequently, I enjoyed making him nervous by purposely misplacing supplies on shelves and went out of my way to make him look bad. The lieutenant in charge once told me that many men and officers disliked him because of his unpleasant personality and rigid demeanor.

Eventually, I became a tech sergeant after two years at Fort Totten but did not enjoy my assignment. This motivated me to apply for Officers Training School (OCS) in the Transportation Corps in response to a notice informing that I might qualify for one of the non-combat arms of the Army. I was accepted, much to the disgust of my family and superiors. The Colonel called me into his office and said, "I want to tell you something. You don't belong in the Army, and if you go to

OCS, you'll be in the Army six months longer than if you stayed here, where I'll see to it that you get out without delay." The Colonel also phoned my father and said that "I was old enough to know better (age 31)." I didn't take his advice. The day I left, I went to his office to pay my respects, saluting him smartly. Sitting in his office chair, he waved a finger at me, exclaiming, "Young man, I'm going to tell you what's going to happen to you. You're going to go to OCS and become a second lieutenant, one of the dirtiest of words in the dictionary, and then they're going to assign you to troop duty and send your ass overseas so fast you won't know what happened. When the war's over and you come home, if you come home, you'll be in the Reserves, and you're not cut out for the Army, as I told you. Good luck!"

Army Amphibian Forces

I attended OCS near New Orleans where we would go on liberty. I was shocked to observe for my first time the discrimination directed at blacks, who were not allowed to ride on New Orleans streetcars except in the back. After becoming a "120-day wonder" (we took longer than the 90-day wonders of other OCS programs), we were assigned to Camp Gordon Johnson to form a company for transporting amphibious troops and artillery from ship to shore. Camp Gordon Johnson was about 50 miles from Tallahassee, Florida, on the Gulf Coast where blacks were treated even worse than in New Orleans. The 492nd Amphibious Truck Company comprised 170 black enlisted men and seven white officers, consisting of our captain and six of us lieutenants. As an officer, I was responsible for instructing the enlisted men, who often had never driven any vehicle, let alone a truck, which I had never done either. I had to learn how one day, teach them the next.

Often, when our enlisted men returned from weekend pass in Tallahassee, the local bus drivers would intentionally slam the rear doors shut so black soldiers would be late returning from leave and be declared AWOL. We had to set up DUKW (amphibious truck) convoys to regularly rescue stranded black soldiers in Tallahassee. I had had no idea what the South was like in those days or how deprived many of the poor were. Most of the men came from very lowly circumstances. More than half were right off southern farms and some had never worn shoes. I realized what a sheltered life I had led and grew up a lot. Attending venereal disease clinic and getting shots twice a week was a regular routine for many of the men. By the time training was over, however, they became competent soldiers.

In my OCS class was a black man, Charles Berkeley, who had been an Olympic track star and had graduated from the University of California. He was not assigned to troop duty but rather to Camp Gordon Johnson battalion headquarters. One time on entering the Officers Club, he was accosted by a white officer, a "redneck" who made a big fuss about the effrontery of a black being in the OC. When our company arrived on the docks of Pearl Harbor, Lt. Berkeley was there to greet us with a big grin and present us with the 50 DUKW vehicles awaiting us. He announced, "Well, fellows I knew you'd be coming and would need these."

Incidentally, I have been asked about discrimination directed at me in the Army because of being Jewish. Well, in the Army, like everywhere else, there are a certain number of jackasses, both Gentile and Jewish, who create unnecessary havoc, just part of the cross-section of America that makes up the military during wartime. One guy within the first 24 hours of my induction inquired while we were lining up, "What I was?" I said, "I'm an American, what are you?" He replied, "I'm a Yankee!" Then he asked, "What was your father?" I sensed what he was driving at so I said, "Let me see, he was born in New York. I guess that makes him an American." He said, "No, that's not what I mean. What church do you go to?" and I replied, "We don't go to a church." Then, he said, "You're a JB!" Well, I turned on my heel because I wasn't about to strike another soldier and be court marshaled, but I almost wish I had! It's interesting that in the medical detachment, many enlisted men were Jewish and never attained a non-com rating, yet for the most part, they had more education. In OCS, on the other hand, many religions were represented, and anti-Semitism or prejudice was never apparent. I had both Catholic and Protestant friends. Our company commander, a Protestant, became a close friend and we stayed in contact long after the war.

Preparing for Battle in the Pacific Theater

The 492nd traveled by train to Seattle where our captain informed us we would depart the next day and cautioned us not to spread any rumors. He said his sealed orders would be opened after we boarded ship to inform about our destination. That night on leave in the city, we encountered some "Red Cross girls" also traveling on our ship who informed us that "we were all headed for Hawaii." So much for: "Loose Lips Sink Ships."

Our company was assigned to a base outside Honolulu on the north shore of Oahu, along with some Marines and a company of Seabees. It was hard on our men, racially, because the Hawaiian natives wanted little to do with blacks. One of my jobs was teaching the troops under my command to swim (half of them didn't know how). Being in Hawaii to us was "heaven" compared to the swamps of Florida. A good friend of my older brother, Bob Thurston, who came from a family with prominent holdings in the sugar cane industry and a controlling interest in the Honolulu Advertiser and radio station, entertained me on many occasions. The son of a missionary (who sailed around Cape Horn "with a Bible in one hand and a bottle of booze in the other"), he had attended LSU. I would often stay with him on weekends and thoroughly enjoyed the experience. Bob once showed me some family-owned sugar plantations. He assured me that, despite rumors to the contrary, Japanese Americans did not construct directional paths within the cane fields to guide Japanese aggressor aircraft to Pearl Harbor targets.

One weekend, I hitched a plane ride to the "big island" and toured Hilo and the nearby volcano. We spent five months training with our DUKW vehicles, practicing maneuvers daily. One of our maneuvers was to practice landings on Maui ("we invaded Maui"). The DUKW floor boards could be taken up and we used them to surfboard behind the vehicle — we regarded this as a training exercise. All in all, our time spent in Hawaii was like "being in heaven."

Shipping Out

The 492nd shipped out on six or seven LSTs loaded with troops and equipment. Our destination was unknown, and it probably was subject to changes en route, depending on the war situation. Our first land sighting finally occurred off the island of Saipan where a massive ship armada was being formed in readiness for U.S. invasion of the Japanese mainland. While we were aboard ship, the war ended with the dropping of two atomic bombs followed shortly thereafter by the surrender of Japan. At that time our ship flotilla was lying just off the Japanese mainland near Wakayama, which is situated at the entrance to the Inland Sea and Kobe harbor.

Our 492nd DUKW unit disembarked from the LSTs and headed for the beaches off Wakayama. I was the first member from our fleet to set foot on the Japanese mainland. I recall the beach being totally deserted, with no sign of Japanese people. We observed that the Japanese shunned the American soldiers, hiding in their homes behind drawn blinds. However, the children were curious and gradually approached us, quickly learning to ask us for "chocolade." We ended up giving the children rides in the DUKWs.

The channel to the Inland Sea had been completely obliterated by intense American bombing and shelling in an effort to destroy the heavily fortified harbor entrance to the Inland Sea and Kobe. As we made forays from the beach, the hiding villagers gradually overcame their fears and began to accept us as friendly troops. Our company was housed in some partially intact factory buildings nearby. We built a latrine ("slit trench") which was partially screened from the villagers who would venture into camp and scavenge everything, including our sewage. The populace evidently had suffered great deprivation during the war.

How I Came to Command an Army Post Exchange (PX)

Eventually, the company disbanded, but I lacked enough points to be rotated back to the U.S. at the time. Being married was one of the criteria, and of course, I was single. So by chance, I became head of one of the first and largest PXs in Japan through another happenstance, one of several after induction into the service.

While strolling the streets of Kobe, I met up with an officer, Dick Lerner, a friend of mine from Columbia who had often visited our family home. Dick was a brother of Alan Jay Lerner of the composer team, Lerner and Lowe. Now he was an Army major stationed in the Kobe area after being transferred from Europe and was disgruntled because his artillery outfit had been sent to Japan. When he inquired what I was doing in Kobe, he said, "Don't worry, I'll get you a good job!" Later, he called me in Wakayama on an Army phone line and said to come to Kobe for an interview with his colonel, who happened to be a West Pointer and very strict. The colonel needed an officer to establish a store in Kobe, which required a qualified field grade officer, i.e., a Major or higher with merchandising experience. My friend said, "You're only a First Lieutenant, but I know from your wealth of experience in the family business and at Macy's that you are qualified to manage a PX." Little did he know my inexperience, but we laughed and I went along with it. So, the colonel assigned me the task of establishing and heading up a new PX.

My first chore was to search out a leading Kobe department store suitable to meet the Army's needs. When I visited the store, the manager served tea in a formal Japanese ritual, then "waltzed" me around the building. He offered rooms in the basement of the building, but the PX I was envisioning required ample space, good lighting, and easy accessibility. Finally, in frustration I said, "I've got orders. Goddamit, if you people hadn't attacked Pearl Harbor, I would still be working at Macy's in New York City! We need prime first floor space. Now are you going to give it to us nicely?" I indicated that I didn't want to be there (in Japan) and acted "very warlike." The proprietor quickly got the message, and the PX was on its way to becoming one of the largest in Japan. We started with only a limited number of items like food supplies, film, cigarettes, magazines, and beer but expanded rapidly to serve the needs of GIs and their families. That was the closest war-like duty I experienced in the military. Serving as the manager for about one year, I saw it develop into a full-fledged department store, Army style.

We were housed in the Silk Building in downtown Kobe. I encountered several German nationals who had spent the war years in Japan. One was a German selling medical supplies and equipment in Japan. While I was wandering around taking photos of bombed areas of the city and the Inland Sea from vantage points in the suburbs, a German man emerged from an elegant home and introduced himself. He invited me into his home where I remarked that he had a copy of *Life* magazine on the table. He took this opportunity to complain vehemently about the bombing and destruction of his city of residence in Germany by the United States. A couple of days after that, an article appeared in the *Army Times* reporting that the man had been picked up by the U.S. Office of Strategic Services (OSS), the forerunner of the CIA.

Another German national I befriended in Kobe, a Mr. Lowenstein, was a nice man who had fled the Nazis but had had to abandon his business in Germany. He became a close friend and told me that he had served in the German army during World War I, but was threatened under the Nazi regime for being Jewish. He finally escaped through Russia, reaching Japan where he was able to pursue his hobby of photography. After the war, I also attended a family wedding in New York of another former German citizen by the name of Rothschild whom I had met in Japan.

Epilogue

In late 1946 I was finally rotated back to the States on a troopship headed to Seattle. We were greeted at the docks by the USO and stayed overnight before taking the train back East. I was separated from the Army at Fort Dix, New Jersey. I signed on to the Army Reserve but never attended a meeting (fortunately) so avoided being called up during the Korean War.

I met my future wife Shirley at a visit to the Lane Bryant store in Cleveland where she had a good job. She was 26 while I was 36 years of age, but she "took a chance!" We were married nearly 40 years. She died of cancer at age 64, and I had an endowment fund established in her memory at Mt. Sinai Hospital. Most of our married life we lived in Highland Park, Illinois with our five children, three of whom are graduates of the University of Vermont and reside in the Burlington area.

A common query is how members of American forces reacted to the dropping of the atomic bombs. Well, I can state with confidence that most of us were glad. I don't care what the stuff printed in some of today's newspapers may indicate, if invading forces had had to land on the beaches around Wakayama, most of us would not be here today to tell of it. I inspected the Japanese gun emplacements directed at the beachhead where we would have landed. They were perfectly placed to mow down American troops as they disembarked from the ships. Their artillery was well concealed and we would have been "sitting ducks in our DUKWs." Of course, we would have eventually prevailed, but at great cost of lives.

The U.S. Navy heavily bombarded the shoreline and the main entrance to Kobe. The devastation wrought by the B-29 bombers in Kobe and Wakayama was extensive. That the Japanese people came to tolerate us Americans is sometimes difficult to comprehend. I am one of the fortunate ones who came out of the Army and can relate mostly funny anecdotes rather than horrible events like men who saw combat. I do not mean to make light of war, but sometimes think it's best to spin funny stories.

Growing up in New York City, Charlie attended Rutgers and Harvard Business School before entering limited Army service due to poor vision. Assigned to the Medical Corps, he volunteered for OCS, becoming a second lieutenant in the Transportation Corps in charge of an amphibious landing unit. Serving in the Pacific theater, he ran a PX in Kobe, Japan after the war. He established a successful business in the Chicago area after the war where he lived with his wife and five children.

HOW I CAME TO LOVE JAPAN

★

George Pasti
U.S. Navy

George Pasti, left, and Navy regional commander

IT IS OFTEN DEBATED whether the United States should have dropped atomic bombs on Japan, while the extreme brutality of the Japanese military during the war has been largely muted and is rarely discussed today. Following the war, our two nations have developed common interests and alliances in opposition to the rise of communism and in support of free enterprise. My career was significantly affected as a result of the evolving relationships between Japan and the U.S.

Prior to college, I had been working to earn money for my education in a defense factory that was building airplane parts, but wanted to get the Japs. After completing officers training at Northwestern, I was assigned to a ship, *LST 953* (Landing Ship Tank) in Hawaii. Our first mission was to transport supplies between Saipan and Guam. The Mariana Islands had been invaded and retaken by U.S. forces in June of 1944 in order to enable B-29s to strike the Japanese mainland. An aircraft required 7,000 gallons of gas for the round trip to Japan, a distance of over 5000 miles. We carried many barrels of gas from Guam to Saipan.

Invasion of Okinawa

After that, we joined the Okinawa invasion forces. This battle proved to have the highest casualties of the entire Pacific campaign. Against our naval forces, "kamikaze" pilots began attacking in waves of suicidal assaults, carrying high explosives and crashing into our fleet lying off shore. One bit of humor was a sign on one of our LSTs in large letters saying, "This Way to the Destroyers" with an arrow pointing towards the much larger escorting warships. Although our LST fired anti-air-craft guns at attacking Japanese airplanes, our ship was never a primary target. The sign must have worked.

Ashore our forces patrolled the many nearby caves. Japanese soldiers retreated to the hidden caves, and many committed suicide rather than be taken prisoner because they had been told that we would shoot prisoners. The story was told of an American yelling into a cave to a Japanese soldier, "Come out and surrender." A voice replied, "Come and get me, you souvenir-hunting sonovabitch." I came home with two samurai swords. Some of the souvenirs were more macabre. A friend had buried a dead Japanese soldier on the beach, and before his ship departed, he dug it up, cut off the skull, and scraped off the flesh. Ever since then he has displayed it as a souvenir on his desk at the college where he taught literature.

Following the brutal battle of Okinawa, our ship returned to Guam heading for the invasion of the Japanese mainland. When the atomic bombs were dropped on Hiroshima on August 6 and Nagasaki on August 9, we cheered. The Japanese quickly surrendered, and war finally ended August 15, 1945 (August 14 in the U.S.).

The Aftermath

We were among the first ships to arrive in Nagasaki harbor after hostilities. The devastation was horrible, shops were abandoned, the town mostly empty. For a year until May, 1946, our ship plied the Japanese coastline, carrying supplies, returning Japanese soldiers to their homeland, and hauling all types of equipment. During my several months in occupied Japan, I grew to appreciate the Japanese people and their culture. I wasn't the only member of our military to undergo a change of heart, as over 10,000 GIs ended up marrying Japanese women during the postwar months. The Japanese populace was found to be caring and very appreciative of acts of kindness. I became enchanted with the Japanese culture, and developed an interest in Zen, Japanese art, and Japanese traditions.

By spring 1946, I had enough points to be discharged from the Navy, but first we had to dispose of our ship. I served as executive officer and navigator. First, we sailed to San Francisco, then were ordered to San Diego, and finally through the Panama Canal to New Orleans. For six weeks we got to enjoy the local cuisine and culture and closed the legendary Pat O'Brien's bar most nights. The officers tried to hold the ship's complement together during this period, because most of the men had enough points to be eligible for discharge and wanted to go home. They were a restless and carefree bunch.

One day while on watch, the seaman on duty at the gangplank yelled up, "Scrambled eggs coming." This meant that senior officers with gold braid on their hats were coming aboard. Quickly, I dispatched someone below decks to "police the area" (clean up the mess) while I greeted our visitors and took them topside. As we passed through the chart room, there on the megaphone leading up to the control deck was a pair of pink panties. Ever since, I have disliked the color pink.

The brass were inspecting to see if they liked our ship well enough to have us take it to Texas where she would be used for Naval Reserve Training. They did like it, so we assembled the crew once more and sailed. When we got to Galveston, Texas, we were loading barrels of oil, and because we were operating with a skeleton crew, I helped. A barrel fell on my toes. I was shipped to the Naval Hospital at Great Lakes, to be patched up.

Ahead lay one final escapade before discharge. A fraternity brother and shipmate showed up at the hospital and explained that he needed help with a personal problem. It seems that his girlfriend and her family expected the two of them to be married, but he was happily cohabitating with her and not interested in marriage. So he concocted a story that our ship had been struck by a bomb, and as a consequence he now was having an operation at the Naval Hospital because of a wound he had received in the incident. The result was that he no longer could have children, so he regretted he could not marry her. The corpsman fixed him up with bandages, he borrowed my wheelchair, and when his girlfriend visited the hospital, he played the role of patient although in fact he was only a visitor. Alas, she called the hospital the next day and discovered there was no patient by his name in the hospital. I was called in by the commander of the hospital and informed that if it were not for the fact that I was being officially discharged, I would be court-martialed. Clearly, the days of fraternity antics were over.

The Japanese Culture

After the war I pursued graduate studies of Western Civilization. However, as I began teaching, I became increasingly interested in comparative studies and wondered why the East Asian cultures, especially China and Japan, had not modernized, given their impressive contributions to civilization. Indeed, they had discovered printing, writing, the compass, and much more that lent itself to transforming a traditional society into a modern progressive society. So at the age of 40 years, after a year of post-doctoral work at Harvard, I began a two year study of the Chinese and Japanese languages, in an effort to better understand this dilemma. For the next 30 years — with a brief interlude in college administration as a dean — I happily read and taught Comparative History of the East and West.

And so my love affair with Japan grew from first only knowing the Japanese as brutal warriors, to a fascination with the Japanese people and their culture, beginning with the U.S. occupation after this terrible war ended.

Born in Chicago, Illinois, George attended Northwestern University and received a commission in the U.S. Navy in 1943. Following the war, he pursued graduate studies in Asian civilization, learned Japanese and held professorships at East Carolina University and State University of New York, Plattsburg.

Dual Armaments and Line Officer

★

William Tobey
U.S. Navy

F ROM SECOND GRADE ON, I lived and grew up in Rye, New York. On December 7, 1941 while enrolled in the MBA program at Harvard (Class of 1943), I was visiting my alma mater Amherst College. A young fraternity brother dashed into the room, shouting, "The Japs just bombed Pearl Harbor!" That afternoon we returned to Harvard, and shortly thereafter I signed up with the Navy Reserve Officer Training Program (NROTP) at the college since I had been classified 1-A by the Selective Service. We received commissions as Ensigns in the Naval Reserve while attending Harvard. This involved an obligation to take some courses in military science and rudimentary military protocol, such as drilling, marching to class, etc. We were forced to march around in "pseudo" military attire for a while because at the time there was a shortage of full uniforms. We were not paid for these reserve commitments in school.

Military Service

Following graduation in March, 1943 I did not immediately go on active duty. For a short time I held down a construction job at the White Plains airport. On induction several weeks later, I proceeded to Fort Schuyler, the U.S. Merchant Marine Academy site on Long Island Sound in the Bronx. There we received some instruction in the proper demeanor of a naval officer ("Navy stuff so we didn't make fools of ourselves!"). We spent about a month there before reassignment to the Boston Navy Yard where we roamed around Boston Harbor in small boats, the main purpose of which I don't really recall.

Shortly thereafter, I was assigned to the gun factory at Anacostia (Washington D.C.) Navy Yard to learn naval ordnance. It involved mostly classroom instruction about large guns and how to maintain and fire them. After two months, I was sent to Pontiac, Michigan to a General Motors plant. There, a contingent of "out of work" automobile dealers had been assembled to instruct us about various types of weaponry, including 5-inch, 40 mm, 20 mm, and other guns being produced by GM in place of automobiles. From there, we moved on to Great Lakes Naval Station for a week or so, and I recall firing weapons ranging from handguns, rifles, submachine guns, to 40 mm guns. Next, I was sent to Pocatello, Idaho to a "big gun" factory to assist in assembling so-called advanced base materials for shipment, offloading, and storing on Pacific islands, such as ordnance, ammunition, and other naval supplies.

Shipboard Duty

I received orders to join a ship under construction in Tacoma, Washington at a Kaiser plant that was building navy aircraft carriers. During WWII, Kaiser produced around 50 carriers at the plant. I was assigned to a new ship, and our task as officers was to assemble a crew and ready the ship for commissioning. During that time, we lived in barracks until our "shakedown" cruise in Puget Sound, which involved learning how to perform some demanding vessel maneuvers at sea and while docking.

We sailed the ship, the *USS Windham Bay*, to the San Diego Navy Base where we loaded aircraft for delivery in the Pacific. This included a shipment of "night fighter planes" which we transported to the island of Saipan, then returning to San Diego with some captured Japanese aircraft on board. I was next assigned briefly to the commissioning of the aircraft carrier, *USS Lunga Point*, but shortly thereafter, was relieved of duty on that vessel "because of having too many ensigns assigned."

The USS Cape Gloucester

I was next assigned to the aircraft carrier *USS Cape Gloucester* (CVE109) which was nearing completion at another Kaiser plant located in the city of Astoria, Oregon. Once more, we had to ready the ship for commissioning, starting with assembling a crew. At that point, I had been promoted to Lieutenant Junior Grade. We sailed for San Diego where we picked up a marine flight squadron. Their aircraft comprised torpedo bombers and some fighters with a new "gull wing" design. This design innovation enabled planes that had larger engines and bigger diameter propellers to fly from carriers. We transported the marine flight contingent to the Philippine war zone after stopping over in Pearl Harbor. I recall this was in 1944 when MacArthur's campaign to recapture the Philippine Islands was getting underway. Possibly, Dick Austin who piloted a torpedo bomber on a carrier during the Philippine campaign was in that invasion force. His story about carrier flying in the Pacific Theater is related in this volume.

We did not see much battle action in the Philippines, as our ship was assigned to service with the 9th fleet. This constituted a reserve fleet composed mainly of aging battleships along with a group of escort carriers, as opposed to the 5th and 7th fleets, which were made up of more modern warships. We arrived off Okinawa sometime after the invasion of that island had gotten underway. It is interesting that "Tokyo Rose" (the infamous female broadcaster of propaganda to American troops for Japan radio) had erroneously reported that our carrier had been sunk by the Japanese because the *Cape Gloucester* was the only carrier believed to be in the harbor at the time. The fighting on the island at this point had largely shifted to the northern and southern ends of Okinawa but remained fierce. Japanese aircraft had actually hit the *USS Pennsylvania*, which was severely damaged. Marine pilots aboard our ship were flying combat missions and reported shooting down several Japanese passenger aircraft.

The *USS Cape Gloucester* next approached the Japanese coastline in anticipation of the impending invasion of mainland Japan. The first atomic bomb was dropped on the city of Hiroshima while our ship lay off shore of the coast. There were also a British carrier and a hospital ship accompanying us. Our ship was tied to buoys in the Sasebo harbor while the cruiser and hospital ship docked at the port loading piers near the railroad station in order to receive freed Allied prisoners of war. At this point the war was not officially over, but a Navy information officer went ashore to view and document the extensive damage to the city of Sasebo, which had been heavily firebombed by American bombers. The POW camp was just outside the city limits and the liberated inmates were entrained to harbor side. We made preparations to take aboard the troops from the area prison camps and set up cots on the hanger deck of the carrier. We were able to accommodate some 500 POWs for transport to Okinawa for processing and treatment, and hopefully, quick passage to the U.S. The prisoners all appeared very thin; the most emaciated POWs were taken aboard the hospital ship rather than our vessel.

While anchored off shore near the Sasebo naval base, we were able to go ashore. There was unbelievable devastation of the city! I recall only one building being more or less intact and left standing — what appeared to be a concrete bank building. We hiked around the hillsides and viewed the immense destruction of the inner city, all caused by saturation bombing by American planes launched from Okinawa as well as other more distant Pacific islands. The area resembled an uninhabited moonscape, a sight never to be forgotten. It's a vivid memory that I will carry to my grave.

Our ship weathered a series of Pacific typhoons. One was a severe storm while we were anchored in Sasebo harbor awaiting the freed

POWs. Our CO (known at Captain "Shaky" Harris) had quite a reputation for being excessively nervous and jumpy. The *Cape Gloucester* had been moored in the harbor to two anchor buoys with three steel lines (a 1-inch, a 1.5-inch, and a 2-inch cable). During the gale, the cables began to part. It was a period of high stress on the bridge. I reported for duty on the bridge to relieve the Officer on Duty (OOD) for dinner. When I arrived, the scene was utter chaos. I found the OOD entangled in his headphone connectors, which I had difficulty untangling and transferring to my head. In his state of distress, the OOD had donned the earphones of the seaman, who functioned as messenger, while the phones were still attached to him underneath his foul weather gear. I finally disentangled both of them and took over command of the bridge. The OOD proceeded to take one of the longest dinner breaks on record. Fortunately, the ship sustained no further difficulties with the anchoring buoys while I stood that watch.

However, a problem arose from the Captain's subsequent decision to have the steel cables run out of three separate chocks. That made the tension on the lines uneven, and two lines finally snapped during the gale. The ship swung around and almost ran aground before the Captain finally dropped anchor. Fortunately, the ship then held its position and the storm abated. After delivering the prisoners of war to Okinawa, the *Cape Gloucester* returned to off shore Japan but we had to weather another typhoon en route. A third typhoon struck us during our return voyage later to the U.S.

Our captain, "Shaky" Harris, was replaced before the ship departed Japan for return to the States. Our new CO, Capt. Burrows, was an entirely different breed of man and officer. As a consequence, encountering our third typhoon en route to San Diego, the crew suffered a much lower stress level. Capt. Burrows was a decisive leader but in a low key way. I recall one instance when the ship was instructed to perform a particularly tricky maneuver to bring two ships in line (together) while I was serving as OOD on the bridge. He came up and instructed me in a gentle manner, "Bill, do so and so." All went smoothly.

While my Navy training was to function as the ship's ordnance officer, in addition, I willingly accepted the duties and responsibilities of a line officer while serving on the *USS Cape Gloucester*. This turned out to be necessary because of the ship's size and limited complement of officers. While many of my fellow officers in ordnance training school moved on to advanced positions and remained in the ordnance field, I enjoyed the dual responsibilities of "being a ship driver" in addition to acting as the gunnery officer.

Epilogue

I had met my wife Marty in 1943 while assigned to the Pontiac, Michigan GM plant while she was a student at the University of Michigan. After a six-week whirlwind courtship, Marty and I were married in the Episcopal Church in Waukeegan, Wisconsin, at which time I had been assigned to the Great Lakes Naval Station. She accompanied me to my next assignments up until the time I shipped out of Tacoma, Washington. Marty then returned to her studies for another year at U. Michigan. We were reunited on my return to San Diego after my first Pacific tour of duty on the *Windham Bay*. She accompanied me when I was reassigned to the *USS Gloucester* in Astoria, Oregon. Marty was able to follow in our car as the ship cruised down the West Coast headed to San Diego. There we were fortunate to rent a pleasant converted gatehouse and entertained many of our Navy colleagues at wonderful parties before wartime duties once again interceded and I sailed for the distant Pacific on the *Gloucester*. My return to San Diego was not until late 1945. Shortly thereafter, I returned to New York where I was discharged at the 3rd Naval District facility in Manhattan.

Bill grew up in Rye, New York, attended Amherst College, and enlisted in the U.S. Naval Reserve. Serving on aircraft carriers in the Pacific, he married his wife Marty before leaving on his first cruise. After the war, Bill and Marty resided in the New York metropolitan area with their five children, and Bill enjoyed a 30-year career that led to becoming a corporate officer with Home Life Insurance Company.

Farm Boy to Admiral

★

Narvin (Moe) Wittman
U.S. Navy

MOE GREW UP ON A FARM and enrolled at the University of Nebraska as an engineering student. When Charles Lindbergh returned in 1938 from a trip to France and Germany after observing Hitler's Luftwaffe, he was so impressed with the strength of European air forces that he informed President Roosevelt of the urgent need for more aviators in the United States. The President toured mid-western college campuses, encouraging young men to learn to fly. Moe promptly signed up for Civilian Pilot Training (CPT) and dropped out of the University of Oklahoma as a junior student to enroll in advanced CPT flight training in St. Louis. After completing flight training, he was asked to join the military and choose a branch of service. He elected the Navy and went to Pensacola, Florida where he finished his flight training and earned his Navy wings in June, 1941. He was assigned to a flight squadron in Norfolk, Virginia to fly PBY amphibian aircraft. His squadron was sent to Bermuda to patrol the Atlantic for German submarines. On Pearl Harbor Day, his squadron was immediately ordered back to Norfolk and reassigned to Hawaii.

Wartime Duty

His squadron was flown to Hawaii, and the Pearl Harbor airfield was still smoldering when he arrived so his aircraft was diverted to an airbase in Kaneohe on the leeward side of the island of Oahu. From 1942 to 1943, Moe's flight group flew bombing missions from Hawaii to Midway Island, Alaska, and the Solomon Islands. He took part in the battles of the Aleutian Islands and Guadalcanal and served as a pilot in the Navy's first B-24 squadron. For his wartime service, he earned the Distinguished Flying Cross as well as Air Medals for combat.

From October 1943 until March 1944, Moe was a B-24 instructor in San Diego, California. He then was assigned to the Navy Postgraduate School in Annapolis, Maryland. While there, he took some engine courses at Pratt Whitney in Hartford where he met and later courted his wife to be, Verna. Verna had left a teaching position when the war began in order to get involved in war production, and ultimately, in manufacture of jet engines in East Hartford, Connecticut. Since the Navy required pilots to log a certain number of hours each month to maintain their flying status, Moe was only too happy to fly up to Brainard Field, Hartford to take Verna to lunch on many occasions, then fly back to Annapolis.

A Post-War Career in the Navy

In 1945 as WWII was ending, Moe was sent to the Massachusetts Institute of Technology to pursue a Master's degree in Aeronautical Propulsion. Moe and Verna were married on December 23, 1945 while he was attending M.I.T. Moe served in the U.S. Navy for 33 years, including two subsequent conflicts, the Korean and Vietnam wars. Moe and Verna lived in many different locations during his years of military service, including two years in Japan where they built their own house, as well as considerable time spent in the San Diego area. In his Navy career, Moe rose from the rank of Ensign to Rear Admiral. In 1970, he was awarded a second Legion of Merit for his contributions on behalf of the Navy to the investigations of the controversial F-111 fighter project, including the often heated Congressional hearings on this multi-service project. He also led a development team that produced a combat-ready multipurpose guided missile. Moe's final duty was as Vice Commander, Naval Air System Command, Washington, D.C. After his Navy retirement, Moe and Verna enjoyed farming in New Hampshire and moving to Wake Robin.

Born in Hooper, Oklahoma, Narvin (known in the Navy as Moe) earned his Civilian Air Patrol license prior to Pearl Harbor and completed Navy Flight Training at Pensacola in June, 1941. He was a bomber pilot involved in several Pacific battles. He was awarded the Distinguished Flying Cross Medal and Legion of Merit and later rose to the rank of Rear Admiral during 33 years of military service. Moe and his wife Verna settled on a farm in New Hampshire where they resided for 20 years before coming to Wake Robin. Moe suffered a stroke leaving him with aphasia, so Verna recorded this summary of his Navy career.

The
European
Theater

The Fighting First

★

David H. Ackerman
U.S. Army

I N THE FALL OF 1943, I was drafted and became a candidate for the ASTP (Army Specialized Training Program). This program, familiarly referred to as "All Safe 'Til Peace," was proffered by the Army to qualified high school graduates for an initial year of college studies prior to military duty. Subsequently, the Army disbanded ASTP due to the need for additional troops. Those ASTP recruits headed for a profession, such as medicine, dentistry, etc., were allowed to continue their college studies, but the rest of us received orders to report for active duty. I was sent to Fort Benning, Georgia for 15 weeks of infantry basic training, then Camp Livingston near Alexandria, Louisiana for another 15 weeks of infantry basic training. Finally, I was assigned to the 86th Infantry Division (Black Hawks Division) where we underwent 15 more weeks of basic training because, as our Division cadre said to us, "we lacked sufficient expertise in creeping and crawling" to survive in battle!

Heading to Europe as an Infantry Replacement

Following what amounted to a total of 45 weeks of basic infantry training, I was transferred to Fort Meade, Maryland to be processed along with other replacement troops for assignment to the European Theater. We were loaded on a troopship at Camp Shanks on the Hudson River above New York City and landed in Liverpool, England. Subsequently, we were transferred to Southampton, a port on the English Channel. We boarded a Belgian ship, the *Leopoldville*, bound for Normandy and landed at Omaha Beach. I recall that the ship's officers and crew were all Congolese and only French was spoken. We later learned that the ship was sunk in the Channel with 800 lives lost during a similar crossing. We were transported by the "Red Ball Express" (an Army transportation scheme) from the coast of France to the battlefront near Aachen, Germany where I joined the First Division ("The Fighting First"), 18th Infantry Regiment, Company I, as private first class.

The Fighting First[1]

When we replacement troops arrived in the 18th Regiment, our commander informed us that "few of us would make it back home!" At that point I began to regard myself as a fatalist, a belief that was strengthened by subsequent battlefront experience. The city of Aachen, a cultural and historic landmark, was also an armament and coal-producing center and a key point on the Siegfried Line opposing the Maginot Line of the French. Aachen, considered by the Germans as a symbol of heroic resistance (as had been Stalingrad for the Russians), was taken by American forces after fierce fighting involving the First Division in late October, 1944. I arrived as a replacement in Company I shortly thereafter. In Aachen, we performed mainly guard duty among the captured bunkers of the Siegfried Line, which were in the hands of Allied forces.

---

[1] *The Fighting First*, a booklet published by the First Army Division before the war's end and distributed to each member of the outfit, with foreword by Clift Andrus, Major General, US Army Commanding, 1945.

From that point on, however, I led the life of a real foot soldier, riding on trucks and tanks when available, but mostly walking everywhere the battlefront took us. The 1st Division moved into the Hurtgen Forest, a treacherous, muddy, and snow-laden woods. Fighting was heavy and the German artillery and mortar fire deadly. This was my first sighting of dead German soldiers. The 18th Infantry Regiment was engaged in house-to-house fighting in Heistern. When we were not marching, our lives were spent mainly in foxholes in the forest. I recall being served a hot turkey dinner in a foxhole on Thanksgiving Day, 1944.

The Battle of the Bulge

By mid-December the 1st Division assembled in the Hauset-La Calamine region of Belgium for a well deserved respite, which proved to be short-lived. On December 16, 1944, the great German counter-offensive that became known as the "Battle of the Bulge" started, aimed at Antwerp and Brussels and the enormous Allied supply dumps around Liege and Verviers. Initially, German parachutists were air-dropped to create havoc and interrupt movement of Allied forces. Even barrages of the new weapon in the air wars, German V-1 buzz-bombs, were launched, producing more chaos and a continual din. The attack resulted in great confusion among Allied forces, with administrative and service units of the Army streaming backward away from the front. It seemed that only the Fighting First was moving towards the front.

Despite repeated attempts by SS Panzer Divisions and infantry, the Fighting First prevented the Germans from ever occupying the strategic town of Butgenbach, a key northerly point anchoring the Bulge. The 18th Infantry Regiment was positioned around Weismes, and in close quarter fighting, repelled repeated German attacks, all of which were unsuccessful. Our patrols reported seeing "enemy dead as common as grass" after these German thrusts into the 1st Division lines. The weather was getting steadily worse, with soupy fog and mud. Fortunately, Christmas Day dawned bright and cold so that for a brief period the artillery could see what they were shooting at, and air cover could resume to disrupt German supplies and troop movements, providing much welcomed but only temporary respite from the fierce fighting. By December 30, temperatures plunged to record lows, however, and snow was piled four-to-five-feet high, with cutting winds and enormous drifts.

By mid-January, the German counterattack finally ground to a halt, and the 1st Division went on the attack. The Germans were determined not to give up any ground they had won without a hard battle. The weather became so inclement that the enemy could not believe that the 1st Division continued to move forward. The 18th Infantry went into the teeth of battle around Klingelberg Hill. Company I was ordered to advance across a snowy meadow. Nearly everyone in my platoon was struck by enemy fire, pinned down in a withering crossfire. Only two of us remained unscathed, and we were forced to lie motionless to avoid drawing fire. I was struck by an enemy bullet which spun around between my helmet and liner, and emerged to penetrate my backpack, shattering its contents. I lay in this position on the ground for several hours until reinforcements finally arrived. The two of us who escaped unhurt in this onslaught were rewarded with a three-day pass to Paris.

On return from our brief respite, my buddy and I rejoined the snow-laden troops during one of the coldest spells of winter on record, in skirmishes to retake the lost ground in the Battle of the Bulge. The 18th Regiment advanced relentlessly through the towns of Moderscheid and Hepscheid. With the German offensive of the bulge washed up, the 1st Division turned eastward, pushing into Hunningen, the last of the enemy held towns, and Honsfeld on the German border. The 1st Division was up against the Siegfried Line for a second time.

The Final Thrust into Germany

Breaching the Siegfried Line, now heavily mined, under inclement conditions took almost three weeks of continuous attack. The 18th Regiment was engaged in the assault on the town of Ramscheid, which required clearing roads and corridors through anti-personnel and anti-tank minefields and bringing up heavy artillery to put pillboxes out of commission. An Associated Press release by correspondent Hal Boyle from the front commented on the 1st Division's relentless attack: "They should pin the Silver Star on every doughboy and tankman fighting in near-zero weather to erase the remaining Belgian salient. It is a wonderful demonstration of the American civilian soldier's courage, initiative, and endurance — this grinding winter battle which for hardship and suffering has made a Valley Forge of the forested, snow-covered Ardennes battle. Nothing saps fighting spirit like exposure to cold. That's why steady progress made by the 1st Division in reducing the Belgian bulge is so remarkable — it is a testimonial to inner resources of heart and spirit — which drives men through hip-deep snowdrifts even as their weary bodies cry out for rest...."

From there, the 1st Division rolled on to the Rhine River. The 18th Infantry was involved in taking the towns of Norvenich and Gymnich, as German resistance stiffened on approach to the Rhine River, finally reached in early March. The 18th Infantry was thrust into the effort to expand the Remagen Bridge "beachhead" across the Rhine. This was one of the last major German counterattacks on the western front. Fierce fighting by the 1st Division was required to clear the enemy from remaining positions, with the ultimate defeat of five German divisions and the capture of over 4,000 prisoners.

Our unit was based at the Remagen Bridge, which previously had been partially destroyed. Nearby was a winery containing many large wine casks in its cellars. We proceeded to tap them by removing the bungs and filling our containers with the valuable contents. These wine casks received "considerable use" during our stay in Remagen. The tapped barrels would be left open and drained their remaining contents onto the cellar floor. Before long, the lower cellar area was totally flooded with wine, and we had to resort to tapping wine casks on higher floors of the winery.

Our next engagement involved the Harz Mountains, a heavily wooded region with few roads. German forces had congregated in this nearly impenetrable forest as a last ditch defense to prevent any push on to Berlin. Again, fighting was fierce, the terrain formidable, but the Fighting First overcame enemy forces, and the 18th Infantry alone accounted for the capture of some 8,000 prisoners. With the wind-up of the Harz mountain campaign, the war was essentially over. The Division had moved into Czechoslovakian territory by the time the cease fire was finally declared May 7, 1945.

My return to the U.S. was considerably drawn out by the sheer numbers of troops awaiting transport. I was afforded an opportunity to attend school at Shrivenham (American) University, some miles west of London. I believe I took some standard freshman college courses. It also provided me with the chance to visit relatives in England and Scotland. When the opportunity came to board ship for home, the trip was via the aircraft carrier *USS Lake Champlain*. All of the aircraft had been removed and the entire hangar deck fitted out with stacks of bunks, six in each row, one above another, on which one couldn't even sit down. The return voyage was exceedingly rough, creating widespread seasickness, and the latrines were plugged up, adding to our misery!

Epilogue

My army experience had a profound and lasting influence on my life. It is difficult to convey in words all of the effects this had on me, but it reinforced my aversion to stress of any kind. Starting out as an infantry replacement on the European front, I became a squad leader in I Company, forging strong bonds with my fellow GIs in The Fighting First. Many of them were not as lucky as I in escaping injury. Entering the army as a private, I was discharged two years later as Sgt. First Class, having been awarded two bronze stars, two purple hearts, and several Battle ribbons.

Born in Passaic, New Jersey in 1925, David spent summers at his grandfather's cottage on Buck Island, Lake Placid, New York. After graduating in 1943 from the Northwood School in Lake Placid, he was drafted into the Army. While fighting as a foot soldier in Europe, he kept a detailed personal record of events and memorabilia. After the war, David attended Princeton and joined American Metals Co., where he was involved with mineral exploration throughout North America, the Caribbean, Africa, and Australia.

Convoy Duty on a Destroyer Escort

★

Duncan Brown
U.S. Navy

Following graduation from Harvard in 1942, I went almost immediately into Naval Officer training, first for 30 days at Notre Dame in South Bend, Indiana, and then for three months in Chicago (V-7 program) where I graduated as an ensign in the Naval Reserve. I was then assigned to the SubChaser Training Center in Miami, at which time the Navy destroyer escort program was just getting under way. I applied and was accepted, then sent to Norfolk, Virginia for duty as part of the pre-commissioning detail for the *USS Dobler* (DE-48). From there, I was sent to Philadelphia Navy Yard where my ship was under construction. On its completion we were sent to Bermuda for training in escort convoy duty. At that time, the German submarines were constantly attacking U.S. coastal shipping, so the *Dobler,* which had originally been built for the British, was kept in the U.S. Navy and assigned to mid-Atlantic convoy escorting — Norfolk to Gibraltar, and later, to the Mediterranean.

Life aboard the Dobler

When I came aboard, I was the junior officer any way you looked at it — age, rank, and date of birth. My commanding officer was a lieutenant commander, a "mustang" (an enlisted man promoted to an officer through performance and ability). He was Regular Navy and had the usual scorn for "reservists." But he decided that I might make a good officer and assigned two career petty officers to the task of making me into one. They undertook to give me practical training with his supervision. I was not yet 21 years of age, the youngest officer on board — and a Harvard graduate to boot. This instruction served me well for the next three years while I was on active duty. For example, I learned from them that a good officer makes surprise visits to the enlisted men's mess to check on the quality of the food being served. I did that all during my active duty days, reporting to the captain when I thought food preparation left much to be desired. I was the only officer on board who did that and the enlisted men knew and appreciated it; they reciprocated by assisting me to become a good officer. I also learned that the officer relieving the watch does well to arrive when he is supposed to, and not one minute later; that makes for better relations in officer country.

Service in the Mediterranean

The *Dobler* was initially assigned to U.S. to Gibraltar convoys. At "Gib" (as we called it) we turned over the convoys to the British who conducted them to their Mediterranean destination. Later on, we escorted the convoys directly to Sicily and North African ports. Previously, our escort group had gone to Casablanca to await a U.S. bound convoy. This was to be my first real taste of war. The big French battleship, *Jean Bart*, had been scuttled in the harbor and had settled in the mud until her deck was awash.

Our convoys usually consisted of around 100 ships plus a naval escort of destroyers in the vanguard with the destroyer escorts (DEs) on the flanks. The former had speed with which to pursue attacking subs; but the DEs only had a maximum speed of 23 to 25 knots so were somewhat limited in attack capacity. Nonetheless, if we could force subs to submerge, we could give them a hard time as their underwater speed was usually less than 15 knots and they could maintain that speed for only a limited period.

We were operating in mid-Atlantic and the U-boats in the main tended to operate further north where they could disrupt shipping to Russia and England. They deemed the Mediterranean Theater less threatening since the major campaigns were the battles being fought in France and Russia. The Russians were desperately fighting German land forces to prevent them from reaching Moscow and knocking Russia out of the war. This would have had very serious consequences for the Allied cause.

The Luftwaffe Moves In

As we penetrated further into the Med, the Luftwaffe by means of air strikes undertook to prevent Allied shipping from reaching its destinations. Our division was assigned to air guard work. The division skipper was a Naval Academy graduate who had forsaken the Navy to practice law, which he did until the Navy called him back to duty. He knew that in the Med we would be subject to heavy air attack, and he drilled us endlessly on defending against threatened air attack. This proved to be valuable on our first escort duty to Sicily when we delivered a convoy without loss or damage to a single ship. In the process our convoy shot down 19 German aircraft in one dusk attack, for which we received a Navy commendation. Our division record was that we never lost a ship nor had one damaged during the war, a record of which I am still proud.

Two Remarkable Coincidences

The first was a chance encounter with my father, about which neither of us knew at the time. He was an Army lieutenant colonel with UNRRA (United Nations Relief and Rehabilitation) serving the area from Casablanca in the west to Yugoslavia and headquartered in Cairo.

We did not actually meet but came close to it. He walked out of the Officers' Club in Bizerte just a few minutes before I walked in the same evening. He outranked me by a good bit so, by custom, he would have had to buy the drinks. From Cairo he relocated to Athens when the British occupied Greece. He had a notable career there and was rewarded by the Greek government with the highest decoration conferred on non-Greek citizens.

The second was one of those strange things that can happen from time to time. After the war was over, my wife and I moved to Burlington, Vermont. One day a man walked into my Church Street office. We knew immediately that we had seen each other somewhere before. It turned out that he, Luther Bridgman, had served on the *USS Decker* (DE-47) sister ship to my ship, the *Dobler* (DE-48). Both ships were assigned to the same division of DEs. The rest of the story is that Luther elected to cast his lot with me, and we formed Brown Bridgman & Company which, while located in Burlington, operated mostly out of New York City. Luther and I had a very happy 30-year relationship until his death here at Wake Robin. We both loved the Navy and going to sea. Brown Bridgman & Co. outlasted us both until it was finally absorbed by a larger company after our retirement.

How can you beat that for a nice war-related ending?

After the war, Duncan married and lived in Burlington with his wife and five children. He spent a career in the insurance and financial counseling field and was active in politics, serving leadership roles with a number of commissions for the state of Vermont.

POEM IN TIME OF WAR

★

George Clay
U.S. Navy

D URING THE WAR, George served in the Navy on a destroyer, part of a small "Hunter Killer" squadron that sank four German U-boats.

Harry One

I forget why we called him
Harry One.
His last name was Heinz
and he came from Wilhelmshaven.
He had been sunk on the U-boat
we'd sunk that morning,
a junior officer.
Showered, in borrowed clothes,
but still stinking

of the oil slick
we'd fished him and the others
out of,
he sat at the wardroom table
building
a quite recognizable replica
of our destroyer,
out of dominoes,
then smashing
it against the bulkhead
with a swipe of his hand.
He'd pick up every last domino
and begin all over again:
leering,
building, smashing,
build, smash.
I was in charge of him,
so I brought him some ice cream
from the galley,
and he invited me
to Wilhelmshaven after the war.

After the war George became a successful writer for the New Yorker, New York Times Book Review, Best American Short Stories, and other journals. His first book, Family Occasions, was published in 1955. Best known for his authoritative work on Tolstoy and "War and Peace" he was the father of 7 children and died at Wake Robin in 2007.

Naval "Cruise" in the North Atlantic

★

Joseph Furlong
U.S. Navy

Aᴛᴇʀ ɢᴇᴛᴛɪɴɢ ᴍʏ ᴅᴇɢʀᴇᴇ in Electrical Engineering, I worked in manufacturing vacuum tubes for radar equipment until I entered the Navy. I became an "instant ensign" in that I was commissioned before my Navy training. My orders were to report to Fort Schuyler in the Bronx, New York. Since I lived in Queens across the Tri-Boro Bridge, it was not a long distance. My father was in Pittsburgh on business so I probably was the first Ensign whose mother drove him to report to duty on the first day.

Our group was all engineers assigned to the Ordnance Bureau. After we learned how to march and identify ships and planes, we were sent on our way to various locations for further training. Since I had some experience in radar, in the perverse logic of the military it was logical that I received my training in anti-submarine ordnance, i.e., depth charges and torpedoes. Interesting work but we thought we should be afloat, being Navy officers.

Watch Out What You Wish For

I was ordered to Destroyer Escort 191, *USS Coffman,* to see how the equipment we had been studying worked in practice. Next I went on to the Brooklyn Navy Yard. It turned out that the DE was part of a Hunter-Killer Group which normally consisted of five DE's and one Kaiser class aircraft carrier. In our case, the carrier was the *USS Core* which had been ferrying planes from the U.S. to Europe. Our ship was first ordered to proceed from Brooklyn to Casco Bay, Maine. This took 10 days, then we were ordered back to Brooklyn so scheduled work could be done on our DE.

The word was that the Group would be going to Bermuda to engage in training exercises with a submarine. This was around the New Year, and it was bitter cold in New York so Bermuda sounded pretty good. I had, presumably, completed the cruise but had received no new orders. At this point, the Captain wanted to send a deck division officer to Damage Control School and suggested I stay aboard to replace him. Having received no other orders and thinking Bermuda sounded good, I agreed. The repairs being completed, the five DEs left New York harbor amid large ice chunks which scraped the newly painted hulls of the ships. Then came the blow! Instead of bearing southeast toward Bermuda, our Group headed northeast into the North Atlantic. Not the place to be in the winter months. One of the duties for officers was to stand Code Watch. The decoding work was done in a very small cubicle and was not too challenging, once you got braced against the violent movements of the ship. The incoming weather report messages advising of low lows and high winds of 120 knots, day after day got to be pretty tedious. The weather men, however, turned out to be remarkably accurate.

Life in the North Atlantic — Afloat

The crew could not work on the outside (weather) decks except during the rare periods of relative quiet. The ship became covered with ice. The objective of all this effort was to find a German submarine that was sending periodic weather reports to its base in Germany. We could hear it but never long enough to get a fix on its position.

The group stopped at Reykjavik, Iceland over night. There was a tumultuous welcoming that night and a welcome respite from the storms. The next day the ships left the harbor in a column with signal flags blowing. It made a brave sight, but then the wind blew and the waves rose and fell, and we were back to where we had been before. Finally, the Code Watch bore some good news. I brought the message to the Captain that we were to return to port, and spirits picked up. After we returned and the ship was in dry-dock, we discovered that the starboard bilge keel had been peeled back about halfway by the ice hazards. The ocean waves had really done a job on it.

All in all, the episode had been interesting and instructive, but when I got back to Washington, with all this accumulated experience and valuable information, all they bothered to ask me was where I had been.

After that, my service was shore-based in connection with maintaining electronic stations for Ordnance. Next, I received orders for the Pacific theater and took a train from Long Island to San Francisco to join Base Hospital 4. Then, the unit moved on to the island of Okinawa where two typhoons demolished many buildings on our base around the time war came to an end. Eventually, I received orders back to Washington DC for separation from active duty.

The lesson from the cruise in the North Atlantic: "Never put any credence in scuttlebutt."

After completing his MBA at Harvard in 1948, Joe married, raised a family, and worked 38 years with the Hudson Gas & Electric Corporation in Poughkeepsie, New York. Always involved with community service, he has continued to be active with Rotary and SCORE after moving to Shelburne, Vermont.

WW II's "Secret War"

★

Hervie Haufler
U.S. Army

IN 1942, I ENLISTED IN THE ONLY MILITARY SERVICE that would overlook my poor eyesight: the U.S. Army Signal Corps. The Corps trained me to be a cryptographer and in 1943 shipped me to England as one of some 500 Americans assigned to the British code-breaking program. As I later found out, we Americans were divided into three groups, each located at a different place, and each delegated by the British to take on a different task.

The Manor House, Bexley, England

My group's assignment was at a station whose task was to intercept and copy down encoded German radio messages for delivery to the British code breakers. We worked and lived in Hall Place, an ancient manor house in Bexley, Kent, with radio aerials strung incongruously over its slate roofs. There I found that the word "cryptographer" can cover a variety of duties besides code breaking. We cryptographers in Bexley were split into three small teams, each working a different eight-hour shift in our Detachment's round-the-clock monitoring. As cryptographers, we received highly secret information from the British that we used to guide our large contingent of expert GI radio intercept operators when listening to their assigned German networks.

Cryptography and Need to Know

In military intelligence, you're informed about only that small part of the whole that you "need to know" in order to do the job. My need to know back then was very slim. For a frustrating example, we cryptographers policed the coded messages our operators copied in scrambled five-letter groups. We then passed these messages on to the British at "Station X" without ever knowing whether they were being broken. There were times, such as the terrible surprise attack of the German army on our Allied troops in the Battle of the Bulge when we believed, in despair, that they were *not* being deciphered, that they were just piling up in a warehouse someplace in hopes that a code breakthrough *would* come. Else, how could Hitler have so fooled our commanders? We GIs at Hall Place had to sustain our faith that somehow what we were doing was making a positive contribution.

Life in England

Although the work there quickly became routine and boring, we did it carefully because — who knew? —it might help some guys in the front lines. We were aware of being fortunate in many ways, not the least of them being the opportunity we gained to familiarize ourselves with Britain. Our British neighbors were kind to us, inviting us into their homes and initiating us in the fine art of British tea. In addition, from Bexley we could entrain to London in just over an hour. On my off-duty days, I roamed the London streets, fed the pigeons in Trafalgar Square and saw a lot of good theater — Olivier, Gielgud, Ralph

Richardson, Terence Rattigan. I bought a bike and toured the English countryside.

We had one disadvantage. Our location in Kent was directly in the path of German bombers, and later in the war, V-1 and V-2 rockets, aimed with not very good accuracy at London. We got our fill of hearing air-raid sirens and of recoiling from the blasts of British anti-aircraft gunners trying to bring the Luftwaffe planes down on our heads. We spent a good many off-duty hours at bombed sites trying to find victims under the debris or helping to clear out rubble. We ourselves almost became victims when, in September 1944, a V-2 landed close enough to make the walls of Hall Place tremble, some of the ceilings crack, and several windows to be smashed. Two of our guys received Purple Hearts from injuries suffered in the bombings. All this was scary but also balm to our egos: sure, we were rear echelon troops, but we weren't completely immune to the bloodletting.

The Secret War

When the war was over and I was back in the U.S., ready to be demobilized, I had to sign a pledge never to reveal what I had done in the war. I and some 10,000 others involved in this British program kept that pledge for 30 years after the war's end. Then, the British authorities themselves began to let the wall of secrecy come down and to allow books to be published about their code-breaking triumphs.

Suddenly, I learned in detail about that "secret war" I'd been involved in. The new books informed me how British geniuses, such as Alan Turing and Gordon Welchman, had solved the Enigma code machine in which the Nazis had placed so much faith that all three of their services — Army, Navy, and Air Force — had relied on it. That was when, for me, "Station X" became Bletchley Park (BP), and those thousands of messages that had passed through our hands could be seen as among the decrypts that enabled Allied commanders to know exactly what their German counterparts were planning. The rush of new information filled me in on the enormous hoax the Allies had played on the Germans by making them think the main D-Day assault would fall not on Normandy but on that jut of French land that pushed out into the English Channel — the Pas de Calais. It was a deception so convincing that it made Hitler order his best army, under Gen. Erwin Rommel, to remain on the ready in Calais rather than in coming to smash the Allies' tenuous hold in Normandy.

Also unfolded was the answer to why the Allies suffered their bloody setback in "The Bulge" of the Ardennes: there were no German radio messages to reveal Hitler's plans because he forbade the use of radio in carrying out the attack. Nazi communications were by telephone or motorcycle couriers only. Allied generals were so used to having BP hand them the Nazi intentions that they refused to take seriously reports from the Ardennes front warning of a huge build-up of German armor opposite the front lines.

Genesis of a Book

Reading these books by British writers about cryptography during WWII, I noted one big oversight: none of them included mention of the three-phase American contribution to the effort. In addition to our intercept station, another American unit operated the complex machines that Alan Turing and Gordon Welchman had invented to help break the Enigma, and the third group worked directly at BP on various capacities relating to the code-breaking. I began thinking about and gathering material for a book that did justice to the Americans' role.

This decision led to research at the U.S. archives on WWII on file at College Park, Maryland, and then to England to explore the files at Bletchley Park and the marvelous records of Britain's National Archives in Kew. My proposal for a book won the agreement of agent Richard Curtis to market it, and he secured me a contract with Penguins' New American Library. My *Codebreakers' Victory* was published in 2003.

In the process of amassing information for the book, I became aware of another intriguing aspect of the secret war. This was that the Germans believed they had established a productive network of spies in Great Britain, never realizing that every one of them was actually a double agent under Allied control. Penguin agreed to publish this story too, but gave me so tight a deadline for finishing the script that I had to do it without ever returning to England. Instead, I hired a fine English researcher who specialized in WWII. He supplied me with all I needed to write the account, and it was published as *The Spies Who Never Were.*

Hervie is best known for publication of two books about his war service as a cryptographer. He is a professional writer who worked for General Electric as Manager of Corporate Editorial Services and later founded a communications consulting firm. He is married to Patricia Haufler whose article appears in the "Home Front" section of this volume.

THE "LUCKY" HERNDON

★

James Hunt
U.S. Navy

MY STORY OF LIFE ABOARD THE DESTROYER *USS Herndon* is derived from an account of the ship's history written by Jane Moore Roberts, the daughter of the Herndon's skipper, Lt. Commander Granville Moore. The book combines dialogue with the Herndon's crew against a background of concurrent events in the Battle of the Atlantic and the Invasion of Sicily.

The Battle of the Atlantic was a violent and deadly cat and mouse game between Allied surface vessels and German submarines. The battle lasted throughout World War II, seriously threatening survival of the Allies. The U-Boat wolf packs of Admiral Doenitz sank some 3,000 Allied ships — representing a loss of 14 million tonnage of vessels, in addition to the tragic loss of lives and materiel. Although 85 German U-Boats were sunk that year, Hitler considered this a triumph of his submarine force.

The Sea War Begins

The United States was at war with Germany in the North Atlantic several months before America's entry into World War II officially took place. I know because I was there — at sea, off the coast of Iceland on the *USS Redwing,* an old World War I mine sweeper converted to a rescue and salvage vessel. In September 1941 before the war with Germany, the destroyer *USS Greer* hunted for German U-Boats and was in turn attacked unsuccessfully by a U-Boat. On October 17, 1941 the destroyer *USS Kearney* was struck by a torpedo, and on October 31, the four-stack destroyer *Reuben James* was sunk by a U-Boat with loss of 115 men. This all happened before Germany declared war on the United States December 11, 1941 (four days after Pearl Harbor).

While the *Redwing* was patrolling around Iceland in January 1942, the U.S. Coast Guard cutter *Alexander Hamilton* was struck by a torpedo. The *Hamilton*, a beautiful ship with graceful lines and painted all white, was taken in tow by the *Redwing*. However, we had to cut her loose because she took on a lot of water, and she finally capsized and sank.

Letter to Secretary of the Navy James Forrestal

A letter to James Forrestal, Secretary of the Navy from Vice Admiral Jonas Ingram, Commander-in-Chief of the Atlantic Fleet stated, "The mission of the Atlantic Fleet was to keep the sea lanes open and protect Allied shipping. The Battle of the Atlantic is going to go down as one of the decisive battles of the war because if the battle were not won, the war in Europe would be lost." In early 1943, the letter went on to say, "when the Germans had as many as 450 subs available, it was just nip and tuck. If they had kept up this rate of sinkings the remainder of the year, I doubt if there would have been the Mediterranean or Normandy invasions, or if there would (even) be a Great Britain."

Jane Moore Roberts added the observation that the sailors of the Battle of the Atlantic, the brave men manning convoy ships and escort warships, were responsible for sustaining the war in Europe. Without it, critically needed troops and supplies for the subsequent invasions of North Africa, Sicily, Italy, Normandy, and southern France would not have gotten across the Atlantic Ocean.

Transfer to the Destroyer Herndon

I was transferred to the brand new destroyer *USS Herndon* in October 1942 and served on her as a Chief Gunners Mate until August 1, 1945. As soon as the Herndon was certified for sea duty, little time was lost. Our first convoy duty was to the Mediterranean, similar to my duty on the *Redwing* except that the *Herndon* was a new ship, well supplied with the latest navigational and battle equipment. The sonar gear was especially vital and could detect submerged objects, even whales. This was put to good use in the two weeks we were at sea en route to the North African coast.

We quickly learned to be alert for the enemy submarines, especially at night and most especially on moonlit nights. Most of the attacks came at night because the subs could surface and sneak up to a no-miss range. The clanging of the general alarm spurred us to our battle stations regardless of where we were, or what we were doing — eating, sleeping, or whatever else. It was very demanding, but effective. The *Herndon* was in the Mediterranean around May 1, 1943, headed for Gibraltar from Casablanca. One time when we were off the coast of North Africa, two shipmates and I watched two torpedo tracks cross our stern about two seconds apart. We were also fired upon another time, and two torpedoes went underneath the ship, too deep for any damage. No wonder we began to think of ourselves as aboard the "lucky" *Herndon*.

The Invasion of Sicily

Despite the rigors of escort and convoy duty, I had never had any real battle experience before assignment to the *Herndon*. The Invasion of Sicily was a military operation of monumental proportions. The Allied Fleet, comprised of some 3,000 vessels, was at the time the largest armada in history ever assembled until the Normandy invasion. The Sicily invasion marked a major point in the Allied march toward victory over the Axis powers. It was the first assault on "Fortress Europe" as well as the culmination of the North African Campaign.

When the *Herndon* reached North Africa in June, 1943, the harbor at Algiers was crowded with ships of all types. Close to the dock was a large fenced area guarded by armed American soldiers. Inside the fence were several thousand captured German soldiers — remnants of Rommel's Desert Corps. They didn't look like supermen to us. We spent several monotonous days shuttling back and forth along the 200-mile stretch of North African coast between Oran and Algiers, escorting ships, patrolling for enemy submarines, and taking part in invasion rehearsals. Our home port was Algiers, and while we were in port, our liberties in that exotic city were interesting and sometimes disastrous! On the Fourth of July, we had to "dress ship," and a 48 gun salute took place from the shore honoring our 48 states before then dining in style.

Plans for the Invasion

The invasion of Sicily was agreed to at the Casablanca conference between the Allied chiefs of state, Roosevelt and Churchill. It was dubbed "Operation Husky" under the command of the major Allied commanders — Eisenhower, Patton, Montgomery, and Doolittle. It was to be an attack on the "soft underbelly" of Europe. However, soft underbelly proved to be a misnomer. We were to face stiff Nazi resistance in the Sicily and Italy campaigns.

The *Herndon* was assigned to Task Force 81 Gela Attack Force (code named "Dime") along with eight other destroyers of the same class, known as Destroyer Squadron 17. Seven of the nine skippers of Squadron 17 were members of the Annapolis class of 1927. There were 90 other vessels ranging from battleships to landing craft, and it included 19,250 embarking infantry troops. Two other Task Forces, 85 and 86, were of similar magnitude. In addition, there was an entire paratroop force of 3,460 paratroopers from the 82nd Airborne Division.

The battle plans had been meticulously drawn up. The American landings were to take place on the southeastern coast of Sicily. Our Task Force "Dime" from Algiers was in the central position with the other two Task Forces on the right and left flanks. This magnificent armada was one mile wide and 60 miles long.

Dispatch to the Fleet from the Commanding Officer

We are about to embark on the most momentous enterprise of the war. We will be striking at the enemy for the first time in his own land. This is the first move toward the rapid and decisive defeat of the enemy. In the light of our duty, great risks must be accepted. On every officer and rating rests the individual duty of ensuring that no flinching in determination will hamper this great enterprise. I rest confident in the resolution, skill, and endurance of all of you to whom this great enterprise is entrusted.

— Admiral of the Fleet Sir Andrew B. Cunningham, RN

Personal Logs of Officers and Crew

Our skipper, Lt. Commander Moore, wrote that, "Operation Husky was underway from the ports of North Africa on the 6th of July, 1943. Objective Sicily."

Excerpts from personal logs recorded by shipmates:

We steamed out of Algiers this morning as a large convoy with escorts moved in. Finally by evening, the harbor was full of ships moving out. It was a magnificent sight and one not easily forgotten.

About 10 o'clock that night we started to come out (from the port). Cruisers, cans (destroyers), troop transports, LSTs (Landing Ship Tanks), tugs, and everything. We had PT boats and planes around us all the time. We picked up Liberty ships every hour. We had a convoy as far as the eye could see.

Each transport has a barrage balloon to protect it from low flying planes.

July 8: Today we saw many Flying Fortresses that may have been returning from a bombing raid on Sicily. At this time nobody knows where we are going....

Prelude to Battle

During the morning of July 8, 1943 the great Armada closed ranks and proceeded in an eastward direction through the Tunisian War Channel — a 50-mile long and 10-mile wide mine-swept sea lane. Once through the channel, the armada diverged, and on July 9 the Herndon turned northward. The Plan of the Day gave orders for everyone to have his shirt sleeves rolled down in case of powder flashes. We also got instructions for becoming a prisoner-of-war — to say nothing except give one's name, rank, and serial number.

We had steak and eggs for breakfast (battle breakfast). They told us over the loudspeaker to get as much sleep as possible because there was going to be a tough grind ahead. During the evening of July 9, the invasion was threatened by the high winds and rough seas of a mistral — a violent and cold wind blowing down from the Alps. Unfortunately, we had many violent attacks of seasickness aboard. The invasion proceeded as planned despite the rough weather, which as we learned later, surprised the enemy and delayed their response because they thought we would not continue until the weather changed.

The Battle Is Joined

For us, the battle began the night of July 9 when we were called to General Quarters at 11:30 PM We could see flares lighting up the sky miles ahead of us and the town of Gela all lighted up with fires started by our bombers. Our planes were dropping paratroopers. From his battle station, one shipmate declared "that the shelling was spectacular — red, orange, and white tracers were flying every which way. The sky was a mass of anti-aircraft (AA) fire and flares." The Invasion of Sicily was on.

At three AM on July 10 the transport ships began lowering boats to land the troops on the beaches 10 miles away. Enemy flares from planes were lighting up the beaches aided by enormous search lights on the waterfront. The first boat wave landed at Gela at 3:50 AM The enemy searchlights were also turned to spotting our ships. One of them homed in on us and our director immediately took a range on it and would have fired, but it was too far away. Closer ships successfully knocked the light out. Thus continued the *Herndon's* good fortune. At four AM, two cruisers and two cans bombarded the town and disabled the shore batteries.

One of the crew wrote on July 10:

> I am on the high pressure air compressor which is on automatic so I could stand at the hatch and observe it all... At about 4:15 AM I was standing outside the hatch with a buddy, and we both agreed that we were like a couple of kids watching fireworks at a county fair. We knew that our wives have probably been listening to the radio and were hearing about the new European Front that is being opened up. Little do they dream that we've been standing here watching it and eating candy bars.

The Air War from Hell

My report on the battle in the sky is culled from the personal logs of various crew members. Early in the morning of July 10, 1943 planes came in from seaward without any identification. Our first concern was whether they were enemy aircraft, which indeed they were — Heinkel III bombers, Focke-Wulf FU-190 fighters, and Messerschmidt ME-109 fighters. Also, there were Stuka dive-bombers, JU-88s, which had sirens that were activated when they started to dive-bomb. The screaming sound was supposed to terrorize the enemy below.

At around 5:30 AM there was a flash and tremendous explosion. The *USS Maddox* from our Destroyer Squadron 17 was hit and sunk within two minutes, with only 74 survivors out of a crew of 284. The German planes seemed to attack whenever our planes returned to base to refuel. At 10:00 AM one of our LSTs was bombed by an ME-109 and burned on the beachhead. It must have been loaded with ammunition as it blew sky high. At 12 noon, another LST was struck and burned on the beach.

The sky was filled with anti-aircraft fire from all the ships. As it was growing lighter, we could discern that there was some firing on our own planes. This was the first time we had ever seen an Air Force Mustang fighter plane. We did not have any recognition information at that time. British Spitfires were in dog fights with the FWs. Chaos was everywhere, and in the state of confusion our men didn't know what they were doing. They were just firing at whatever came in view.

Inland near Gela, naval fire was still effectively shelling the enemy. The destroyer *Shubrick*, sister ship of the *Herndon*, fired on a column of Italian tanks approaching Gela from the north. A shore fire-control team directed the *Shubrick's* fire, and several tanks were put out of commission although about 10 managed to reach Gela. The Rangers who had landed took them out with bazookas, and the remaining tanks beat a hasty retreat.

The *Herndon* meanwhile spent July 10 (D-day) as part of the anti-submarine screen that patrolled to seaward of the transport vessels five miles offshore from Gela. This meant that we were more or less removed from the worst of the fighting, although mines were still a problem. On July 11, transport ships were moving in closer to land their troops, and we accompanied them. The Germans staged a fresh air attack primarily aimed at the troop transports. This continued on through dawn until nightfall of July 12. We were one of the first ships to be spotted in the enemy flares and a stick of bombs was dropped 100 feet from our fan-tail, just missing us. The whole ship heaved and shook, but again it was the luck of the *Herndon.* Our anti-aircraft guns were going full blast, shooting at planes and flares. We think we got one of the planes.

One of our crew, a 19 year old gunner, wrote in his log:

> A plane flew over our starboard side about 75 feet off the water. I started firing my 20 mm gun and emptied two and a half magazines into the plane. I could see the tracer shells hitting into the body of the plane as it went down and crashed into the water. Later we found out about the flight of the air transports. In my own mind that plane could have been one of the American planes. If it was, it had already dropped its cargo of men and was heading back to base since it was

going seaward toward Africa at the time I fired on it. I didn't know why anyone would fly troops through an air raid to get to the beach instead of flying around the trouble.

This was not one of the Herndon's lucky days. It was a terrible tragedy, but the gunner really couldn't be blamed. We all had to play for keeps on very short notice. It was either them — the enemy — or us. Another incident was described by two crew men:

A German ME-109 dived at ships near the beach and dropped a bomb, and then went up again to shoot down a barrage balloon. We had the 40 mm guns under director control, and I opened fire on the plane. This was the first time I ever fired on an enemy plane. The other wrote: The Herndon opened fire on a ME-109 as it was banking to shoot down a barrage balloon. The Army shore batteries opened up on him and hit him. You could see him spiraling around and down and exploding in flames as he hit the ground.

The air raid finally ended in what seemed an endless two hours. We never knew how many Germans were shot down, but apparently only two of our LSTs were hit.

Struck By a Mine

Commander Moore wrote that at dawn on July 12 radar blips were reported to westward, thought to be the Italian Fleet approaching. The *Herndon* and *Gherardi* from Destroyer Squadron 17 departed at high speed to investigate, but nothing was found. On their way back, the *Gherardi* picked up two fortunate U.S. airmen floating in the water. *Herndon* picked up a drowned American. While still on the way back, a mine went off very close to our hull. The rudder was nearly collapsed by the explosion, and the starboard main propulsion shaft had a kink. Both generators were out and both engines were dead. The bridge reported that the steering engine was not responding. The ship rocked and seemed to be going down at the stern. Men were quietly putting on their life jackets. Miraculously, thanks to the skill of the crew, everything was at least partially fixed in 15 minutes, and we were back underway — the "Lucky *Herndon*" lucky yet again.

Always alert and patrolling, we steamed back to Algiers for rest, repairs, and resupplying July 16.

We arrived in harbor, and shortly thereafter, the most horrible thing happened. We were thrown about by six terrific explosions, presumably from bombing. Not far away three ships were being ripped apart — a tanker and two cargo ships. Half of the tanker had been blown up onto the shore. Ammunition was exploding, and men on fire were jumping into the water. We went to General Quarters and backed out of there in a hurry. We were too close to those burning ships for safety. There must have been a great many dead and wounded. Ambulances were carrying them away all afternoon and evening.

July 19 found us patrolling off the southern coast of Sicily near Gela. On July 22 we went back to Algiers, and the end of July we were transferred to Task Force 88 along with Squadron 17 to take part in operations on Sicily's northern coast. The *Herndon* was assigned fire support and screening duties on July 31, and offensive patrol on August 1. It was exasperating to see enemy trucks and tanks moving along the roads and not being able to fire on them because the range was too great. It would have been foolhardy to go closer because enemy minefields had been reported closer to shore. Enemy artillery opened up, and we dodged shell splashes with high speed maneuvering. One of the most anxious moments I recall during the entire operation at Sicily was our assignment with another destroyer and a cruiser to patrol the northern coast of Sicily to establish whether the Germans were reinforcing or evacuating the island.

The Worst Daylight Air Raid So Far

Nearly 50 German planes evaded Allied radar detectors, and after dropping flares, unloaded about 60 bombs, which exploded with more violence and noise than any we observed in the entire Sicilian campaign. Railway cars on shore estimated to contain at least 900 tons of ammunition of the Allied forces caught fire. Shell fragments rained down for the next four hours.

The cruiser *Philadelphia* was also a primary target, and planes dive-bombed her, with bombs dropping all around us, all near misses. The radar reported that groups of planes with no identification except electrically transmitted IFF (Identification Friend or Foe) were coming from all directions. They were everywhere, and the calm clear sky was cluttered with AA fire.

A crewman wrote:

> Just at day break on August 1, a high-level two-engine bomber flew over the center of our ship from stern to bow at a height of about 25,000 feet. It was following our every move. The Herndon delivered intense AA fire but the shells were exploding below the aircraft. We could not reach the altitude of the bomber. Suddenly, there was an explosion just beneath the plane. A shout of joy went up from the crew. When the smoke had cleared, the plane was still following us. I then noticed Captain Moore standing beside me, watching the plane's every movement. All of a sudden he yelled "Right Full Rudder!" The Herndon, making about 20 knots, did a hard right and a load of bombs dropped harmlessly into our wake. This is the closest I ever want to get to a bomb. I could not believe how calm the Captain was. He watched every movement of the plane and he gave the order to turn just as he saw the bombs being released from the plane.

Another crewman wrote in his log:

> At about 3:30 PM we heard a terrible explosion. Just behind the Philadelphia we saw water burst up into the air even higher than the ship. We saw at once it was dive bombers — 12 of them. They were coming for us and I wasn't going to stand on the fantail and watch. I was scared to death. We got underway at full speed, zigzagging all over the place. Suddenly, four planes came in from the north and we opened fire on them. One plane dipped his wing to show its British marking (the Spitfire Bullseye). It was our own fighter protection coming and we almost knocked them down. We did a hurried retreat

from the coast, covered during our run by the British Spitfires. We could see that it wasn't healthy for us to stick around. I was really glad to get out of there. If we had stayed, there wouldn't have been anything left of our three ships.

The *Herndon* claimed two planes downed in this raid, which brought our total to six.

Homeward Bound

From August 2 to 7, the *Herndon* headed back to North Africa, patrolling or screening ships all along the way. On August 10, 1944 exactly one year from the start of the Sicily invasion, the *Herndon* and what was left of Squadron 17 headed for New York to prepare for their next role, the invasion of Normandy. Our rudder that had been damaged in the mine explosion needed further repairs. The starboard main propulsion shaft never did get properly fixed and continued to make odd noises.

For her part in the Battle of Sicily, the *USS Herndon* received a Battle Star. The men all received the European-African-Middle Eastern medal. Was the *Herndon* truly a lucky ship? She was a destroyer that emerged from the invasion of Sicily virtually unscathed despite many near misses. I am convinced that she was indeed a lucky ship. Her sister ship *USS Shubrick* was an unlucky ship (it was hit in the Pacific, destroyed by a Japanese kamikaze). I once heard luck defined as: "opportunity meeting preparedness." I can't really agree with that. There is little, if any, control over luck. The Herndon was lucky from the time of her commissioning — all through the many convoy trips, the enemy planes at Sicily, and shore batteries at Normandy. Her luck held even when she was an escort for the ship carrying President Roosevelt to Yalta. She was really lucky that the war with Japan ended before she was dispatched there for picket duty. Some have said, on the other hand, that the luck of the *Herndon* was actually the skill and competence of her Captain, Commander Granville Moore. Herndon went on to many further engagements with me aboard. However, I end my story here with her part in the dangerous, violent, and bloody but finally victorious Invasion of Sicily campaign.

A Proud Aftermath

There is a town in Virginia named Herndon. The town and the *USS Herndon* were both named to honor the great naval hero, Commander William Lewis Herndon, a brave, intelligent and dedicated servant of our nation. Because of his dedication to the safety of his crew and ship, he lost his life when the ship he commanded sank at sea in 1857. On September 18, 1982 the Mayor of Herndon proclaimed that day to be *USS Herndon* Day to commemorate the same dedication, bravery, and heroism of her entire crew as had been displayed by Cmdr. William Herndon. All surviving members of our crew were made honorary citizens of Herndon, Virginia. The Herndon Depot Museum proudly displays the badly tattered but perfectly beautiful Stars and Stripes that flew from the mast of the *USS Herndon* during the invasion of Sicily.

Jim enlisted in the Navy right after high school, remaining in the service for 20 years. After his Navy career, he taught school, worked for an engineering company, and headed an economic development corporation.

ENSIGN TO OFFICER OF THE DECK — OVERNIGHT!

★

Richard M. Ketchum
U.S. Navy

Barbara and Richard Ketchum

ON APRIL 23, 1943 I GRADUATED from the Midshipman School at Northwestern University and was commissioned Ensign. That afternoon I boarded a plane to Pittsburgh, my home town, where I was welcomed by my parents. They drove me to Sewickley, the home of my fiancée, Barbara Bray. We spent some time (though not much) inspecting wedding presents and eating dinner, after which my parents and I left for home, about 20 miles away.

The next evening we returned to Sewickley where Barbara and I were married. After dinner and dancing, the two of us drove to the William Penn Hotel in downtown Pittsburgh, where we spent the night. Early the next morning, we went to the railroad station, boarded a train for Sea Island, Georgia, and arrived there the following afternoon. We spent a week at the Sea Island resort before I had to report for duty at the Submarine Chaser Training Center (SCTC) in Miami, Florida.

So, in the short space of two weeks, I received my commission as an officer in the U.S. Navy, inspected our wedding presents, was married, went on a honeymoon, and reported for duty. The reason I had not married earlier, I might add, is that I had signed up for what was called the V-7 program while I was an undergraduate. This permitted me to finish college — I had one more year to go — and get my degree, in return for which I agreed not to marry until I was commissioned.

Trip to Brazil

After completing the program at SCTC, I received orders to report to the *USS PC 493* in Recife, Brazil. Leaving my bride in Miami (she went to Nashville to visit one of her mother's sisters) I flew on a DC-3 to Brazil. It was not a luxurious flight: steel seats without cushions, once-a-day stops for food and fuel, then more flying. The only break in the routine was when the pilot dove down to fly just above the treetops of the Brazilian jungle, where the natives threw spears at us. Clearly, the pilot had done this before. The plane was hardly at risk from spears, but I wondered several times what would have happened if we had been forced to land.

Finally, I was in Recife, where I went at once to the officers' club to find out where I should find *PC 493*. "Try the docks," the dumb newcomer was told, and sure enough, there was my ship baking in the sun. When I went aboard, the outgoing commanding officer was just leaving. That was unfortunate, I thought, because he seemed like a very good guy, and I sensed that his successor was a different sort of bird. And so he was, as I learned the next day. I was informed that night that the convoy we were escorting would shove off early the next morning, and I was to be Officer of the Deck (the man in charge of taking the *PC 493* to sea). I did not sleep well.

In Charge of the Ship

My task would begin with taking the ship out of the harbor, zigzagging back and forth, and keeping watch over the ships in the convoy, to make sure that no German subs sank any of them. Since I had never before had anything larger than a canoe under my command, this did not bode well. The Captain was nowhere to be seen. Fortunately, however, an Irishman named Lew Cassidy, who said he was the Engineering Officer, appeared on the bridge and told me to do what he told me. For the next four hours that's just what I did.

"Come right to one oh five," he would say, and I would say, "Come right to one oh five," in a voice loud enough for the helmsman to hear. Ten minutes later, Lew whispered, "Left to three five oh," and I repeated in an authoritative voice, "Left to three five oh." And so it went until I was finally relieved by another ensign, who seemed to know what to do.

Lew accompanied me below, and we had a cup of coffee. I thanked him profusely. "Oh, that's all right," he replied. "You'll get used to it. Captain never shows up the first two days at sea. He's always plastered and has to be poured aboard the night before we leave. It's kind of tough on a new man like you. Thought I'd better give you a hand."

We were sitting in the wardroom of the ship. A lieutenant named Joe joined us, and Lew introduced him as the Executive Officer. I didn't notice it at the time but not long afterward I observed that often when Joe was talking, his head would drop, and he would be sound asleep. This was my first exposure to narcolepsy. So, I had a captain who was a drunk and an exec with narcolepsy. Happily, neither one caused us any serious problems, and both were transferred before doing us any damage. But as long as they were on board, I never felt what you'd call easy.

Convoy Duty

We had what was said to be the second longest convoy run in the Atlantic — from Recife around the hump of South America to Trinidad and back again, and it was what you'd call b-o-r-i-n-g. It entailed anywhere from five and six weeks at sea. Only a couple of times did we see any battle action. One memorable episode gave me a real feel for the people we were fighting. Our convoy unit of a destroyer and a number of sub chasers sank a German sub on one trip and picked up some of the survivors. When we got to Recife, the tide was out when I went ashore and I happened to see a German sailor who had lost a leg, who was attempting to climb up on the dock. An American sailor leaned down, holding out his hand to help the German. The German prisoner looked up at him and spit in his face. That was my introduction to the Nazis.

Dick was a writer and editor most of his working life. Following the war, he edited American Heritage Books, and then was editor and co-owner of Blair & Ketchum's "Country Journal." He has written many books of non-fiction on American history, with a special focus on the American Revolution.

The 10th Mountain Division

★

Gordon Lowe
U.S. Army

As a high school ski racer in North Adams and with the recommendation of the National Ski Patrol, I applied for the 10th Mountain Division shortly before Pearl Harbor Day. I was accepted in early January 1942, and underwent infantry basic training at Camp Roberts, California. During that time, we practiced loading and offloading techniques using rope ladders for making transfers from ships to landing barges. I thought, "Why are we doing this? I want to be a ski trooper!" After completing basic training, I went on to join the 10th Mountain Division, 87th Infantry Brigade, which was undergoing training at Fort Lewis, Washington. Our Division then went by troopship to Alaska as part of a convoy with a large naval escort heading for the Aleutian Islands. We were to make an amphibious landing on the island of Kiska. Arising before dawn, we consumed a large breakfast, and were issued live ammunition and hand grenades for the first time.

The Aleutian Campaign

During the voyage we were told for the first time that we would be landing on the beaches of Kiska to retake the island from the Japanese. The men descended rope netting into landing barges, wearing rain gear and a good pair of boots. Provision for suitable outerwear resulted from prior experience when Army troops invaded the island of Adak lacking proper equipment, leaving many men disabled from exposure to the elements. It was very foggy and rainy. Instructed to advance to the top of a mountain, we dug foxholes and settled down for the night, unable to see more than vague shapes in front of us. Come to find out, all the Japanese troops had fled Kiska the previous day onboard submarines. The only shooting we encountered was from our own troops because of the poor visibility, which resulted in some inadvertent injuries ("friendly fire"). Since we encountered no hostilities, we were relegated to standing guard duty in the miserable Alaskan weather.

I encountered only one dead Japanese soldier, whom we came upon when searching an abandoned hospital room. We did discover that the Japanese had been building landing strips on the island to prepare for possible invasion of the U.S. mainland. The Aleutian campaign was the only WWII episode when a foreign power invaded U.S. territory. The Alaskan campaign was referred to in the Army vernacular as "JANFU", standing for "Joint Army and Navy Foul-up" (except one word was slightly different). After a time, we were issued tents with stoves so we could keep warm and dry. Shaving involved using one's helmet filled with water heated on the stove. It was rough living on Kiska, but fortunately for me, my tour there lasted only about four weeks.

I and a few other selected troops who were accomplished ski racers and jumpers were summoned to headquarters and informed we were being sent back to the States for a new assignment. There was a barge loaded with coal in the harbor whose captain told us we needed to unload a large load of 50-lb. bags of coal before we could ship out since there were no facilities for transferring supplies. Because it was no longer fully loaded, our Liberty ship pitched and rolled in the rough seas, and many of us suffered from seasickness. The ship made several stops to pick up mail along the way before we finally landed at Fort Lewis, Washington after a month.

In Seattle, we joined others destined for mountaineering training. Our group included experienced skiers, mountain climbers, and rock climbers. We were assigned a Pullman car, which was hitched and unhitched to different trains as we proceeded pokily across the continent. We had no idea where we were headed, but the food was good and we enjoyed sightseeing along the way. Three days later, we ended up at Fort Devens, Massachusetts where our mission was revealed to us but remained a war secret. It turned out that one of the men in our contingent had a mother in Lincoln, New Hampshire, and when he phoned her, she informed him, "You're coming up here for training!" She even knew what hotel (The Lincoln Hotel) we'd be staying in. Since it was autumn, we thoroughly enjoyed the New England fall scenery.

Mountaineer Training

On arrival in Lincoln, we were informed that our mission was to teach rock climbing and mountain rescue work, such as evacuating the injured and wounded in mountainous terrain. Our students coming from places like Texas had no idea what a mountain even looked like. We had to teach them how to climb, tie ropes, and the like. Half of each day we received instruction in Norwegian from two female teachers, one an old school teacher from Washington, D.C. It was all very hush, hush, and nobody was permitted to talk about it. Later, we found out that some contingents of the forces we were training had boarded troopships dressed in winter gear bound for England. The Germans erroneously surmised that the Allies were preparing to invade Norway, which was held by the Germans, in part because of the Norwegian language training program; they shifted large numbers of troops to Norway as a consequence. In the meantime, the forces we had trained who were bound for England changed uniforms and gear en route and participated in the amphibious landings in North Africa. It was a diversion that actually worked, apparently. In spite of all the warnings, people could be counted on to talk so that most everybody was aware of our "secret" training operation.

After about two months, we were given two-week furloughs and orders to Elkin, West Virginia. There I met my former captain in Kiska by the name of Ed Bailey, who lives in Burlington and is now 88 years old. I had been his jeep driver. River crossing and other water maneuvers were being taught at the school in West Virginia. Following this, I was assigned to Camp Hale and served as a ski instructor there for about a year. Camp Hale, located in Leadville, Colorado, was a terrible camp situated on a hillside overlooking a deep valley. Three locomotives were required to pull cars up the mountain to the camp. Smoke hovered in the air constantly from the stoves and furnaces which all burned soft coal, and we constantly were coughing up dark sputum. I was housed on the top of the mountain in a training area that had a T-bar lift. We taught troops to ski down the hill carrying a 90-lb. back pack. Many were complete novices because the 10th Mountain Division was pressed to reach its full complement of 15,000 men.

From Colorado, I returned to Camp Swift, Texas for additional training to qualify for the Medical Battalion of the 10th Mountain Division Battalion and was promoted to staff sergeant on completing training. Our unit functioned as the Medical Corps for the 10th Division. My responsibilities involved transporting wounded to and from field hospitals.

The Italian Campaign

The Division shipped out for Italy in early 1945. I spent Christmas Day 1944 on a troop train leaving Camp Swift, Texas bound for Newport News, Virginia where we boarded ship. We disembarked somewhere in southern Italy near Naples, then travelled overnight by LCI (Landing Craft Infantry) up the west coast to the area around Pisa. Our unit was assigned to support a field hospital in mountainous regions of northern Italy above the Po River valley. I never did get to see Rome.

The German army had retreated to this region of Italy, and our Division was going up into the mountains to finish them off. It was a terrible assignment. The Germans would set up near the summit of the mountains, establishing a last line of defense, and put down withering fire. The commanding officer of the Mountain Division, a General Wolf, had not earned his third star as yet, so he decided to make a name for himself by wiping out the German troops even though the war was winding down. If we had only waited them out for another couple of months, the war would have been all over without the terrible bloodshed our troops incurred. Our Division had a reputation as an elite outfit, and our leaders wanted to show off our stuff. We did defeat the tenacious, dug-in German army but lost 997 men and three times as many wounded. I was fortunate to escape injury but many comrades did not. We achieved our objective and World War II in Europe ended soon thereafter.

My outfit then was loaded on troopships destined for Japan. I was looking forward to the trip through the Panama Canal, another free tour thanks to Uncle Sam. While en route in the Atlantic Ocean, we sensed there had been a change of plan as the whole convoy headed northward. We learned that the first atomic bomb had been dropped at Hiroshima and we were being re-routed to the States. After a furlough, I reported back to Camp Hale, Colorado. On arrival in Denver, I was diverted to another Army camp and separated from active duty. At the time, they asked me to reenlist, but I replied, "Please, give me my discharge!" Five years of service was enough for me. I never was really an "Army guy" but I must admit I did have some wonderful experiences in spite of it all.

During infantry basic training at Camp Roberts, California, we were given an IQ test and I scored 110 or something like that. This qualified me to apply to OCS, and I inquired, "What are my chances of getting back to the 10th Mountain Division?" I was informed, "Not very good." I elected to stay with the Mountain Division and take my chances. Things worked out OK for me by so doing. I earned sergeant stripes, which had its advantages, and I commanded a platoon at times. Best of all, I met many good guys and shared a lot of beers with them!

One story involves an experienced skier from civilian life who eventually became a Second Lieutenant. His former good buddies grew to dislike him intensely because he began ordering them around with "you gotta do this, or you gotta do that!" all the time. The bar on the shoulder can change you sometimes. Another episode describes a Stowe, Vermont friend of mine, head of the Mt. Mansfield ski school. He was in charge of a light 50-caliber machine gun group whose officers all became casualties. He assumed command of the group, receiving a field commission as second lieutenant and was awarded a bronze star and two purple hearts.

Epilogue

A book has been written about the Mountain Division, entitled *The Boys of Winter*, which describes the deeds and travails of this famed outfit.[1] Fighting during the last four months of WWII in the rugged Apennine Mountains cost the Mountain Division 5,000 casualties, one of the highest rates of the war. Alumni of the Mountain Division include a president of the Sierra Club and a co-founder of Nike. Perhaps the most famous was Robert Dole, who overcame serious injuries and became U.S. Senate majority leader. The "broken down mining town" discovered by members of the Division at Camp Hale led to the ski resort Aspen, and the post-war skiing industry flourished with the opening of other world class resorts at places like Vail and Sugarbush.

Born in Schenectady, New York, and growing up in North Adams, Massachusetts, Gordon was a ski racer in high school. He joined the famed Mountain Division, serving in the Aleutian and Italian campaigns. After discharge he helped develop Dutch Hill ski area in Stamford, Vermont and managed several Mt. Mansfield facilities, including the T-bar, Spruce Peak lift, and the State of Vermont ski lodge. Moving to North Hero, he and his wife raised Highland cattle for 33 years. Interested in politics, he served in several town offices and as Town Selectman.

---

1. *The Boys of Winter.* Charles J. Sanders. Boulder, University Press of Colorado 2005.

No Sailor for This Boat

★

Robert Middleton
U.S. Army

IN LATE 1943 WHILE STATIONED IN THE ARMY at Fort Benjamin Harrison, Indianapolis, Indiana, I was sent to Camp Gordon Johnson in Florida for training in something called "Harbor Craft." This branch of the Army was set up to train units that would be called on to operate seaport facilities in Europe after the liberation. It was assumed that damaged ports would be in dire need of repair.

I had no idea why I was selected to be sent to Harbor Craft school since I had absolutely no prior experience with any sort of boat. I underwent various training exercises. One of the trials entailed attaching a tug boat to a barge. While I was manning my tug boat, it failed to stop and I managed to ram the barge. I was immediately relieved of that task and re-assigned to company headquarters, which was fine with me. I hated boats.

My company deployed to England, and after a few months, we were sent to the port of Antwerp, Belgium where I worked in the headquarters group. In Antwerp I met several people who had grand pianos, and I was able to continue playing. I never did go near a tug boat or barge again!

Recently, in going through some old letters, I came across one written to my mother from Europe. It showed that it came from XXXX (censored). My letter stated in the text: "I first went by truck to XXXX (censored), then by box car to where we are now living in XXXX (censored)." Another letter to my mother mentioned my going to an opera in Brussels, and afterward attending a party at a private mansion in XXXX (censored). My mother had scribbled on that letter: "Doesn't sound much like war, does it?"

Robert Middleton, composer, pianist, and teacher, resided after the war in Pough-keepsie, New York and New Hampshire. He was Professor of Music at Vassar College for 32 years and composed the opera, Command Performance, *performed in 1961 at the Vassar Centennial Celebration.*

Under Fire in Cannes, Mishap in Carolina

★

Bradford Patterson
U.S. Navy

D URING MY SENIOR YEAR AT HARVARD, I switched to pre-med and graduated in 1942 with a BS in Chemistry. I decided to accept a position as chemist at the DuPont plant manufacturing explosives in New Jersey, just across the Delaware River from Wilmington. This was significant because prior to our marriage, my wife Helen, who was employed across the river, and I took turns commuting by ferry when dating, which was frequently. In those days there was no Delaware River Bridge. My wife, a graduate of Radcliffe, was employed at Merck Sharpe Dohme in Wilmington. We married in 1943 and spent our honeymoon at the Helen Ross House, Weybridge, Vermont.

Receiving a U.S. Navy Commission

At Dupont, I was employed in an "essential" position in an explosive-making plant, granting me an exemption from the selective service draft. However, I had an epiphany one evening when my wife and I attended the movie, "All Quiet on the Western Front." We both were so moved by the film that we agreed to my enlisting in military service. Consequently, I applied for, and was granted, a direct commission in the U.S. Navy. A family friend, Admiral George Russell of Charlotte, Vermont was instrumental in facilitating my application and its subsequent approval. I received orders to Fort Schuyler, New York on the Hudson River for basic training, and then was assigned to PT boat training in Melville, Rhode Island, an island in Narragansett Bay.

On completing training, we were sent by troopship to join a PT squadron in Cannes, France. En route, the ship encountered a big storm and most of the troops suffered extreme seasickness. The ship's captain ordered all of the officers to go below decks to prevent full scale mutiny of the men because they were "very restive" and needed close monitoring. I recall that the deck and the gutters were running with vomit, and conditions were truly awful.

Patrolling the Coastline around Cannes

We arrived in France after the Allies had liberated much of France, but the German army still held northern Italy. Our job was to patrol from Cannes eastward to Leghorn, Italy, near Genoa, along enemy-held coastline. At that time the Sixth Army was pushing the Germans northward out of Italy toward the border. We generally patrolled about 10 miles off shore. In those days there was only primitive radar and most of our patrolling was visual. One night we must have wandered a little closer to shore than planned because we were fired on by German shore batteries, kicking up water sprays about 100 yards from us.

We enjoyed time spent ashore in Cannes, but not in Leghorn where there were few amenities. In Cannes, we were billeted in the villa of Marion Davies, situated in the nearby seaside resort of Golfe Juan. Marion Davies' personal chef prepared the food for us, and we enjoyed wonderful gourmet meals, a far cry from the usual Navy grub — shore duty in Cannes was no hardship. With the war in Europe rapidly coming to an end, some of us were transferred back to the U.S. for reassignment to form a new PT squadron at our home base in Melville, RI.

Adventure on the Inland Waterway

The new squadron was being organized in anticipation of the pending invasion of the Japanese mainland. New PT boats manufactured by Higgins Boat Company were transported to our base in Rhode Island in an LST (Landing Ship Tank), carrying the PT boats inside. The new Squadron (MTB Squadron #22) was to be based in Miami, Florida, so we proceeded with the new boats down the inland waterway, a relatively shallow and sheltered coastal water route for small boats, which extends from New York to Florida. I was the second in command of my boat.

The group proceeded to go roaring down the waterway at near maximum speed, much to the distress of shoreline residents who objected to the backwash and noise of small boat armadas such as ours. On a straight stretch of water we typically would attain speeds over 30 knots (about 40 mph). One morning when we had reached Currituck Sound in North Carolina, a large body of shallow water with a marked channel across it for navigation, I was below deck seated backwards and starting to enjoy lunch. Suddenly, without a sound the boat lurched from full speed to a dead stop over a distance of less than one boat length. Naturally, my meal ended up in my lap! Fortunately, neither I nor any of the crew was injured, but we were fast aground in a mud bank adjoining the channel. It turned out that the navigational officer and crew in charge had missed a channel marker and failed to change direction at the appropriate moment.

At the bow our boat was resting in about one foot of water, with the stern riding free. Attempts were made to dislodge the boat by another PT boat, and then by engaging a seagoing tugboat, neither of which was successful. However, this managed to rip some mooring hardware off the stern. With no prospects of imminent rescue, the crew offloaded, leaving one man on board to stand watch, and sought respite at a nearby inn along the waterway. That night there was a "neap tide" which is an unusually high tide that occurs when the moon's orbit is closest to the earth. There was also a fairly strong wind coming across the sound with lots of wave action. Sometime during the night the boat floated free, and the crewman standing watch started the engines and backed out of the mud. He proceeded to cruise down to the inn where we were quartered for the night. We awoke to the surprise of our craft moored at the dock. So this episode ended our much vaunted trip down to Florida.

Around the time of our mishap, the dropping of the first atom bomb at Hiroshima occurred. We were ordered to return to Fort Schuyler, New York on the East River where I happened to be stationed on V-J Day. Helen had joined me by this time, and we spent the evening in the city, naturally migrating to Times Square amidst the teeming celebrants. It was a memorable occasion for all to remember and celebrate. The war was finally over.

Epilogue

Our PT squadron was disbanded and I was ordered to report for duty at Green Cove Springs Navy Base near Jacksonville, Florida. The base was located near the mouth of the St. Johns River, which drains much of central and northern Florida and is an important aquifer of the state. The base was involved in decommissioning naval ships, mainly LSTs. My job was to supervise enlisted men who spent all their days "chipping paint." This boredom lasted about six months before I was discharged from active duty as Lieutenant, Junior Grade, USNR.

My undergraduate degree met all the requirements for medical school except for one course, which Harvard allowed me to take while awaiting matriculation, and I took the required course at UVM summer school. My family had a summer camp on Long Point, Lake Champlain and I commuted to the campus daily. Following my surgical training and private practice in the Boston area, my wife and I decided to move to Weybridge, Vermont where I specialized in cancer treatment and practiced in the Rutland area for a decade before retiring from medicine.

Born June 25, 1921 in New Rochelle, New York, Brad grew up in West Hartford, Connecticut. While enrolled in the accelerated wartime curriculum at Harvard, he found time for diving on the varsity swim team. After graduation, Brad was a chemist at DuPont before enlisting in the Navy. After the war, he attended Harvard Medical School followed by a surgical residency at the Peter Bent Brigham Hospital under the tutelage of the renowned physician Francis Moore, MD.

Escapades of a Combat Engineer

★

Benjamin Schweyer
U.S. Army

A T AGE 18 AS AN ENLISTED MAN in the Army Reserve Corps, Ben Schweyer decided he wanted to go on active duty sooner rather than later, and wrote a letter requesting activation. While in the Army special Training Program (ASTP) at Norwich University, he was taking an engineering course. That was all it took — he soon found himself enrolled in a 17-week combat engineer course at Fort Belvoir, Virginia. Quickly he became a Private First Class in Company C, 303rd Engineer Battalion. The 303rd was being readied to take on engineering projects that confronted the 78th Infantry Division during the fighting in the Europe.

These events were taking place in late 1944 when Ben's battalion shipped out of New York Port of Embarkation aboard the *USS John Ericksson,* flagship of a convoy headed for Southampton, England. Their stay in England was short-lived, however — just long enough to receive additional equipment, trucks, jeeps, and other supplies needed for the tasks ahead.

On November 19 they crossed the English Channel and quickly moved up to the front near Herderen, Belgium, where they were issued weapons, ammunition, bazookas, and grenades. So armed, they moved on to Rotgen, Germany, where the first contact with the enemy took place. Their initial assignment was to assist the 78th Division capture the largest and most important dam on the Roer River, the Schwammenauel Dam. If the Germans breached this dam, a wall of water — more than 22 billion gallons — would go pummeling down river and wash out the attempt at Allied river crossing. This could potentially cut off a bridgehead on the far side of the river, putting advancing troops beyond rescue. Allied troops could not safely bridge the river until the dam was taken and secured.

Breaching the Siegfried Line

Capturing the dam was a tough assignment for the 78th Division and our Engineer Battalion. Reaching it would require blasting a roadway through Germany's Siegfried Line, the defense line opposite the French Maginot Line. The objective assigned to C Company was to slip into the fortifications and blow up the pillboxes, a task made extra-dangerous by extensive use by the Germans of hidden mines and booby traps, in which they were expert. Most hated of the Nazi weapons was the "schu" mine, which contained just enough explosive to blow off a foot when stepped on and set off.

It was December, bitterly cold, with heavy snows. Ben and a mate drew the assignment of being escorted by some infantrymen driving a Weasel snow vehicle to the Roer River five miles downstream from the dam. There, the Engineers were to measure the speed of the current — information needed in order to know which military vessels could withstand the velocity of the flowing water. Despite being spotted by German soldiers on the far side of the river and subjected to mortar fire, Ben and his crew made the trip unharmed and returned with the vital data.

Both the 78th and the Engineers had many men maimed and killed in the effort to pierce the Siegfried Line. But then, the effort had to be put on hold because Hitler and his general staff launched an offensive in the Ardennes, a desperate last ditch effort to defeat the Allies which became known as the Battle of the Bulge.

Battle of the Bulge

The 78th Infantry Division was in a pivotal position along the upper corner of the Bulge, opposing the attacking German troops and weapons. Their job was to anchor that region of the breakthrough and prevent the Germans from making progress northward. By then, the Americans in the region were under the command of General Bernard Montgomery ("Monty"). Monty was a defensive-minded leader and issued orders to hold the line at all costs. He wanted in-depth minefields laid to block the Nazi push. And of course, it was the job of the Engineers to place the thousands of mines required to accomplish this. To dig the mines into the frozen earth was too much to ask. Ben and his fellow engineers simply positioned the mines and let the snow cover them over. These resourceful units constructed sleds on which to transport the mines instead of having a hard slog in heavy snow on foot.

Montgomery's strategy placed the Division and its Engineers directly athwart the path Hitler had plotted for his troops to move north to the coast, reviving German hopes in the war. His plan was to drive north to Antwerp, Belgium and insert a wedge between the American and British forces. By isolating the British, he hoped to massacre their forces and so dishearten the British people that they would withdraw from the conflict on the continent. It was the scheme of a desperate madman, with scant chance of success, especially as the German tanks rapidly outran gas supplies and were denied access to the large Allied fuel dumps.

Capturing a Dam

After the Ardennes drive was repulsed with great losses of troops on both sides, the 78th with the 303rd Engineer Battalion resumed the offensive and attempted to take the dam. Now, the Nazi resistance was weaker but still tenacious. With the Engineers blasting the German pillboxes out of the way, the 78th was able on February 10, 1945 to seize the dam and remove the Roer's potential threat to Allied thrusts into German territory. Before the Roer could be crossed, a bridge had to be built, another job for the Engineers. They had to accomplish this under artillery fire coming from the far side of the river. With the bridge in place, Allied infantry poured across the Roer, and as the Battalion's official history puts it, "without the great number of casualties that usually accompany a river crossing."

A race to the Rhine River now began. The Germans were in such rapid retreat that they could no longer lay minefields. The result for the Allied forces was a high-powered plunge to the last major natural barrier on the way to Berlin — the Rhine River. At this point, the weary combat Engineers were relieved to find they would not be called on to build a bridge over the Rhine. This was to be the job of the Corps of Engineers, which had the necessary heavy equipment. The Engineers also benefitted from the historic capture of the Remagen Bridge over the river — the bridge that the retreating Germans succeeded in only partially destroying and which would be used for the crossing of thousands of Allied troops along with their armor.

End of the War in Europe

Ben's unit crossed the Remagen Bridge amongst the very earliest troops and awaited their next assignment there. Along the Rhine River they found many abandoned German boats. They tinkered with two of the larger ones, got them to working, and used them to ferry wounded men across to medical facilities on the western side.

Their next duty was to protect the left flank of the U.S. Army in the drive to encircle the vital Ruhr industrial valley. In 11 days, the Allied encirclement netted more than 47,000 German military, including several Nazi generals. On May 8, 1945 Germany surrendered.

As the war approached its end, the Army tried to woo GIs into signing up for post-war reserve corps by offering them promotions. Ben was promoted to corporal and then to sergeant. But he resisted the Army's blandishments — he had had enough of the military for a lifetime. More deservedly, he received the Army Distinguished Unit Badge as an added adornment to accompany his battle ribbons. Taking advantage of the GI Bill of Rights, after the war Ben earned his college and law degrees and practiced law for 45 years before retiring.

Born in Owego, New York, Ben grew up in Burlington, Vermont, enrolled in Norwich University, and enlisted in the Army. He served in the European theater as a combat engineer. A graduate of the University of Vermont and the University of Pennsylvania Law School, he was partner in a Burlington law firm, a director of the Merchants Bank, and an adjunct Professor at UVM.

THE CAISSONS GO ROLLING ALONG

★

Leo Spellman
U.S. Army

AT AGE 95 YEARS, Leo Spellman is among the oldest Wake Robin residents and a veteran of World War II. These are some of his reminiscences related in an oral history, to which he added, "I may have gotten things a little mixed up:"

I was the first one to be drafted from my section of the country — the Lake Placid region. I lived in Elizabethtown, New York. At 28 years of age and unmarried, I was classified as 1-A in the selective service and was among the first to be drafted. I was inducted into the U.S. Army at Fort Dix, New Jersey. That winter New Jersey was very cold so we were issued heavy long underwear. We were all lined up outside the tent at Fort Dix, and stood in line; there were 81 of us. The Second Lieutenant came along the line and said, "You're going to the 8th Army, and you'll go to the Field Artillery."

Field Artillery

So I went to North Carolina in the field artillery, 8th Army, A Battery. The guns were brand new, never used World War I weapons. Can you imagine? We got a 240 mm cannon. It took seven tractors to move the darn thing, plus I don't know how many men, I couldn't count them. I was given the job to work the phones (for positioning the gun on enemy targets). I was asking how to run the phones, they were always fouled up. We went out into the field with this big gun, but they finally figured out that it was no good. After a year or so, they threw out the 240 mm guns and brought in light artillery instead.

This was before Pearl Harbor. We stayed there for quite some time. I had gone directly to the Field Artillery but new soldiers after that had to first go through basic training, and that was tough. I was happy to avoid that. Since we were in North Carolina, I could go to the beach every weekend, and we had great times. I liked the seashore. I was there for a year or more. Then, they sent us to Tennessee in the mud. We stayed there about another year.

We went overseas on the liner *Queen Mary* to somewhere off the coast of Ireland. We waited there off shore for some time before an okay was given to go ashore. We got into smaller boats and were taken to England where we were under English command, for some reason. We had kidney stew — it was terrible! I felt sick when I ate it. I had a chance to get hold of some Hershey bars so I bought a lot of them and lived on them.

Arrival in Europe

It was just before the breakthrough — when the Germans attacked and broke through into the Netherlands. The U.S. Army was also fighting in Italy at the same time. We had moved across Europe in trucks in a blackout. That was a nightmare. The truck I was riding in slammed up against another truck and really shook us all up, all 12 or 14 of us in the back. I wasn't hurt too bad, but they did bring us to the hospital. The drivers were drunk.

We went to the Netherlands to fight the Germans in the mud. I got sent into battle by air, at night, in a glider. We were fortunate, for you know the Germans had "barrage balloons" to interfere with flying craft. The gliders were attached to a big plane, and we were unhooked and dropped off. Our guns also were dropped in by parachutes. I landed in an apple orchard in a tree somewhere in France. It was winter and the trees were bare. Some Frenchmen came by and helped me, I was hurt. After I got better, they told me I should go back in the Army so they got in touch with the Americans. I returned but was assigned to another Army outfit. It was hard trying to find a place to sleep in the mud. Somehow, I got through all that stuff. It was quite a battle and lasted pretty near a year.

I was part of General Patton's army then. Somehow I got into the headquarters group. I was a typist, so instead of a gun, I carried a typewriter with me. We lived in a French settlement and were housed in a great big building. Patton was an old soldier, and had been in the army when they had horses and mules. What a character he was. He wore those high cowboy boots. He was not very popular with the soldiers, especially the West Pointers. I didn't like him. I was in the unit under a General Lentz. He was a West Pointer and a serious guy. He was writing a series of articles on the Army field artillery. I took all this down in short-hand because before I was in the Army, I had gone to Albany Business School for a short time and learned it there.

We moved wherever Patton went. He was an awful guy. I don't think Patton was one to worry about the men under him. I remember one time we were riding in a jeep with no top on it, going down a road. For some reason, he told his driver to stop. He stood up and opened fire with his pistols, I don't know why. Patton always had a dog with him. The dog was well trained, of medium size, with short hair, and rode in the jeep.

Patton's Army went down into Germany, then into Czechoslovakia. He was powerful and could do almost as he pleased. He was preparing for a big push all the way to Moscow. Eisenhower or some of his lieutenants heard about this and shut off his supplies of ammunition.

They even restricted his food supplies, and we had to go on war rations. They kept us on that for a few days so he would change his plans. He was nuts!

End of the War

The war in Europe finally got over, and the Germans had surrendered. I spent quite a while in Czechoslovakia. I was in a family home where we had living quarters. The meals were prepared in the central part of town. We spent a long time there. Just to keep busy, they gave us lots of time off, and had light airplanes fly us to England. I went on one of those trips, and that was enough, I didn't want any more of it. I never got out too much in a social way.

When we were leaving, I went to France because they wanted to show us Normandy. From there we went back to England, then home. It was an awful trip on a converted ship that went on for days and days. I heard later that others in my outfit had come home by air while I went through this terrible trip by boat. I don't know why they did that to the soldiers that had been fighting over in Europe so long. We were down in the lower decks where there were bunk beds about four or five feet high. The waves were coming into the bathroom, and the water washed down the stairs right into the bunkrooms. It was punishment being on those old ships.

Epilogue

I had been a sergeant in the Army. Some fellows in my outfit were much better off when they got a commission. I was glad to get out of the service because I was sick and tired of it. I never went back to France, I never wanted to.

Note: Leo Spellman died April 9, 2008.

Stateside
Service

Training Pilots: a WAVE's Story

★

Elise Barash
U.S. Navy

I WAS 28 YEARS OF AGE WHEN I JOINED the Navy in December 1943. At the time I had been working in New York City as a secretary for *Town and Country* magazine. With the war underway, I felt everyone had to try to do something to be of service. So I was one of the earliest women to join the WAVES (Women Accepted for Voluntary Emergency Service). This uniformed military service of the U.S. Navy was authorized in Congressional legislation signed by President Roosevelt July 20, 1942 to alleviate projected shortages of uniformed personnel. As a result Lt. Commander Mildred McAfee became the first female commissioned officer in U.S. Navy history. The demand for women was great, and in the first year 27,000 women enlisted. By war's end, nearly 100,000 women had served in the Navy, including 8,000 as officers.

WAVES Training

The Navy was prepared to accept large numbers of enlisted women in the WAVES and needed female commissioned officers to supervise them. I was in the first group to graduate from WAVES Officer Training School. It was an entirely new and different experience for all of us, and we just took each day as it came along. Most of the rules they laid down for us candidates had to do with preventing us from going into the men's barracks or officers' quarters.

When I joined the WAVES, I was assigned to the U.S. Naval Training School in Cedar Falls, Iowa, for basic training. Then I was sent to Link Trainer Instructor School in Atlanta, Georgia. Next, I entered the Officer Training School in Northampton, Massachusetts, where I received my commission as an Ensign. Finally, I was assigned as a Link Trainer Instructor in Miami, Florida.

Link Trainer Instrument Flying

The purpose of the Link Trainer was to provide future pilots their first taste of being in an airplane cockpit and having to rely on instruments to fly. Each Trainer was an airplane fuselage-shaped piece of equipment on a pedestal with a simulated cockpit. About 50 Link Trainers were set up in a large gym-like space in our Miami facility. My job was to program the flight simulators and monitor performance; monitors were enclosed and fully darkened with no external light, so that the future pilots could get the feel of a cockpit and learn to operate "blind" and strictly by instruments.

Most of the young men we trained were just kids, 19 or 20 years of age maybe, and were generally scared. We were supposed to assess which ones might become good pilots. I made sure they knew what they were getting into. They would have to learn to land on a moving aircraft carrier, a very risky business. That was part of the simulation experience. I tried hard to be sure that they developed the best possible skills so they could take the next step, which involved having to fly in over the swamp and learn to land on a carrier deck. The swamp was enormous, with the carrier just beyond it and cruising back and forth. So they were scared about flying a plane for the first time, and also the possibility of going down into a huge swamp. A lot of them did go down, but we were able to rescue them all.

One young man in particular sticks in my mind because he made many mistakes in the Link trainer. If it had been a real plane, he surely would have crashed. I'll never forget it; I was so concerned about him, I reviewed his "jacket" (personnel file) to learn more of his history. Flight training was serious business, because what he did could mean someone's life, his as well as another's. I discussed this with him and talked with my superior. We decided to meet, and we three sat around in a circle. The whole time he was fussing with his hands and crying. We finally learned that it was his father who so badly wanted him to become a pilot, not himself. He was scared to death that his father would be angry with him if he washed out of pilot training. We counseled him to give up becoming a pilot, and recommended him for another assignment in the Navy to allow him to serve honorably and make his father proud.

Social Life of a WAVE

During training time before officer candidate school, the other WAVES and I had a lot of fun. We would go out with officers or men in training. Mostly, we dated officers because we were older than the enlisted men. We went out dancing often, and maybe joined the men for dinner in the mess hall, all pretty informal. My close friend Sue Ahn, a Korean American, was also a Link Trainer Instructor. I was most impressed by her and her family. They had some very tough times because of being Korean-American. I loved her spirit, and we stayed in touch for the rest of our lives, seeing each other on occasion after the war ended.

The toughest part of my job as a WAVE officer who was responsible for training future pilots was the realization that some of these boys would not be coming back. We all tried not to think about that — we avoided reflecting on the future. That's why having fun mattered to us. It helped us avoid thinking about the horrible things that might happen later to these men when they were in combat.

I was called upon at some point in my career to deliver by hand a written message to my superior officer at his residence. It was late in the evening and he met me at the door in his pajamas.

"Shall I salute you, sir?" I asked.

"Darned if I know," he replied.

My official date of separation from the Navy was December 23, 1945, well after the Japanese surrender and the war's end. I was discharged from the Naval Reserve November 19, 1952; we all were kept in the Reserves up to 7 years, just in case. I still see in my mind's eye my days as a WAVE — people, places, and things from 60 years ago.

After her three years service in the U.S. Navy, Elise worked in the journalism field for several magazines and newspapers. She has a long-standing interest in historical research and had served as a board member and chair of Pennswood Village, a retirement community in Bucks County, Pennsylvania before becoming a Wake Robin resident.

German POWs in Appalachia

★

Bruce Campbell
U.S. Army

As members of the elite German Afrika Corps marched along Route 60 in West Virginia to a prisoner of war (POW) camp, Italian prisoners from the same North African campaign were leaving the camp to be transferred to another location in the mid-West. The two groups purposely were hidden from each other by a mound separating them on Route 60, so that the two contingents would avoid seeing each other in passing. There was known animosity between members of this elite German Corps and their Italian counterparts, whom they regarded as quitters.

That was my introduction to the POW Camp 1514th Service Unit at White Sulphur Springs on the grounds of the resort Greenbrier Hotel, which had morphed into Ashford General Hospital. It was 1943, the year of my induction into the U.S. Army. At the POW camp were GIs who formerly had been classified 4-F because of a medical deferment but later were reclassified 1-A (fit for limited duty). Most of us had undergone no formal basic training. We were housed in a former Civilian Conservation Corps (CCC) campsite left over from the Great Depression days. Only two of us were college graduates; the rest from West Virginia and Kentucky had very little education. This was the lot of those of us who had once been 4-F.

Military Drills

The detachment Colonel decided that this raggle-taggle group lacked training and needed drilling in how to march in formation properly. All men not on guard duty lined up near the front gate outside the prison compound. Our Company Commander, with the Colonel over-seeing, ordered:

"Line up two by two!"

And then yelled:

"You have to face in the same direction!"

The he barked out:

"I said by twos, not threes!"

By this time a large audience of German POWs was lining the fence, intrigued by the goings-on. They started to laugh. Our CO next shouted:

"About face!"

Some men turned correctly, some the wrong way. More and more prisoners lined up at the fence, and their rollicking laughter rose to a din. Just then fog rolled in from the hills of West Virginia as we received the order:

"Forward march!"

A dense mist enveloped the group of marchers, who marched off, gradually disappearing from his view in the fog. The CO roared:

"Halt! Halt!"

The last utterances we could hear were:

"Stop, stop! Oh, to hell with it."

In apparent disgust, the Colonel stomped off as the marching drill abruptly ended. The company never was reassembled for marching drills during my two years there.

A Surprise Visit

Ashford General Hospital with its airport, golf course, and magnificent swimming facilities was a prime spot for R&R for WWII brass. The PW Camp contingent was surprised when we learned that the Duke and Duchess of Windsor had asked to visit the camp. We were instructed to stand at attention along the road and salute as the Duke and his Duchess passed by. They approached the Greenbrier riding in a large convertible touring vehicle with the Duchess waving and the Duke standing. I noticed that our men up the line were snickering. By the time the car passed me on the gravel road, the snicker had turned into full laughter. The Duke's fly was wide open, and he and the Duchess were quite unaware. To this day, I shall remember the Duke of Windsor, the former King Edward VIII who renounced the throne of Britain for the American divorcee Wallis Simpson — with his fly open.

German Prisoners

The prisoners were treated by prison staff with respect: they were paid a modest sum for working in the hospital or harvesting apples in the nearby orchards; they were permitted to have their own cooks; they were provided reading materials. They could hear the constant drum of nearby rail traffic on the Chesapeake & Ohio Railroad carrying coal to supply our Allied forces. They thought the war news to be all propaganda until they were required to view footage taken at the liberation of the German concentration camps. They remained stunned in total silence.

Most of the POWs spoke little English. One prisoner who spoke creditable English worked with me at the 1514th headquarters translating into German any orders for the prisoners. I had little social interaction with this very taciturn man, who did his job in silence most of the time. Two prisoners escaped into the West Virginia countryside while I was at the camp. These two returned within 24 hours, voluntarily, after finding the Appalachian countryside daunting.

I was very happy at the end of 1946 when I was mustered out of the Army, having spent three years at the camp. I looked forward to getting on with married life.

Bruce grew up in Cleveland Heights, Ohio and graduated from Allegheny College. After the war he married, residing in Cleveland with his family, and became Director of Sales for the Automotive Paint Division of the Sherwin-Williams Company. He is the author of two books, Scotland: A Field Guide to its History *and* British Rulers and Their Queens. *The latter volume enjoys continuing sales since the year 2000 in the bookshop of Westminster Abbey in London.*

Incident at 8,000 Feet

★

Rudyard Colter
U.S. Navy

THE YEAR IS 1944. Early morning sun shines roseate on the silver fuselage of my twin-engine plane as it rises over the Chesapeake, banks a two-needle width turn and heads out over the ocean. It's the start of a routine Naval Air Transport Service flight to the island of Bermuda. Having climbed to 9,000 feet to take advantage of the favorable winds aloft, I turn the controls over to the copilot and tune into the Berlin Philharmonic playing Beethoven's Seventh. All routine.

Some three hours later, the sharp-eyed copilot abruptly levels binoculars on the forward horizon. "Submarine — submarine — bearing 025 degrees!" Rapid thumbing of the ID silhouette cards confirms a surfaced German U-boat's conning tower, crash-diving. Break radio silence! Warn Bermuda control! Enemy sub position, course and speed go out in clear language. With the message confirmed and transmission completed, the plane resumes its scheduled course and lands at Kindley Field, Bermuda.

Meanwhile, the call for "General Quarters" shatters military routine throughout the armed island. U.S., British and Canadian navies scramble patrol bombers and deploy anti-submarine ships. Then follow three harrowing days of the deadly cat and mouse game: hunting — finding — depth charging — losing — seeking — wounding the quarry. Finally, leaking fuel and losing seaworthiness, the U-boat is forced to surface. The crew scuttles the vessel, and all are taken captive, including the captain.

Several weeks later, after interrogation, the U-boat commander is ordered under marine guard to a POW camp in South Carolina. By coincidence, the same plane and crew that had spotted the U-boat is again in Bermuda, ready for the return flight to Patuxent River Naval Air Station in Maryland. Among the passengers are the U-Boat captain and his guard.

Another routine flight? Not quite. The passenger configuration of that workhorse plane of WWII, the rugged, dependable DC-3, features two lines of unpadded aluminum bucket seats along the sides of the fuselage. Up forward, just aft of the cockpit door, are four leather, upholstered, so-called MacArthur chairs reserved for VIPs. On this run they are occupied by wounded servicemen with a medical corpsman attending. The prisoner and his guard are assigned two of the bucket seats.

Cleared for takeoff, as pilot I take the U.S.-bound plane to the designated altitude of 8000 feet. Then we level off, correcting the course, throttling back to cruising rpm, trimming for straight and level attitude, and leaning out the fuel/air mixture for optimum cruising speed and fuel consumption. Flying over blue water, all pilots are conservationists. However, on this particular flight for some reason the plane refuses to trim down to a straight and level course, but instead gently porpoises up and down, a gas-wasting motion. After adjusting the trim tabs again and again, finally in frustration the copilot heads aft to investigate a possible cause in the cabin. Returning, he reports that the U-boat commander is stamping up and down the length of the compartment citing the Geneva Convention and demanding a MacArthur chair as befits his rank. His constantly shifting 200 pounds is enough to upset the weight and balance ratio necessary to a perfectly trimmed, level flight.

Again, the copilot is dispatched to restore order and quiet. However, angry and arrogant insistence upon his rights of rank is the only response. The plane's porpoising continues. At this, I yield the controls to the copilot. I two-block my tie, don my Lt.jg. uniform jacket and gold braid hat, strap on my ammo belt and 38-caliber Smith and Wesson service revolver, and dramatically throw open the cabin door, then march down the aisle, right quarter-turn before the marine guard and the now seated German prisoner. Jerking my head up, I lead the rising marine in a formal salute.

"Sergeant, if this prisoner gives any further trouble — shoot him!" Both salute, with only the marine catching the broad, private wink. Then I march back to the cockpit, knowing, as the guard knows and all in earshot know, this breaks U.S. Navy regs. The prisoner, however, knows only Nazi customs.

The rest of the flight? Routine all the way.

Born in Washington D.C., Rud grew up in New York City, attended New York University and George Washington University, and pursued a career in advertising and marketing. He and his family lived in Madison, New Jersey, and enjoyed skiing and boating.

WAVE under the Weather

★

Marianna Grimes
U.S. Navy

T HE DAY JAPAN BOMBED PEARL HARBOR I was a freshman at
Antioch in my hometown of Yellow Springs, Ohio. I was studying
in my dorm room, with the NBC symphony playing on the radio. Sud-
denly, the music was interrupted by news of the attack on Pearl Harbor.
Two years later, my scholarship having expired, I enlisted in the U.S.
Navy as a WAVE. In early September I was on the train bound for
New York along with other enlistees headed for basic training at the
Bronx campus of Hunter College. At Grand Central station a WAVES
officer met us and herded us up the stairs to catch a subway to the
Bronx. There, she abruptly barked, "Up against the bulkhead, Seamen!"
— our introduction to Navy lingo and discipline.

Induction into the WAVES

Our quarters were in an apartment building adjacent to the campus
— six of us in one large room, five from various states and the sixth, a

refugee from Nazi Germany. We all spoke with different accents. Our six weeks of training comprised daily marching drills, learning Navy history, military protocol, and viewing films like "Why We Fight." Our graduation ceremony was on the football field, where our marching smartly down the field validated the weeks of drilling. I was told I would be assigned to shore patrol duty. On one occasion, I was in the lobby of the Paramount Theater on Broadway where a WAVE contingent was attending a Frank Sinatra performance. I vividly recall the screaming and boisterous carryings-on of the excited audience, mostly young girls.

Next, I received orders for training to be a weather observer, and in November I reported to the training school in Lakehurst, New Jersey for Navy and Marine male and female seamen. We had a crash course in the basic physics of atmosphere, learning how to read and repair instruments for recording temperature, humidity, wind speed and direction, and barometric pressure. We became proficient in identifying cloud formations at different altitudes. Receiving data by teletype from weather stations around the country, we learned to prepare weather maps. This involved laboriously recording tiny symbols and numbers on pre-printed maps that showed the location of the reporting stations with a small circle. Later a meteorologist officer would analyze the data and prepare the weather forecast.

During the weekly inspection ritual outdoors ("Captain's Inspection"), I recall standing in formation next to the flag-bearer with Old Glory flapping in my face on cold, dreary days of late autumn. Another time toward the end of training, as I was alone studying in a classroom, the radio in the next room started playing the national anthem. Suddenly the classroom door burst open, and a petty officer cried out, "On your feet, seaman!" I scrambled to my feet, my hand over my heart.

I spent one weekend in New York City, away from Lakehurst. The USO provided me with a ticket for a Sunday afternoon concert at Carnegie Hall. The conductor, Bruno Walter, was indisposed and was replaced by his assistant, a handsome, energetic young man who received a tumultuous response from the audience. We had a marvelous view of Leonard Bernstein's debut as a conductor.

First Duty Assignment

I was promoted to Aerographers Mate, Third Class (petty officer) and was assigned to the Naval Air Station outside Clinton, Oklahoma. Five seamen and one meteorologist (a Lieutenant) comprised our office staff. By late January 1944 I was confident about participating in the daily weather observations and map-making.

We experienced some extreme weather events: thunderstorms, dust storms, blizzards, even tornados close by. During the thunderstorms, ball lightning hit the ground, seeming more threatening to me than the familiar streak-lightning. During dust storms, grit seeped through tightly closed windows and doors, covering every surface, including clothing, bedding, and all our weather-observation equipment, even aircraft in the hangars. These storms were a great nuisance, though it made for some gorgeous, rosy sunrises and sunsets. A terrible blizzard struck at the end of March. Gale force wind sent tumbleweeds rolling across fields at breakneck speed. No planes could fly — it was nearly impossible to walk outside in the storm.

One evening the weather office told the station captain there was a tornado in the area, headed our way. He issued a Red Alert, which meant that planes had to fly out of danger or else be tethered to the ground. I was asked to join the control tower operator to watch for the tornado, but we couldn't see anything beyond the heavy rain lashing the windows. However, we could hear the storm's howling and feel the building sway. It was the scariest few hours of my life. The tornado didn't strike us directly, but there was significant damage in a nearby town, including ripping off the roof of the movie theater.

On one lovely spring day I flew in a plane equipped with weather-measuring instruments, flying high up in the atmosphere. In a jump-suit, wearing a helmet and strapped into a parachute, I climbed into the open cockpit seat behind the pilot. We climbed to about 10,000 feet, then slowly headed earthward, so for a few seconds we were look-ing down at the cloud formations I had had to learn about as well as the Oklahoma countryside. No plane trip I've taken since has been as thrilling. Later that spring, I contracted measles and spent two weeks in a darkened room in sick bay, forbidden to read or have visitors. My only contact with the outside world consisted of the nurse and the radio (sadly, no VPR).

Washington, D.C. Duty

Soon after D-Day, two men from our weather office were shipped to the Pacific, and shortly thereafter I was transferred to Washington, D.C. Naval Intelligence had taken over a private girls' school near American University. We were quartered in a colony of newly-built barracks across the street from the school, four to a cubicle, each containing two double-decker bunks. We worked in eight-hour shifts, changing shifts every two weeks. The work was weather-related, but we conducted no observations of our own; we were engaged in decoding Japanese weather forecasts for the Pacific region. Since neither the office nor the barracks was air-conditioned, the climate in summer was often almost unbearably hot and humid. During one shift I was sleeping fitfully in the afternoon when someone woke me to say that President Roosevelt had died.

In 1945, the Navy began to recruit negro women. Those who came to WAVE Quarters D were all housed in one barracks and all of them, regardless of qualifications, were employed in the mess hall. Many women of southern origin in our unit were agitated by the influx of blacks, including one in my cubicle from Mississippi.

We enjoyed lots of sightseeing around Washington and other leisure activities. A group of us took an overnight ferry-boat round trip from Washington, D.C. to Virginia Beach, the only time in my short Navy career that I was actually at sea. I attended a concert of the National Symphony Orchestra at Watergate on the Potomac River near the Lincoln Memorial, where the orchestra played on a barge anchored on the river and the audience sat on the river bank. It was so hot I took off my uniform cap (against protocol). As at every public performance, the national anthem was played, and I heard a person behind me inquire, "How do you know whether to salute or not?" The man answered, "It depends on whether you think you're outside, or not."

In September after the war ended, I was transferred to the Naval Air Station in Willow Grove, Pennsylvania. I was the only seaman in the weather office, and worked the shift from 0600 to 1800 hours (12 hours), making weather observations and preparing weather maps. One weekend, I visited the family of a college friend in a suburb of Philadelphia. We went to hear the Philadelphia Symphony Orchestra and enjoyed the fabulous acoustics of the fabled Symphony Hall.

One weekend after I had returned to Washington, I visited relatives of another college friend. I rang the bell and was stunned to see an arm with three gold stripes on its sleeve reaching to open the door. She hadn't warned me that her father-in-law was a Navy Vice-Admiral. Seeing my obvious embarrassment, he quickly put me at ease, and I went on to enjoy the evening. The next day I attended a piano concert in Constitution Hall. The man next to me nudged me a couple times to offer me his opera glasses, but I declined. Afterwards, he said he had wanted me to observe President Truman seated in the loge below, following the score in his lap as he listened to the music.

On December 7, 1945, Pearl Harbor Day, I was discharged from the Navy at the Great Lakes Naval Air Station in Chicago, exactly four years after the attack. I returned home to Yellow Springs. That was some weeks prior to the return of my Army brother from Europe and my Navy brother in the Pacific, both of whom had served their country much longer than I.

Marianna, who was born and grew up in Yellow Springs, Ohio, attended Antioch College before the war. After military service and graduation from the University of California at Berkeley in 1948, Marianna worked with UNESCO in New York and Paris for over 29 years. In her retirement years in Vermont she served as Brookfield, Vermont librarian before becoming a Wake Robin resident.

How I Became a Mathematician

★

John W. Heisse
U.S. Navy

On Pearl Harbor Sunday, I attended a party with my parents, and while there, news of the attack was broadcast over the radio. My father, a Regular Army major who was assigned to Fort Holabird, Maryland realized he would be reassigned immediately. A University of Pennsylvania graduate, my father was promptly transferred to the Pentagon where he spent the remainder of the war as a colonel. During the first semester of my final year of high school, my father's superior officer, a general, presented his staff with a complicated mathematical problem that no one could solve. My father brought it home and over one weekend I solved it to the general's satisfaction. I have always thought this might have had something to do with my military career always being pointed towards mathematics.

When I was a senior in high school at age 16, I enlisted in the Navy with my parent's permission, with the proviso that I would be allowed to graduate before going on active duty. My father had advised me to enlist early and to join the Navy rather than be drafted into the Army because he had been an infantry officer who served in France during World War I. Based on his experience, he strongly advised that I avoid ever having to sleep in a foxhole by becoming a foot soldier,

Following high school I entered the Navy as Seaman, First Class (equivalent to Corporal). I was assigned to Johns Hopkins University as a freshman, essentially as a civilian college student. Because I had scored very high on achievement tests in school, the Navy wanted me to major in science and to take several mathematics courses. After completing a year at JHU, I received orders for Navy basic training at Great Lakes Naval Station.

Great Lakes was awash in sailors who were arriving there for Navy basic training. We had to learn the basics of marching (I was the guide-on), weapons use, and some gunnery. I recall vividly that one of our training activities was firing guns from shipboard out on Lake Michigan. On completing basic training, I was given two weeks' leave and took the train home to Washington to see my father and spend time with the family.

Training in Electronics

My initial schooling in electronics took place in a Chicago high school that the Navy had taken over for the duration of WWII. There were about 200 students housed there in the gymnasium of the school. There was a cooking crew assigned to our school, and of course, we all drew KP duty! WWII ended while I was stationed at that facility.

After two months of training, I received orders for the Navy base at Gulfport, Mississippi. The base was located on godforsaken swampland that one of the Mississippi Congressional representatives in Washington D.C. had sold to the government! It was cold, wet, muddy, and required plank boardwalks between most of the buildings. It was the coldest and most miserable I can ever remember. One good thing about Gulfport was the fact that Italian POWs prepared all the meals, and the food was generally great. I spent about six months there for additional schooling in how to troubleshoot and repair electronic equipment. Generally speaking, civilians we encountered in the South were not very friendly or supportive, unlike Chicago where meal checks and drinks were usually picked up by the non-military folks we encountered. In Gulfport there were about 60,000 military and only 10,000 civilian population. My favorite recreation was to check into a Gulf Coast hotel, either in New Orleans or Mobile, Alabama, and spend the weekend bathed in luxury (after all, I was making $44/mo. pay with room and board provided!). Family friends in Mobile also were very hospitable when I was in town.

Next, I was ordered to the Naval Research Laboratory, located adjacent to Anacostia on the Potomac River below Washington, D.C. This naval base actually sits atop the sewage disposal area for DC (perhaps it was part of a ruse to locate it there?). On completing training, I was promoted to petty officer rank, Electronic Technicians Mate, 3rd Class (comparable to Sergeant). My time in the Washington area I recall as being pleasant. My father was stationed there while the rest of my family remained in Baltimore, so we two often spent free time together. My duties included being the company driver for officers at the Research Labs who needed transportation off-base. I found it interesting that most senior officers remained reticent en route, while junior officers tended to be talkative. One of our activities at the base was to build TVs for the high ranking officers. TV was just becoming available to the populace, and the admirals wanted to watch boxing, which at that time was one of the mainstays of evening TV (along with the Milton Berle show, "The Texaco Hour").

My one bout of "sea duty" came about when a destroyer coming up the Potomac River somewhere near Mt. Vernon required repair of the ship's radar in order to receive permission to proceed further up river. I took a small boat from the Naval Research Labs downriver to the destroyer and spent perhaps half a day making repairs. Other duties at NRL included standing guard duty periodically on the one escort ship permanently stationed at the naval labs. Because of my duties as company driver, I did not have to do guard duty as often as the other enlisted men.

Epilogue

Once basic training was over with, I enjoyed my military experience, in part because it offered a structured environment and was very goal-directed. My technical training involved a good deal of study. We were often given practical problems where a component had been removed from a radar or piece of equipment, and we had to figure out how to diagnose and repair it. Perhaps, one can compare it to medical practice where clinical problems can be daunting and often require astute diagnosis. When my tour ended in 1947, I thought seriously about staying in the Navy because I liked the life. By and large, my whole experience in the Navy was positive. In any event, the military experience proved to be for me a valuable experience. I would favor a compulsory service experience for all young men following high school graduation and before going on to college or into the work force. When I went on to college, the competition proved to be intense because of the numbers of returning veterans who were dedicated to gaining a good education.

Born in Baltimore, Maryland, John attended Friends School, enlisting in the Navy in 1944 in his senior year. Following graduation, the Navy sent him to study mathematics at Johns Hopkins University for a year prior to becoming an electronics technician. After discharge in 1947, he returned to Johns Hopkins, attended medical school at the University of Maryland, and completed a residency in ear, nose, and throat. He joined the Mary Fletcher Hospital medical staff, became a Burlington resident, married and had two children who are Vermont natives.

From Pillar to Post in the Air Corps

★

Sanborn Partridge
U.S. Army Air Force

From left to right, David, Sanborn, and Charles Partridge

I WAS PRACTICING LAW, an avid pilot, and owner of an airplane when World War II began. I had a keen interest in navigation and radar, the latter a technology at the time only alluded to in aviation magazines and little understood by most. Of military draft age, I was fortunate to "draw" a high lottery number for the military draft so I was not called up immediately and had time to look around. Consequently, I looked into the U.S. Navy in January and February 1942 and was on the wait list for photo interpretation, but I flunked the Navy physical in Washington for "nearsightedness and too high arches." It happens that my selective service number (drawn out of a fish bowl in Washington) was five from the absolute end, so that my chances of being drafted seemed remote. I tried for the Navy once again in Boston, but flunked the Navy physical for, more accurately, flat feet! Then I learned of an Army Air Corps series of eight-week courses that could lead to flying status and pursued this opportunity to join the military.

The Army Air Corps

I decided to enlist in the Army Air Corps (subsequently, it became the U.S. Army Air Force). I joined in Rutland, Vermont with the rank of private when I finally succeeded in passing the physical exam given by the Middlebury College doctor. Initially, I was stationed at Middlebury College for ground school and practiced flying at the Bristol airfield. After that, I was sent to Northeastern University in Boston for a brief period of study in ground school, and continued flying out of Concord, New Hampshire. Next, I was assigned to the air base at Barnes Airport, Westfield, Massachusetts to study navigation. Following my time there, I moved on to Enfield, New York (near Binghamton) to gain proficiency in the Link Trainer in order to learn instrument flying. On completion of training, I was eligible for leave and used the time to gather additional information in Washington, D.C. about career options for me in the Air Force. The essence of what I learned was that I might be too old to qualify for Air Cadet training but more likely would be assigned to duty as a flight instructor.

Next, I was sent to Fort Devens, Massachusetts for a brief time before proceeding to North Carolina for army basic training. This was followed by a stint at Fort Knox where I did additional army basic training before finally being assigned to the Second Army Airways Communications Service in Cincinnati, Ohio. While there, I recall spending one day in Detroit and flying a large single engine aircraft. The base in Cincinnati turned out to be a Signal Corps cryptography school and not an opportunity for achieving flying status. I was still interested in a military flying career, and after being promoted to corporal (a requirement for being accepted to Officer Candidate School) I was accepted to OCS. On graduation in Miami Beach, I became a "120 day wonder," and was commissioned as Second Lieutenant in May 1944.

My Career as Intelligence Officer

I was then assigned to Orlando, Florida for a two-month Intelligence course, followed by a week of military leave which I spent in Vermont. I received orders to report to Colorado Springs where they reassigned me the following day for two weeks' duty at an air base near Sioux City, Iowa, the name of which I do not recall. Next, I was assigned to the Dalhart, Texas airbase where a B-29 bomber group was just being formed. I was assigned to the 346th Bomb Group Squadron intelligence and sent for one month to Norfolk, Virginia for radar intelligence training at Langley Field. In January 1945, I was assigned to the CPM branch of the Air Force in Washington, D.C. for a two-week course at the Pentagon. This among other things involved instruction about distinguishing escapees from prisoners of war. We had to report to the Pentagon daily and then be escorted to a secret establishment somewhere out in the Washington countryside. During that time I was fortunate to be able to live at the DC home of my sister Frances.

Following this, I rejoined the bomber group in Pratt, Kansas. This was shortly before V-E Day. While there, I was promoted to First Lieutenant. Our group was scheduled to be flown to the Orient to join the war in the Pacific. V-J Day intervened, changing everything. Plans to fly to the Pacific theater were cancelled abruptly. A shuffle of assignments occurred — I proceeded to Everett, Washington in late August 1945, then down to San Francisco, then back to the Central Valley to Chico Army Airfield. With the war's end I was reassigned as "base survey officer" at Smoky Hill AFB in Salinas, Kansas. This proved to be largely a make-work assignment and a job of little note. I was finally discharged from the Army at Fort Devens in late 1945, without ever achieving my original goal of earning flying status with the Army Air Force.

Born in Proctor, Vermont in 1915, Sandy attended Amherst College and Yale Law School before joining a Rutland law firm. He was a scoutmaster, piloted his own airplane, and enlisted in the Army Air Corps. After the war, he pursued graduate studies in geology. Returning to Vermont, he served 20 years in the State Legislature as one of the group of "Young Turks." Sandy was on the University of Vermont Board of Trustees, including one term as Chairman.

Bill is Missing in Action

★

Frank Smallwood
U.S. Army

MY FATHER CALLED ME JUST AFTER SUPPER — it was February 1944. He read the just received message in a very direct tone: — "The Secretary of War desires me to express deep regret that your son, Second Lieutenant John W. Smallwood Jr., has been reported missing in action since 25 February over Germany. If further details or other information are received, you will be promptly notified."

My brother, Bill (John William Smallwood), had completed his sophomore year in college in 1942 and volunteered for the Army Air Corps. Once our family received this news from the War Office, the next few months were harrowing for us all. It was not until May 1944 that we finally confirmed that Bill's plane had landed in Austria following a raid over Regensburg, Germany. The lengthy delay occurred because an Austrian doctor had performed surgery that saved Bill's life but necessitated a prolonged recovery. Following rehabilitation, he was shipped to a prison camp, Stalagluft One, in northern Germany.

At the time Bill was captured I was completing my junior year at the Lawrenceville School in New Jersey. Although I still had a year to go, I immediately began to speculate on how I might rescue Bill from the Germans. As it turned out, I was way ahead in my planning. On May 7, 1945, Germany surrendered, followed three months later by the Japanese surrender. My brother was liberated, returning home while I was still waiting to join the military.

I turned 18 in June 1945, but my big day did not arrive until November 1, 1945 when I was inducted into the Army and sent to Fort Dix, New Jersey. I served in the processing center there for 15 months, helping to discharge servicemen returning home from overseas duty. Here I was, wet behind the ears, advising mature, experienced soldiers how to plan the rest of their lives. I felt far from heroic.

While our two sisters had died many years ago, my brother, recently turned 85, and I celebrated my 80th birthday in June 2007. We both know that we've been extremely fortunate.

Born in Ridgewood, New Jersey, Frank attended Dartmouth College and earned a PhD from Harvard. He served in the Army in 1945–46, and later in the Atomic Energy Commission for five years. He was Professor of Government at Dartmouth College and served in the Vermont State Legislature. He has published several books, including a volume on Thomas Chittenden, the first governor of Vermont.

FLIGHT INSTRUCTOR WITHOUT WINGS

★

Gus Swift
U.S. Army Air Force

IN THE EARLY 1940S, after completing an MA degree in American Studies in the Harvard Graduate School of Arts and Sciences, I was teaching social studies at the Williston Academy Junior School in Easthampton, Massachusetts. Recognizing that my draft number was about to be called up before the next school year was over, I chose to volunteer and visited the recruiting office in Pittsfield, near my home-town of Hinsdale. By volunteering, a recruit could choose a branch of service, i.e., Army, Navy, Air Corps, etc., rather than being assigned to the service of greatest current military need.

From Pittsfield, recruits were sent to Fort Devens, Massachusetts, the major processing center for the area. I chose the Army Air Corps, though astigmatism and requiring eye glasses precluded pilot or navigator training. The Classification Officer asked what I had been doing as a civilian, and discovering that I'd been teaching, said in effect, "We'll show you what to teach." I was assigned to become an instrument flying teacher, or Link Trainer instructor, and sent to Miami Beach, Florida for basic training. We underwent several months of basic training in military demeanor and firearms in Miami Beach during the summer of 1942. This inured recruits to the considerable heat of the Florida summer. It also offered plentiful opportunities to do KP in some of the best Miami Beach hotels, which the Air Corps had confiscated for the duration of the war.

Instrument Flight Training

From Miami Beach I was sent to the instrument flying training program at Chanute Field in Rantoul, Illinois in late 1942. In addition to instruction in the operation of an instrument flying device known as the Link Trainer after its inventor Edward Link, the program included aircraft navigation, flight rule study, and a bit of meteorology. In those decades, the technology of navigating an aircraft by instruments, rather than by visual ground contact, involved a network of radio transmission towers that broadcast an array of radio beams oriented more or less to the four cardinal points of the compass. The beams could be accessed by the pilot's radio. Listening to the radio signals on the beam, the pilot, using his aircraft navigation instruments, could navigate along the beam without any visual contact. Regardless of the weather and degree of visibility, one could follow a flight path that would take the plane to the chosen location. Being "on the beam" became part of the jargon of the time.

Edward Link in the 1930s had devised a simulated aircraft cockpit containing basic navigation instruments. The trainer was mounted on a small platform that enabled a "pilot" in the cockpit to simulate aircraft movement and control. An accompanying device, mounted on a desk, simulated the pilot's flight path, so that the instructor could monitor the accuracy of the pilot's blind navigation using only instruments.

The Link Trainer instructor assigned navigation problems to the student pilot and evaluated his performance. This device became an essential part of instrument flight training.

The Battle of MacDill Field

On completing my six month's training at Chanute Field, I was assigned to MacDill Field in Tampa, Florida, a major training base for heavy bomber pilots in their last phase of pilot flight training before going overseas. The instrument flying training unit included a small cadre of 15 or so instructors, and seven or eight Link trainers. Once fully trained and assigned to a post, an instrument flight training instructor was not allowed to transfer, so I spent three years at "The Battle of MacDill Field," as GI humor referred to it — it was rather far from any theater of active combat.

In most respects, it was a lucky assignment for me, though restriction to one location had its drawbacks. During those years I was married, so part of this time, I was able to live off base in a tiny Tampa apartment. My wife, with her business background, worked as a secretary in the Aircraft Safety unit of the Army Air Force in Tampa. There were many thousands of men and women who like me served roles as specialists in the Air Force, as well as in other branches of military service. The instrument flying training program, though mostly humdrum and uneventful, was an essential part of pilot training. My military service provided me access to the GI Bill of Rights, a major benefit for members of the armed forces and an important step in my lifelong career in higher education.

Born in 1916 in Hinsdale, Massachusetts, Gus was teaching at Williston Academy in Easthampton, Massachusetts on Pearl Harbor Day. Enlisting in the Army, Gus spent the World War II years in Tampa, Florida where he was stationed at the Army Air Force Base at MacDill Field. Following a post war career in academia, he and his wife moved to Weybridge, Vermont on retirement.

HOW I LEARNED THE TELEPHONE BUSINESS

★

Thomas E. Ward, Jr.
U.S. Army Signal Corps

THE WAR STARTED AS I WAS TURNING 18 in my senior year at school in Connecticut. Because of a congenital eye disorder (strabismus) I was unable to volunteer for the Navy, but I was allowed to graduate before being subject to conscription and military service. I was classified 4-F, but I was eligible for service in a non-combat arm of the U.S. Army. Normally an inductee is held less than two weeks at the Fort Dix Induction Center before being given a permanent assignment. Because of my limited service category, I remained there for two months. My memories of that experience involve largely a variety of lowly Army chores.

I was finally assigned to Camp Grant, Rockford, Illinois to begin basic training for the Army Medical Corps. I had applied for and been accepted into the Army Specialized Training Program (ASTP) at the University of Illinois, Champlain-Urbana. This involved another delay because the next term did not begin for two more months. After only two months into the regular college semester, the Battle of the Bulge took place and the ASTP program was abandoned. All of its participants were transferred to military duty with Army units. I was assigned to the Signal Corps in New Jersey. There, I attended Signal Corps training schools at Fort Monmouth, Camp Wood, and Camp Edison as a "buck" private at $50 per month (and all one can eat!). The training included weapons practice with carbines, grenade launchers, and 50 cal. machine guns, firing out over the Atlantic Ocean at Sea Girt where Camp Edison is located.

The Army Signal Corps

After taking courses in telephone pole climbing, telephone line construction, soldering and circuit repair, as well as manual and automatic switchboard operation, I was promoted to the rank of Technician, Fourth Grade. I was assigned service category #232. The Bell Telephone Company was the backbone of the Signal Corps telephone operation. It was affectionately referred to as "Ma Bell."

I was doing KP duty one morning at 6 am when we learned of the D-Day landings in Normandy on June 6, 1944. I moved on to Camp Crowder, in Neosho, Missouri, just south of Joplin. Here I learned how to clean and change relays, detect line problems, and estimate the distance to a line break, using a technique involving 2-wire and 3-wire communication lines. This capability later proved to be of value when I was in the Yukon. When a vehicle got stuck out in a storm, the soldiers would throw a tire chain (frowned upon and against regulations) over a communication wire, thus shorting it out. At the switchboard, we could detect the location of the line trouble and estimate the distance to the vehicle, thereby facilitating rescue. While we were at Camp Crowder, President Roosevelt's death was announced.

I was on leave in New Jersey in August 1945 when WWII ended. This was prior to being sent to Camp McCoy, Wisconsin (a former Japanese prisoner of war camp). In October 1945 we shipped out by train to Edmonton, Alberta, Canada where we were then flown to Watson Lake, Yukon, located on the Alcan (Alaska Canada) Highway. This was a vital artery completed during WWII to connect main-land U.S. and Canada with the Alaska Territory. The Alcan Highway started at Dawson Creek, British Columbia and ended in Fairbanks, Alaska approximately 1,500 miles away. The Yukon population today numbers around 31,600, but the territory is some 50 times larger in size than Vermont. Alaska's population is approximately the same as that of Vermont but the state is 72 times larger. If Alaska were divided into two equal size states, Texas would be only the third largest state.

Watson Lake Repeater Station

We arrived at Watson Lake to relieve troops who had been stationed there for two years or longer. It was a very lonely spot along the high-way, and they were very glad to see us. Watson Lake was one of the Signal Corps repeater stations, which were located every 100 miles or so along the Alcan Highway. The hard wire telegraph lines, which were maintained by the Signal Corps, were vital to Army and Air Corps communications, especially for weather information. There was no FM radio, and AM radio reception was very poor due to interference from the Northern Lights, especially in the winter. I was stationed at Watson Lake from October 1945 to April 1946. Watson Lake had a Canadian air base which was used by the U.S. Air Force in an emergency. The U.S. delivered many fighter planes to Siberia using this route, which continued on to Fairbanks, Alaska, and then on to Russia. Watson Lake is located at Alcan Highway Mile Post No. 600 and is just north of the British Columbia border in the Yukon. It was one of the larger repeater stations, with a contingent of about 15 Signal Corps men.

We lived in a small apartment dwelling with limited kitchen facili-ties and took our main meal each day at the home of a local civilian couple, who were under contract to the U.S. Army. For a meat course, we were often served caribou, moose, or deer. A 65 year old Royal Canadian Mounted Policeman ("Mountie"), engaged in local police work, served as the barber. Some of my more vivid memories include attending evening movies put on by our unit. The local indigenous people (First Nation Eskimos) were invited. You could easily recognize that they rarely bathed. We did not interact with them much except at the film showings. I also took some correspondence courses in mathematics furnished by the Army.

Other recreational activities available to us were skiing using GI (Government Issue) 7-ft. long skis. We walked up small hills in the area, but could have really used a rope tow. On one occasion we swam in the hot springs at Muncho Lake Mile Post 456, 179 miles to the south of us. The air temperature there at the time was around zero degrees Fahrenheit while the pool temperature was at least 90 degrees. We all went skinny dipping and the hair on our heads froze as soon as it got wet.

The northern lights put on vivid displays of flickering curtains of color nearly every evening. It was spellbinding to see the ever changing colors. The coldest temperature we encountered at Watson Lake was around 40 degrees below zero, and some days it never went above minus 20 degrees. At those temperatures, the engines in the trucks would freeze solid so we had to leave the truck engines running all night long. Our only garage, which maintained a temperature of 30 degrees, accommodated only one truck.

Returning Home

I became eligible for discharge in April 1946. My total Army career amounted to 34 months. We traveled the Alcan Highway by bus to Dawson Creek, then by rail via Edmonton, Alberta to Camp McCoy, Wisconsin for separation from the Army. From there, I went to Chicago and caught one of the new TWA Constellation airliners to New York on the way to my home in South Orange, New Jersey. Since I had been accepted as a student at Yale before going into the service and most colleges were now crowded with returning servicemen, I went on to matriculate at Yale. I majored in Industrial Administration, which largely involved taking engineering courses for the first two years, followed by economics and business administration the final two years. The GI Bill paid my college tuition plus $75 per month for room and board. In 1949, I did a summer internship with the Mene Grande

Oil Company, a Gulf Oil Company subsidiary, in Venezuela where I worked mainly in drilling and oil production as a "mud man." I also took a summer course in geology at the Colorado School of Mines in Golden, Colorado.

Epilogue

Some of my positive memories of military service include the excellent technical training in Signal Corps schools that I received before being deployed to the Yukon. I made some fast friends in the Army. One friend I met while I was in ASTP at the University of Illinois introduced me to classical music. We often attended symphony concerts and art museums in Chicago 100 miles distant. When I was stationed at Camp Crowder, Missouri, which is near Joplin, there were many Mormon families who often invited servicemen to their homes and held dances for the troops, which were great fun. My Army experience exposed me to many different types of individuals and social settings, from Eskimos to Mormons, which I would otherwise never have encountered.

Born in Flushing, New York, Tom graduated from Yale and made his career in the oil business. He worked for various oil companies including Standard Oil of California and served as President, Oldfield Equipment Co. Dealing with drilling and mining equipment, he travelled extensively in the Caribbean and South Africa.

Medical Service

The Horrors of War

★

Ralph Blocksma, MD
U.S. Army Medical Corps

RALPH BLOCKSMA, MD WAS A SURGEON during World War II attached to General Patton's Third Army. He helped to liberate Buchenwald death camp before returning from Europe at war's end. His wife, Ruth, a resident of Wake Robin, assembled these excerpts from letters and journals he kept about his WWII experiences:

Buchenwald Concentration Camp

As a physician I am familiar with scenes of suffering and death. But I had never seen such documentation of human tragedy as the stark visages that lay before me that day in April, 1945 when I visited Buchenwald shortly after the capitulation of Nazi forces in the area. I was attached to a medical unit close to the front when called on to care for prisoners in a German prison. An advance patrol of Americans had intercepted an extermination detail at the camp and stopped the killings going on inside.

151

Several miles outside Weimar, a German town steeped in Reich-land history, we came upon an area of bombed-out factories leading to a large gate flanked by two towers. A sign over the entrance said "Recht Oder Unrecht — Mein Vaterland" (Right or Wrong, My Homeland). American soldiers guarded the iron gate, and inside we saw crowds of men milling about, some with striped pants, some with striped coats, all wearing a red triangle on their clothes. Each triangle contained a letter, J, R, or F, meaning Jew, Russian, or French. There was a young Russian boy who was imprisoned for stealing from a German officer. There were children as young as five years of age and up whose only crime in Germany was that they were of the wrong nationality. It is estimated that at one time there were more than 80,000 prisoners in the camp. The day we arrived there were just 20,000.

The stark sadism confronted us on a huge cobbled square just inside the entrance where prisoners assembled daily for roll call and disci-pline. There was a whipping rack in the square, and a kind of gallows where prisoners were hung by their wrists with their arms tied behind their backs. Nearby, guard dogs snarled at us. They had been trained to track down missing prisoners. One-story wooden buildings flanked the square. Each was barely 30 paces long and 40 wide, yet each had housed 1900 prisoners. Inside one of the buildings we saw a triple tier of planks stretching the length of each sidewall. The tiers only two or three feet apart in height were divided into compartments, each about six feet long and 10 deep from aisle way to the wall. Thirty men had to occupy each compartment. Each man got one thin blanket, one spoon, one tin bowl. They were fed once a day, a liter of fluid, three loaves of black bread for each tier. Loaves were one-third the size of those you buy at the store. The stench in these quarters was sickening.

People came to Buchenwald for two clear-cut purposes: work and extinction. There was a stone quarry in the camp, where average size blocks weighed 100 pounds, and two SS men served as over-seers. After a preliminary period of starvation, new arrivals were sent to the quarry. Carrying blocks upon their shoulders, or in their arms, they were compelled to run to waiting carts or to a stockpile. If they did not run, they were beaten with clubs. The strongest were beaten the hardest simply because of their strength. No one was supposed to stay strong in Buchenwald. After a 12-hour work day prisoners returned to their barracks. It wasn't necessary to take time out for meals, because there was only one "meal" a day. Many became very sick.

It was cold in April, the day we came to Buchenwald, and during the winter, the snow had often been five feet deep. Wintry blasts, however, rarely deterred the work schedule. We found many men with pneumonia, many with tuberculosis, and almost everyone had dysentery. Piled one on top of another at night, 30 to a tier in the barracks, prisoners often found it impossible to reach the single latrine outside the barracks door. Sometimes men died in these tiers, and since each tier received rations for 30 men, bodies would be kept concealed for many days so that the living could receive the rations of the dead.

Each barracks was overseen by an SS trooper, his room with its small table and bed occupying a space identical to that allowed to 90 prisoners. Noise in the barracks at night brought him quickly between the tiers with club or whip. If the mood struck him he might decide to order everyone outside to give the barracks an airing on a bitterly cold night. The trooper kept a roster book and put a red cross after the name of each man who died, plus the date. The books I saw were solid with red crosses. March had been a particularly bad month.

After several years, inmates had somehow managed to have one building allotted to them as a hospital. A building the same as the others, except that tiers were four feet in height instead of three, and occupancy was limited to 900 inmates. Half of one side was reserved for active cases of tuberculosis, the opposite quarter for typhus and other infectious diseases. The farthest quarter to the right housed operative cases: men, for example, who had marched from Stalingrad, Prague, Warsaw or Budapest, arriving with frozen, gangrenous feet and legs required amputation. The last quarter was reserved for the SS office, and just beyond it the area for children. Prerequisite for getting into the hospital was for one's illness to be so advanced he or she could no longer walk. In a kind of aisle between the children's and the surgical areas stood a table rather like a kitchen table, on which Russian, Czech, and Polish doctors performed operations. Two men who served as ward attendants assisted; they also removed the bodies of those who had died during the day. An average of 40 bodies was piled at the door each evening.

The Crematorium

At one end of the building, a double door opened into a closed-in porch separated from the main structure. Each day a number of selected men, in good health by normal camp standards, came to this area for "immunization" shots given by an SS doctor. They were ushered into a tiny room, seated on a seat that was bolted to the floor, and given their shot, which probably contained cyanide and brought almost immediate death. As the prisoner fell from the stool, a door opened and the prisoner was pitched backward into a rough stone-floored shed. The doctor would then walk to the entrance and, often with a pleasant smile, invited the next patient to enter. So quick was death that waiting prisoners never heard any outcry, not so much as a moan. The attendant only knew that each day six to 30 men were brought in for shots and that at night he would find from six to 30 bodies in the shed. We were told of one attendant who inquired about what happened to those given shots. He was immediately taken out and beaten to death.

With so much death, the disposal of bodies became a sizable chore. Cremation solved the problem. We found the crematorium building surprisingly neat and clean, a situation we could scarcely be expected to appreciate in view of the naked bodies piled like cordwood just outside. Nearby stood a large cart loaded with some 100 corpses half-covered by a piece of canvas. We looked in momentary awe at the bodies, ranging from the very young to the very old. Ghastly as this was, the crematorium with a pile of charred bone fragments and bodies waiting outside to be burned was only a preparation for what we would see in the basement. Here, spaced about the walls above the cement floor, were more than 40 hooks, like the meat hooks used by butchers. At one end a trap door opened from the outside. The victim was stripped, pushed through the trap door into the basement, where men set upon him with large clubs. He was then strung up by the throat on one of the hooks, a gutter carrying away the blood. When dead, the body was placed on an electric elevator and carried to one of the six furnaces, each of which accommodated three bodies at a time. Thus the crematorium had capacity for over 100 victims every day. A noisy air-conditioning fan in the basement drowned the screams of the men who were being clubbed to death.

For 50 marks, a German family could have the ashes of a deceased relative returned. Actually, we were told, any shovel full of ashes might be placed in an urn. What did it matter? For the most part, however, the ashes were used to fertilize the camp vegetable garden. Total registered deaths for Buchenwald were 51,000. No one knows how many were not tabulated, but men of at least 21 nationalities died there over a period of seven years.

During the three months prior to our arrival, as the certainty of the ultimate fate of Nazidom loomed on the horizon, restrictions became less rigid. SS guards were not placed in the barracks rooms and the inmates had slightly more freedom. In broken English one prisoner told me, "It was much better. We could talk and even tell jokes if we did it quietly."

When American soldiers first approached the area, a special extermination detail had been sent from a city 50 miles away to destroy every inmate so there would be no survivor to tell Buchenwald's awful story. Fortunately, an advance patrol of Americans intercepted the detail. They had not arrived in time, though, to save over 40 British and American airmen who had made forced landings in the vicinity. They had been brought to the camp, whipped, beaten, and hanged before the other prisoners, as an example of the fate accorded those who dared to invade the Reich.

I talked with many prisoners: a lad from The Hague, Holland, whom I found in the hospital; a Czech who had managed to stay alive for years by switching numbers and keeping useful as a bricklayer; several Frenchmen with whom I conversed in my smattering of college French; a Russian youngster from Stalingrad, and many others. I won't recount many of the stories they told me, one hideous tale after another. It is enough to speak of what met our eyes that day. These prisoners, like starved animals waking from a nightmare, could take only bread and water. The simplest balanced meal would make them retch and vomit. Some were so young they had memories only of concentration camp life in Holland, France, Poland, or Russia, and if they recalled anything before that, it was only of bombings, wrecked homes and broken families.

"What will you do with the men?" they asked. "What will the conquerors do?" There was something of a sad reproach in their eyes, because we were soft-hearted men, ill-equipped to deal with such travesties on human decency. We could only shake our heads and wonder whether we'd ever possibly be the same again.

Years have passed since that first day at Buchenwald, and you may wonder why I would recount such ghastly memories. It's because each of us has a personal responsibility. For the same international mistrust, the same greed, the same hatreds that gave us Buchenwald, once more walk the face of the earth. It is something that demands our individual attention and dedication.

End of Hostilities in Europe

As the war in Europe wound down, casualties were fewer, and plans were made to move units to the Pacific Theater. In July the 184th General Hospital located in Mansfield, England was dissolved. I was shifted to the 104th in Bournemouth, with the understanding that the unit would shortly head for the U.S. Two weeks later, I was ordered to report to the 180th hospital based in a Luftwaffe hospital in Frankfurt, Germany, a unit planning for transfer to the Far East. On the London-Paris flight I was seated with a plain-looking English woman wearing a rumpled British equivalent of an American Red Cross outfit. On the way, she turned to me in a friendly way so I introduced myself. I offered my hand; she shook it and said her name was Eden. I smiled and said, "Related to Sir Anthony, no doubt?" She grinned. "Oh, yes, he is my husband. I am on my way to join him at the Berlin Conference." I bit my lip. At least she could have dressed like a VIP.

We continued on to Verdun, crossing the Rhine at Mainz. We were jammed into a filthy, German railway coach once used to haul prisoners and rarely, if ever, cleaned. I slept on the floor with the rails whacking my ears all night. French towns could be identified by the powerful stench of sewage as we jolted through. The camp at Verdun was a huge French military barracks near old World War I trenches and memorials. Thousands of crosses marked the nearby graves of U.S. GIs. There was an impressive memorial where a bomb blast had totally buried soldiers except for their protruding bayonets. Massive collections of bones were being prepared for display, the remains of dismembered soldiers of days gone by. It was gruesome. And the accommodations were just as bad.

On August 9, 1945 we learned that Russia had just entered the war against Japan on the side of the Allies, and on Aug. 14 at 11 PM we were told the war had ended in the Pacific. There was no celebration, just an uncomprehending relief. Our radios described wild celebrations around the world, especially at Times Square in New York. Next day we were moved to Camp Philadelphia near Rheims, France where we encamped in tents and wondered when we'd be sent home. The camp was a muddy field, once an airport, and we had thousands of tents, nine men in each. It was a three-quarter-mile walk to the mess hall, 50 yards to the latrine, and 200 yards to a washstand. It looked endlessly monotonous and our superior officers saw no relief ahead.

Four of us wangled a leave to England, first on a weapons carrier to Paris, then by boat-train to Dieppe and London. My friend Tony Burke paid for our dinner and provided some luxuries. He was easily the most affluent officer I ever met; he was an accomplished gambler and had $7,000 in francs stashed in his trench coat pocket.

Dieppe had been well worked over with explosives and its fortifications along the sea looked impregnable. Here thousands of brave English soldiers lost their lives in a daring raid as a prelude to D-Day. In London we luxuriated in clean white sheets at Grosvenor House, and then went to Bournemouth and its Ambassador Hotel. It was a delightful, posh contrast to the mud of France. On BBC radio we heard President Truman announce the Japanese surrender. Celebration can be an obscenity when the price has been so heavy.

I called my old RAF friend, Michael Christy; I had visited him frequently when stationed at the 97th General Hospital. During the first months of my service in England, Michael had watched me perform skin graft procedures in his capacity as an official British photographer. He was impressed by a terribly burned American pilot who had third degree burns of face, neck and scalp, ears destroyed, one hand devoid of fingers, the other of skin. His burns covered 40 percent of his body. Mike took pictures later published without identification. He said the patient would never make it; I said he would. Michael said if I was right, he would reward me with a super party in London. The burned man was transferred to Plastic Surgery Centers in the U.S. in good condition, and Michael and Pam Christy gave me a party that started at 9:30 AM and ended at five the next morning. It included Les Ambassadeurs Club, the Melroy Club, and a number of others. My friends and I enjoyed it all, but then reluctantly returned to ugly Camp Philadelphia in France. Our entire unit had disappeared, and the camp was deserted. We slept wet and cold, huddled in our trench coats that night. Next morning we traced our missing unit to Sissonne, near Rheims. The hospital was already in operation with 259 patients, and in three days we were up to 800. For the past year we'd been treating trauma almost exclusively, but these last two weeks of September we were busy with hernia repairs, appendectomies, draining abscesses, and performing minor plastic surgery.

At regional army headquarters I tried to pick up information about going home. I knew I had accumulated plenty of "points," but how to unravel the red tape? The miracle was performed by a dentist working in a key position at headquarters. We had worked together on the maxillo-facial team in Germany, and he assured me I'd soon be on my way home. Great coincidence!

Next I was sent to Etamps, 45 miles south of Paris, to join the 19th Replacement Depot ("repo depo") to await orders for shipment home. I first met a Staff Sgt. who recognized me at once. "Aren't you the doctor who grafted my fingers at the 97th General in England?" I admitted I was, and remembered that despite having received a severe hand grenade injury, he had been sent back to France early, when the Battle of the Bulge sucked back into action any man who could handle a gun. "Well, doc, you sure fixed me up just fine," he drawled, "well enough to get my ass blown off while riding a tank near Bastogne. Thanks to you docs I have ended up in this stinking French chateau with plugged toilets and no windowpanes." He urged me to get out and go to Paris for a few days, since the camp was rat-infested, filthy, and sans hot water. I quickly entrained for the Grosvenor Hotel in Paris. The city in 1945 was full of people with nothing, digging in garbage pails, picking up ends of cigarettes, and utterly disillusioned. Paris was a great composite of good and evil, ugly and lovely, in a crazy patchwork.

Two days later I returned to find orders for Le Havre where I discovered I was Medical Officer Number 13 on the shipping list, expected to sail as ship's surgeon on a homeward bound ship. Le Havre was more than half destroyed. Center city and port-side areas were leveled, streets obliterated, trees with their limbs amputated, lifting splintered stumps to the sky. Everywhere were acres of brick and rubble. Crews of POWs were working to bring some sort of order out of chaos. Many sunken ships were in the harbor, some with holes topside, some with superstructure at sea level; a ship at the entrance to the harbor was said to be loaded with explosives. Yet ships came and went all day long.

Homeward Bound

I was called to the Port Surgeon's office and given my orders: I would sail next day though no specific ship was yet assigned to me. It will be a Liberty or Victory ship. That was fast action. I was assigned to the *SS Alexander Graham Bell*, cleared by Customs, my money changed to U.S. dollars. I awaited orders to head for the ship. Capt. B.F. Edwards, a small mustached man from Texas, claimed Texans need double the dosage of drugs that northerners do. He leaves on the *SS Longfellow* about the same time I board the *Alexander Graham Bell*. I carried the stock of a shotgun for him in my bedding roll.

Old Doc Edwards took off early and forgot his important military papers. I rushed down to the dock to be sure they were delivered to him. I was ready to be picked up at noon, until I heard smallpox had broken out on my ship and sailing was cancelled pending investigation. But at one PM all was OK, and we boarded a Liberty ship about two

PM. I had a small stateroom with Col. Elms. As ship surgeon, I ate at the Captain's table and had some privileges. At night I went on deck to watch the phosphorescent gleam from dolphins swimming near the ship. A few days out, we had stormy weather and had to catch falling silverware; water pitchers were a real menace, sliding off tables. I hated seeing rats running along the beams overhead in my bedroom; knowing they can carry typhus didn't help.

On November 8, 1945 we had a real gale of unbelievable fury. No one was allowed on deck after eight AM, not that we wanted to go up there. The wind was screaming through the gear on deck, and the ocean was a seething mass of tumbling foam as far as the eye could see. Enormous waves charged at the ship like cavalry, flinging spume like bullets from their crests. The old ship would shudder from stem to stern under the smashing impacts, then pitch and drive into the trough, then up to thrash crazily in the air. The ship groaned and strained like a wounded animal, dragging itself from wave to wave, rolling, wallowing, and careening through the seas.

Below decks, men were thrown about, piled up in corners; an officer came in and wanted to start a pool on how long it would take for the ship to break up. At dinner a huge lurch of the ship leveled the officers' dining room: food, men, and dishes plus one collapsed table, all crashed to the floor in a messy heap. Many had to be treated for bruises and abrasions, and increasing numbers were seasick. Most of the ship's dishes were broken and the sugar, salt, jam, ketchup, soup and potatoes were all mixed up on the floor. Col. Elms drew a "turn and bank indicator" on the wall with a stylet hanging free to record the degree of list of the ship. He stationed himself in front of it on a folding chair with a pencil; the vessel made on awful roll, the Colonel reached up to mark it, his chair flew out from under him and he pitched full length on the deck. We both laughed until the tears came. The list he was trying to mark was 33 degrees to starboard. Since then we recorded another at 40 degrees to starboard and one at 30 degrees to port.

At dinner in the Captain's Mess I had to learn to grasp the soup bowl firmly with the left hand and alternately tip it fore and aft with the ship's roll; you had to synchronize with the roll or mop off your trousers. I was not seasick! The ship was making almost no headway, laboring mightily, the wind still screaming relentlessly and scooping sheets of spray from every wave. We're just holding our own, headed straight into the wind. I suspected that we were well off course. The wind was reported to be about 65 miles an hour.

In the morning the storm was still intense, with enormous waves, but the gale was now in a southward direction. That night an enormous wave burst over the ship, engulfing it from stem to stern. It went into the funnels, putting out fires in one of the boilers and flooding the engine room. Even the cook's galley was flooded; we were entirely at the mercy of the sea. The crew feared the boilers would explode, but luckily they didn't. However, during the night the entire supply of canned goods broke loose from the stout nets in the supply room adjoining our stateroom. They made a terrific racket as they charged back and forth across the room and piled up with an enormous crescendo on the opposite metal bulkhead. It went on all night, and this morning no one dared hazard an entry to restore order.

Quite a bit of sugar and flour spilled into the No. Four hold. They did not bother to pump it out, just put ballast atop it. Now the spill has been wet for a week and is fermenting and creating a nauseating stench. A different stink has been created by the drain outside our door backing up and spilling sewage on the floor. Some seeped into our stateroom. They finally cleared it out, but the smell was still intense. Then there was the odor of 500 dirty men jammed together in close quarters in the hold, and the smell of food moldering on the floor where the seas dumped it; plus the smell of disinfectant used liberally to try to eliminate the other odors. All together there was a suffocating stench, making life miserable below deck, as the storm made it impossible above. Some of the men went around in a daze; they joked about the weather, but nothing seemed funny anymore.

When I got up on the bridge we were heading west, exacerbating the ship's motion. From up there I could see the size of the waves better; they appeared 80 to 100 feet high, each one a mountain of water. The captain was haggard and unshaven. He had been on his feet for two days and nights, ever since the storm struck. He said a freighter had broken in two a few miles south of us, but another ship was going to her rescue. That night the Colonel and I looked out briefly; still no change in wind or waves and we wondered how long this could continue.

Later the captain came into our stateroom with a radio message from another ship that needed medical advice. The symptoms sounded like pneumonia so I ordered penicillin and cold sponges and fluids; I found diagnosis by radio difficult: Morse code is tedious and slow, but we could never take a patient aboard in these heavy seas. That night was the worst yet. Heavy rolling made it hard to stay in a bunk; I would alternately slam the headboard and assault the footboard. From nine PM to one AM we did everything but stand on our heads. Sleep? I sneaked in a wink now and then from sheer exhaustion, and woke with a stiff neck, sore back and shoulders, but the motion of the ship was less intense. At breakfast we learned the waves were "only" 30 feet high, though the wind was still pretty stiff. I had a haircut completed successfully, despite the lurching of the ship.

On November 11 the sea was much calmer, and we got a decent night's sleep, and by the 12th we couldn't see a single whitecap. We had a final banquet with chicken, carrots and peas, mashed potatoes, olives, cake and ice cream and peaches. Everyone stood and cheered the skipper when he said his goodbyes after dinner; I realized he was only about 31 years old. On November 14 we were home.

On the 15th we arrived at Camp Kilmer, New Jersey. We craned our necks at the sight of bright lights, big and little cars everywhere, and trucks bigger than we could ever remember. Dinner at camp was wonderful, steak and real cold milk. Then we went off to a telephone building to sweat out a long line waiting to call. Over 10,000 long distance calls a day were going out of the camp. At last, it was my turn. I heard Ruth's voice, then Mary's, then Dewey said "Hi." I'd been dreaming of this moment and the joy it brought is beyond telling.

After the war, Ralph completed Boards in Plastic and Reconstructive Surgery before working in Pakistan for five years. On return to Grand Rapids, Michigan, he established a plastic surgery residency program at Butterworth Hospital and spent his last professional years in the British Virgin Islands. He died in 2001.

Not a Nurse

★

Elizabeth Middleton Brown

I WASN'T A NURSE, but anyone seeing us in our smart grey uniforms could guess we were with some special service during World War II. I was serving as an Occupational Therapist with the American Red Cross and stationed at Staten Island Area Hospital in New Dorp, New York. It wasn't long before I discovered that the uniform covered not only my ignorance but also my fears about what I had gotten into. Where were the nurses? Inside the Office, I learned. Yes, we were expected to do all that was necessary short of actual nursing.

Wounded soldiers came regularly to be treated. They were all bed patients. I was assigned to an Amputee Ward. Suddenly occupational therapy became real to me. Never mind looking for an occasion to play gin rummy; what does this guy want? He wants a urinal. My job at this moment is to find a nurse. Sometimes we saw a movie, when again my training might desert me. I might pull a cart alongside a patient's bed and we'd go together to see "It Happened One Night."

On New Year's Eve I went all out, demanding extra sodas from the canteen, more hats, blowers, and whistles. I ran about the corridors whooping it up in a hula skirt; yes, it relieved the boredom, the men sang, they laughed, finally telling Army jokes that dispersed the shadows creeping along the gray cement block walls that they had come home to.

Sometimes the men would practice walking. The hospital was located on the beach at New Dorp and had a short boardwalk. Again, my Washington schooling didn't fill the bill. Carl caught his crutch between the boards — here was a job I could do, grabbing a shoulder, leaning for balance, and he came up, one leg, one crutch, one smile. Another GI, a real smart guy, pegging up to me might say, "Hi! Wanta dance?"

Sometimes work was heartbreaking. Early in the morning as I checked in for the day I would hear a nurse speaking softly on the phone to the CO: "Yes, sir. Corporal Smith managed to escape last night. He crawled down the sand to the water and he drowned." And Oren, a slight figure struggling to accept that his arms were gone: I said to him, "Good night, Oren, we will work those muscles tomorrow." When I went to the ward I saw that his bed was freshly made up — and empty. He had died in the night.

So I had training as an Occupational Therapist in Washington D.C. with plastics and play dough and other useful things to help keep wounded men busy and trying to get well. But I found out a lot more in New Dorp. The cement hospital is now gone. The tides flow freely back and forth on my bit of history.

Born in San Francisco, Elizabeth Middleton Brown received her education in the East at Dana Hall and Connecticut College. After the war she raised a family and taught science in schools in Washington, D.C. and Montclair, New Jersey.

REFLECTIONS OF A RED CROSS
STAFF MEMBER

★

Barbara Dunnington

I AM A LONGTIME, COMMITTED MEMBER of America's Peace Movement. After Pearl Harbor, I went to Washington and volunteered to
work for the American Red Cross. I had said I would work overseas,
but when my medical records showed I had to take a daily thyroid pill,
the officials said they could not send anyone needing medication outside the continental U.S. because they could not guarantee it would get
to me. Previously, I had done volunteer work for the Red Cross, working with parents with a son overseas, so I was sent to the Valley Forge
General Hospital, Phoenixville, Pennsylvania to join the Social Service
and Recreational staffs. The hospital specialized in Plastic Surgery,
Eye Surgery and Neuropsychiatric disorders, but there were patients
with every kind of serious, crippling injuries that the doctors worked
extremely hard to heal or correct.

During 1944 and 1945, I worked with a great many severely
wounded veterans. They had endured unimaginable horrors, and all are

unforgettable unsung heroes. One of the patients survived the infamous Bataan Death March (Philippines) and the many months of inhumane treatment that followed. He later wrote the book, "*Some Survived,*" but as he said memorably, "we endured without losing our humanity."

I was placed on the Social Work staff under a supervisor. I also worked with the Recreation staff, and in that capacity I well remember playing tennis with a tennis-loving veteran who had lost one arm. I also played golf with some blind veterans. In that instance, I would estimate the number of yards to the green, then go up ahead and rattle my club in the hole so they could judge the direction and distance. They often would kid me about my poor judging of distance accurately. Thank goodness a person's sense of humor can transcend the worst of human tragedies. For these casualties of global warfare, it proved to be remarkable. There were even tennis-loving blind patients who wanted to attend tennis matches in Philadelphia. I was delighted to take them, and their level of interest and concentration in a match was phenomenal. Without any assistance, they recognized who was serving and what the score was, often even better than the seeing audience.

I also ran the Intake Office at the hospital, which was always jammed with bath-robed patients. They needed a variety of items and services, such as loans, travel arrangements for the blind, or just friendly conversation, and most importantly, laughter. The Red Cross maintained some rooms upstairs in the hospital where parents of ailing patients approaching death could stay. Our office handled a variety of activities and welcomed the many musical artists, big bands, comedians, and other performing artists who gave of their time so patients could enjoy their evenings. When work schedules allowed, the busy hospital staff were also invited to attend.

Epilogue

Many of our doctors gained fame within their medical specialties. One of our plastic surgeons, Dr. Joseph Murray of Massachusetts, later was awarded a Nobel Prize for performing the first successful kidney transplant. Twenty years after the war, some of us were invited to attend the

National Convention of Plastic Surgeons, a memorable event. I well remember one very special volunteer from Philadelphia who during the war travelled every day from the city to assist both patients and doctors, and the unforgettable speech she made that night. She said what she learned from this experience was that "the human spirit can survive anything," and these casualties of the war mostly did.

Barbara grew up in Minneapolis and graduated from Smith College. As a uniformed member of the American Red Cross, she spent the war years at Valley Forge Army Hospital, Phoenixville, Pennsylvania, a specialty hospital for plastic surgery, eye surgery, and neuropsychiatric disorders of the severely wounded. After marrying and residing in several cities, she and husband Bill settled in Colchester where Barbara was a Board Member of the Vermont Nurses Association

Second Auxiliary Surgical Group

★

W. Philip Giddings, MD
U.S. Army Medical Corps

A T THE TIME OF PEARL HARBOR I had finished three of my four years of surgical residency at the Massachusetts General in Boston, so I was eligible for a spot in the Army Medical Corps. Treating life-threatening casualties as close to the battlefront as possible was an innovation of medical treatment introduced during the Second World War. Groups of well trained surgical specialists were being formed to provide advance treatment of battle casualties to reduce mortality rates caused by delay in administering definitive care. Our outfit was known as the Second Auxiliary Surgical Group. I was fortunate to become a member and join others largely drawn from medical centers in the U.S. — think of MASH, faintly similar.

The typical outfit was composed of teams of six individuals: a chief surgeon and assistant surgeon, an anesthetist, a registered nurse, and two enlisted medical/surgical technicians. We lived and worked in pyramidal tents as close to the front lines as possible. These special units were first deployed in the North African campaign in 1942. The 2nd Auxiliary Surgical Group landed in Morocco in early 1943, and subsequently participated in the invasions of Sicily and the Italian mainland, the Anzio beachhead, and the bloody campaigns fought up the peninsula of Italy.

This new concept of surgical teams assigned to Field Hospitals, but usually detached, expedited care of the wounded because the group was located close to division medics in the frontlines who were evacuating the wounded. It is a story of surgical teams that trudged on day after day following major pushes of infantry units, sometimes even in front of the division command post. It makes a compelling war story, literally of blood and guts, about surgeons operating while under fire battling to save lives by reducing delay between injury and definitive medical treatment.

The Operating Room

This excerpt from *A History of the Activities of the 2nd Auxiliary Group, 1942-1945* describes typical operating room conditions in the mobile hospitals set up near the battlefront to administer prompt treatment of the severely wounded.[1]

The field hospital operating rooms are typically housed in tents. In summer, a tent hospital in the field soon became extremely dusty and passing vehicles on unpaved roads even 100 yards away raised dust clouds which billowed across the area and into the operating tent. Personnel walking through the surgical theater raised more dust, and water for sprinkling the earth was seldom available. It was impossible to control flies and insects. Fitted screens were not feasible so mosquito netting and cheese cloth were used instead. To those trained in the aseptic ritual of a modern surgical amphitheater, the sight was ap-

---

[1] *Forward Surgery of the Severely Wounded: A History of the Activities of the 2nd Surgical Group 1942-1945*. Editors: Luther H. Wolff, chairman; Reeve H. Betts, Paul S. Samson, Robert H. Wylie, Samuel E. Childs, Wooster P. Giddings, co-editors. The Surgeon General, U.S. Army, Washington D.C. 1945.

palling at first. Temperatures could vary from near freezing in winter to almost intolerable heat in summer. The floor was often thick with mud or powdery dust of desiccated, richly manured earth. Flies were a plague in summer and in winter; the roof often leaked, sometimes onto the sterile surgical field below. In spite of the crudity of facilities, the surgeons always observed rigid procedures of aseptic technique.

One would expect under these conditions epidemics of wound sepsis, anaerobic (gangrene) infections, and streptococcal and other wound infections would be rampant. In fact, severe infections were a rarity except as a result of direct soiling of the peritoneal cavity due to a penetrating wound itself. The sulfonamides and penicillin, which had only recently been introduced into therapy when bacterial resistance had not yet developed to these drugs, doubtless aided in the prevention of sepsis.

D-Day: Invasion of Italian Mainland

Teams of the 2nd Auxiliary Group were involved in D-Day, September 9, 1943, landing 10 miles south of Salerno, Italy around 2:30 PM as part of the Fifth Army, which was charged with securing the southern flank of the bridgehead. The diary entry of one of the surgeons of the Second Auxiliary Group describes the battle conditions they faced that day.[2]

The fact that we are going ashore with only one unbloodied, inexperienced American division, the 36th Infantry Division (Texas National Guard), did not worry us in the least. After all, we were anticipating that we would have little or no resistance from the Germans now since Italy had just capitulated. D-Day in fact was memorable; there was no preliminary bombardment, but we soon found out that the Germans were set and waiting for us....our flank proved to be untenable for some period of time following the landings of Allied forces due to fierce 88 mm artillery fire from the mountains.

---

[2] *Forward Surgeon: The Diary of Luther H. Wolff, MD, 1943-45.* Vantage Press, New York 1985.

Hard fighting proved to be incessant as the Third Army slowly fought its way up the Italian peninsula toward its first major target, Cassino. The Germans always put up a tenacious defense. During this time, the 2nd Auxiliary Group teams were affiliated with the 33rd Field Hospital of the Third Army, operating in mobile units that advanced with the front. The Italian campaign was grueling. Shelling by the Germans was constantly harassing, and the weather was often inclement — cold and rainy.

The Allied forces continued to push northward in the ensuing months over rugged country, fighting the Germans who were masters of defensive warfare. Second Auxiliary groups provided forward surgical care in the Anzio beachhead (11th Evacuation Hospital), the Po River and the Apennines (33th Field Hospital), and Po River Valley (32nd Field Hospital) campaigns until final conquest of the German army in Italian territory.

A Close Call at Anzio

My life took an unexpected turn in February, 1944 at the Anzio beachhead. While my surgical teammate was finishing up operating on a current patient, I went into an adjoining tent to pick out the next patient. On my return, I stopped to speak to two nurses chatting together. After a moment, I left them and had taken only a few steps into the operating tent when an enemy shell landed on the very spot where I had been standing moments before. Both nurses were blown up, and a large shell fragment struck me, going in one thigh, then through my lower abdomen and coming out the other thigh.

I had a prolonged recovery in an army hospital in Naples. After several operations over a three-month period, I began to feel that I would recover fully. Then, I was approached by Dr. Churchill, chief surgical consultant of the Mediterranean Theater of Operations, who said my injuries were severe enough that I was supposed to be sent home, but because of a shortage of doctors, and with no replacements expected, might I waive my discharge orders and stay on? I replied that I was willing to return to medical duty, so upon my discharge from the hospital I was able to rejoin my own surgical team. I remained with that team until the war ended.

Record of the Second Auxiliary Surgical Group

On July 5, 1945 after the end of hostilities, the 2nd Auxiliary Group was housed in the Grande Albergo Lido Hotel in Riva, Italy in the lake region near the Swiss border. This was a swank hotel on Lake Garda, although it appeared to be old and down-at-the-heels at that time. The Germans had been using the building as a hospital, so most of the furniture was gone, but there were plenty of beds and chairs to go around.

This day we learned that the Unit would not be going back to the U.S. anytime soon — a bitter pill to swallow and a cause of resentment. It seemed to us a shame to keep 100 highly trained and skilled surgeons and anesthesiologists sitting around doing nothing, with little chance that their medical skills would be utilized. However, this did provide an opportunity to record the wartime experience of the 2nd Auxiliary Surgical Group while we were otherwise idle and stuck in northern Italy. With the encouragement of our superior medical officers we began seriously to undertake writing a surgical history of the Unit. This decision led to creation of two volumes documenting the history of surgical practices in World War II during the African and Italian campaigns, and I was fortunate to serve as a co-editor of both of the books.

A group of several surgeons and I volunteered to stay on at Lake Garda to record the activities of the 2nd Auxiliary Surgical Group in the North African and Italian campaigns. I was delighted to be able to contribute several chapters to this tome and to serve as a co-editor. This effort resulted in producing the volume, *Forward Surgery of the Severely Wounded*, the official account for the Surgeon General's office of forward-based surgical practice during World War II.[3]

---

[3] *Forward Surgery of the Severely Wounded: A History of the Activities of the 2nd Surgical Group 1942-1945*. Editors: Luther H. Wolff, chairman; Reeve H. Betts, Paul S. Samson, Robert H. Wylie, Samuel E. Childs, Wooster P. Giddings, co-editors. The Surgeon General, U.S. Army, Washington D.C. 1945.

A later Army Medical Corps volume on the history of surgery in World War II published in 1955 contained several chapters about expedited surgical intervention for treatment of the battlefront wounded.[4] I regarded it as a privilege to participate in writing and editing these two volumes on treatment of the severely wounded based largely on the experience of the 2nd Auxiliary Group. Hospital teams such as these effectively reduced the delay in initiating therapy with aggressive treatment of shock, a common cause of high mortality, and prompt surgical intervention.

The interval from the time the soldier was wounded until he had been restored to sufficiently good condition for his wound to be repaired was the most critical period he would undergo following injury. Unlike previous wars, early intervention now was made possible by the practice of preoperative resuscitation with liberal use of banked blood (donated by troops) to replace lost blood volume combined with skilled anesthesia. Other important departures in WWII from previous medico-military practice included: 1) routine performance of colostomies for management of abdominal and rectal wounds, resulting in the saving of thousands of lives, and 2) the ability to make thoracic surgical approaches to thoraco-abdominal wounds, which was enabled by the availability of competent anesthetists and suitable anesthesia equipment. Most important of all was "the technical competence, sound professional judgment, and surgical courage of the 2nd Auxiliary Group," as stated by The Surgeon General, Major General S.B. Hays in the introduction to *Surgery in World War II.*[4]

Surgical Experience of the Second Auxiliary Group

The Second Auxiliary Surgical Group comprised 121 medical officers, 11 dental officers, 70 members of the Army Nurse Corps, and 176 enlisted men. The enlisted men were for the most part surgical techni-

[4] *General Surgery Vol. II. Surgery in World War II.* John Boyd Coates, editor in chief; Michael E. DeBakey, editor for general surgery; associate editors, W. Philip Giddings, Elizabeth M. McFetridge. Office of the Surgeon General, Dept. of the Army, Washington D.C., 1955.

cians who had graduated from training schools of the Army Medical Department. The personnel of the group were broken down into surgical teams, 28 of which were assigned to general surgery and the remainder to various surgical specialties. As a rule, each team comprised two surgeons, an anesthetist, an operating room nurse, and two surgical technicians. These surgical teams functioned for the most part as detached units from Field Hospitals and were assigned to Army divisions on the frontlines.

An accurate and detailed compilation of Surgical Group data was enabled by the wise insistence of the commanding officer, Col. James H. Forsee, Army Medical Corps, on maintaining duplicate and complete medical records of all patients. This effort was facilitated by medical staff being assigned to the 2nd Auxiliary Group from leading teaching hospitals whose chiefs of surgery insisted on maintenance of high standards of care.

The 2nd Auxiliary Group performed over 3,000 abdominal operations alone, analyzed in great detail, and a similar number of other types of cases. A tally of surgical intervention of severely wounded soldiers in the North African and Italian campaigns by the Surgical Group totaled:

2,629 intra-abdominal wounds
903 thoracic-abdominal wounds
1,364 intra-thoracic wounds
915 traumatic amputations
2,416 compound fractures of long bones
574 serious head injuries

The case fatality rate for abdominal injuries of soldiers who reached and received surgical treatment at the hospital was 24%. Infantrymen made up 70% of the cases suffering abdominal injuries; eight percent were enemy prisoners. Of a total of 3,154 abdominal injuries treated, high explosive fragments of various types caused 2,123 of the wounds (70%), the majority from artillery and mortar fire.

The most dreaded complication of abdominal wounds in World War I was sepsis, generally due to peritonitis. Hemorrhage was the other major cause of postoperative death. In World War II, in approximately 3,000 cases treated by these specialty surgical teams, only 12% of patients developed postoperative sepsis, and postoperative hemorrhage was uncommon. For all types of wounds treated by the surgical specialty teams, the overall case fatality rate for wounds caused by high-explosive fragments was 23%, and by bullet wounds was 25%. This is a remarkably low figure given the grave nature of the injuries of typical cases assigned to early operative intervention at advance location field hospitals.

Status of Patients at Admission

Preoperative diagnosis of injuries in battle casualties is understandably inexact and based on probabilities regarding entry wound, site of exit wound, direction of the missile or fragment striking the soldier, and the location of the foreign body as demonstrated by X-ray or fluoroscopic examination. Diagnosis was particularly difficult in the presence of multiple wounds of the abdominal and thoracic regions. Surgical exploration was often required to establish the extent of injuries. It was important to determine whether a hollow viscus (i.e., stomach, small or large bowel) as well as liver, kidney, or bladder had been penetrated, requiring closure. It was of utmost importance to establish the presence or absence of abdominal injury associated with most thoracic wounds. Wounds of the chest below the fourth rib were viewed as likely to be thoraco-abdominal wounds, with penetration of the diaphragm. In these instances, the abdomen was almost routinely explored surgically to rule out organ damage in addition to the lung injury.

The preoperative care of a casualty with an abdominal wound included placing the patient on a clean litter, removal of all clothing, maintenance of body heat by blankets placed well underneath, as well as over the patient, making a rapid but complete history and physical examination, blood typing and cross-matching, catheterization, and X-ray examination. As soon as possible, even before evaluation had been completed, resuscitation measures were begun to treat shock and replace blood loss according to guidelines. Penicillin 25,000 units were given by the intramuscular or intravenous route, depending on the urgency of the case. Nasotrachial suction was often necessary to clear the respiratory passageways, and needle aspiration of blood in the lung cavity was employed before surgery as necessary to drain blood or remove air due to lung puncture. These measures were carried out by members of the surgical team, depending on availability of the anesthetist or shock officer, but overall responsibility rested with the surgeon to ensure that preoperative routine was properly observed. Ideally, the anesthetist and shock officer cared for the patient jointly; but if casualties were heavy, the surgeon almost always was occupied elsewhere, and ideal management was often not achieved. It was the surgeon's responsibility, preferably in consultation with the shock officer, to determine the optimal time to operate.

The Enemy Soldier

This memoir would not be complete without a comment about the German soldier who opposed our troops in North Africa and Italy. In *Forward Surgery*[5] the German soldier was described as a formidable opponent:

> The German soldier was generally the best in the world. He obeyed orders implicitly, never gave up without a stubborn and vicious fight, and showed amazing stamina and courage. The Germans were masters of taking every advantage of terrain and were artists of well concealed defenses. Without air support, often with restricted artillery support, and with largely animal-drawn transport, they fought the Allies practically to a standstill in Italy. They were also masters of nasty warfare; booby traps and delayed action bombs were commonly used. One such device was the anti-personnel mine called the 'Bouncing Betsy' by the American soldiers which, on being tripped, jumped out of the ground about three feet and exploded, scattering ball bearings over a wide area. This was first encountered in January 1944 in the taking of Cassino, Italy, and from then on, this vicious weapon blew off many feet and accounted for 90% of leg amputations. Of course, the German 88 became

---

[5] *Forward Surgery of the Severely Wounded: A History of the Activities of the 2nd Surgical Group 1942–1945*. Editors: Luther H. Wolff, chairman; Reeve H. Betts, Paul S. Samson, Robert H. Wylie, Samuel E. Childs, Wooster P. Giddings, co-editors. The Surgeon General, U.S. Army, Washington D.C. 1945.

legendary in its accuracy and effectiveness as a multipurpose weapon and caused many injuries to armor and infantry soldiers.

One reaction of the German soldier that greatly surprised me was the almost craven fear of the soldier when professionally encountering a physician. This fear almost amounted to terror. In trying to understand this phenomenon, I finally concluded that it was the result of barracks tales of the cruelty and lack of regard for pain and suffering exhibited by the German doctors. In truth, this was partially true; many procedures were done without local or general anesthesia, where clearly such anesthesia was indicated.

Epilogue

These battle experiences presented wonderful surgical training, especially for this group of young surgeons just out of residencies at academic medical centers. These products of the teaching programs of eminent medical institutions were recruited to form the Second Auxiliary Surgical Group of the Army Medical Corps and work under demanding battlefront conditions. I was fortunate to be one of those men who served his country by practicing the highest level of surgical care as close to the front as possible where lives could be saved that otherwise would have been lost.

Dr. Giddings was born in Boston, Massachusetts and educated at Amherst College and Harvard Medical School. He served in the North African and Italian campaigns with a group of surgical specialists created during World War II to operate mobile hospitals near the frontlines for urgent care of soldiers with life-threatening chest and abdominal wounds. After the war he practiced general surgery in Bennington, Vermont for 41 years and was a faculty member of the Albany Medical School.

My Husband the Doctor

★

Edgar Hyde, MD
U.S. Army Medical Corps

THIS MEMOIR IS BASED ON EXCERPTS of voluminous correspondence from Edgar Hyde, MD, which was assembled into a journal by his wife, Margaret Hyde. Dr. Ed, now deceased, and Margy were early residents of Wake Robin. Ed served as a physician in the African and European campaigns and describes activities of the 91st Evacuation Hospital from Casablanca and the Normandy landings to war's end, including his revulsion at the sights in Buchenwald. The excerpts are taken verbatim from his letters.

December 12-24, 1942: Sailed from New York City on the Army transport USS Argentina, the former American Republics liner of 33,000 tons displacement. Our convoy consists of 19 transports, tankers, and freighters, and 9 escort vessels, including the battleship New York, the cruiser Philadelphia, and seven destroyers. Dense fog prevented our seeing much. Steel helmets and life jackets were required when outside, and life jackets had to be carried even when going to meals. The third day we were presented with pamphlets on North Africa. On the deck, where we spent much time, there was always something interesting — the intricate zigzagging of the convoy, the catapulting and picking up of the scout planes from the cruiser, gunnery practice, or just the changing colors of the sea. Our 14-knot average speed helped protect us, and with the heavy naval escort we didn't worry too much. On the 12th day we were met by small boats and land suddenly loomed on the horizon; we found we were off Casablanca, French Morocco. We moved into the small harbor past the hulks of a couple of blasted and scorched French warships, mementos of the American occupation six weeks previously.

The 91st Evacuation Hospital took over the hospital established by the medical battalion of the Ninth Division outside Casablanca. Malaria was one of the common infectious illnesses affecting the troops. In April the 91st moved to the coast of the Mediterranean in Algeria and in July became part of the Sicily campaign. On September 8, 1943 all Italian troops surrendered unconditionally. In November 1943 the Hospital unit boarded the *Santa Rosa* and sailed to England, landing at Swansea and moving to quarters in the village of Charfield in South Gloucestershire, England on the Little Avon River.

November 26, 1943: We disembarked at 3:30 AM and boarded a train. We arrived in Charfield around 9:00 AM where we boarded trucks. We had no idea what type of bivouac area we were drawing. You have never seen such an amazed group as when we turned in past a neat stone gate in the Tudor style and drove up to a huge manor house. It was the kind of building one dreams of in connection with England, and occasionally sees in the movies. We climbed out of the trucks with our mouths agape as we viewed the towering stone structure and gazed at the beautiful lawns, shrubs, and trees. The place had over 100 rooms and belongs to the Earl of Ducie, with about 7000 acres in the estate. To make the day perfect, I had about 35 letters awaiting me.

The 91st hospital set up and trained there along with another unit, the 128th Evacuation Hospital. Dr. Hyde was temporarily assigned for a month to run a dispensary for another American outfit that lacked medical officers and was occupying the estate of the Duke of Suffolk. On return he was put in charge of the Shock Ward and an X-ray section of the 91st Evacuation Hospital.

> **February 6, 1944:** The hospital was set up under tentage as it would function if doing a lot of surgery. All wards are of double size with two ward tents laced together. The result is that one can care for nearly twice the number of patients with fewer personnel and less equipment. The operating room combines two ward tents and two large wall tents to make a large cross-shaped tent. There is an anteroom for scrubbing and examining patients, two three-table operating rooms, and a central sterile supply tent. Both of the ORs are lined with white cloth drapes. The nurses made these from sheets and make for much better light as well as improving the looks and sanitation. Also, the double wall will make the tents warmer in winter and cooler in summer.

Orders came through on June 3, 1944 for the 91st Evacuation Hospital to move out toward the coast in preparation for D-Day.

The Normandy Campaign

> **June 6-15, 1944:** (The Normandy Landings): All last night sleep here in our tents in England was disturbed by the continuous rumble of passing aircraft, to support the troops who landed in France last night and early this morning. On June 8, we started for the docks at 3:30 AM and were assigned to a Liberty Ship: 300 servicemen plus our medical outfit, so it took all day to load the ship. We crossed the channel the night of June 9-10 and anchored 2 miles offshore to begin unloading. Couldn't unload vehicles until the captain allowed the crew to work the winches and the men to work as stevedores to unload them. The beach was covered with vehicles, and the Germans had sunk many of our ships in the harbor.

Surviving parachutists told us terrifying stories of what the Germans were doing to the captured: torture and death were quickly dealt them. Our hospital opened June 12, a couple of miles behind the front lines, and we really earned our pay the first day. We had over 400 admissions in 24 hours, most in shock, and I operated for 17 hours. If Americans at home could see their gifts of blood plasma in use here, they'd give even more. We continued to work almost incessantly, until auxiliary surgical teams arrived to help, but we still can't do all the surgical procedures necessary. I can't see when we'll ever catch up, at the rate the casualties are coming in. I'm expected to work noon to midnight, but it's usually 2-3 AM before I get off. German planes fly over every night. Later, some of the captured German infantry we operated on turned out to be aviators who had to shift services because so many of their planes have been shot down.

Hyde's surgical unit moved frequently as Allied forces advanced. In July, after they had been working 12-15 hour days flat out without a break, additional medical staff finally arrived. Dr. Hyde's team no longer had to deal with the less serious injuries, such as broken limbs, and could focus on providing prompt, definitive treatment of life-threatening injuries.

July 25, 1944: Our unit heard a steady stream of Allied heavy bombers overhead, plus a tremendous rumbling of bomb explosions. The German prisoners taken are having a fine time; one told me he wants to move to America and live there after the war. His father and brother were killed on the Russian front. Now and then a woman comes in who is about to deliver a baby, so the Allied doctors have an informal "OB" ward to care for them.

During a break Dr. Hyde had an opportunity to visit Paris. By September 1944, Allied troops had moved into Belgian territory, and on September 14 Allied forces invaded German territory. An American captain he met who had been a German prisoner of war told Hyde that his "incessant daily fare consisted of a cup of herb tea and small piece of black bread for breakfast; dinner was one small potato and a bowl of the water it had been boiled in; supper was a small piece of very salty cauliflower and the water it had been cooked in." He and the other prisoners became so weak they could barely walk. French citizens who offered to help them were not permitted by the Germans to do so. One of the libraries in Belgium liberated by units of his battle group was found to contain many fine new books — every one Nazi propaganda.

Battle of the Bulge and Beyond

November 17, 1944: A big drive began; waves of bombers and fighters overhead kept the medical unit awake all night. Next night waves of casualties were brought in; I have never seen such a string of traumatic amputations of feet and legs in my life. Our boys had to cross heavily-mined fields.

November 19: The shock cases rolled in about as fast as we have ever encountered; I am really whipped at the end of my 12 hours. We had about 18 cases of traumatic amputation from mines. Last night we had more German wounded than our own. Am not getting much sleep with the continual roar of our bombers and fighter bombers going over. It is cold, wet, and very muddy in the field these days. The poor doughboys take a beating in this weather.

November 25: At Liege the 15th General Hospital was hit by a buzz bomb (V-1 rocket), and they had to stop taking patients. The damned Germans are plastering the town with V-1 and V-2 rockets, according to good authority as many as 120 of them coming in every 24 hours. We had patients on litters in halls and in every corner; looked like some of the bad days in Palermo (Italy).

December 17-18: The Luftwaffe came out of hiding and attacked continuously all night long. Today comes news that a bunch of German paratroopers were dropped during the night — apparently for a suicide mission. Planes are buzzing around with occasional bombs and strafing as part of a big counteroffensive by the Germans. They are using a raft of armor and troops.

The German counteroffensive was centered around Aachen, Germany and largely to the south of Liege. The 91st Evacuation Hospital was prepared to pull out with trucks parked next to the building loaded with gas and rations and readied to move at any time. The hospital was able to enjoy a quiet Christmas celebration. In January 1945 snow fell heavily and the German offensive gradually ground to a halt.

January 24, 1945: Today, Col. Hayes was awarded the Bronze Star for the fine work he had done as our Commanding Officer. We were happy to see him get the award, he is a wonderful man and has all the qualities in a CO that one can value and admire.

By February 1945 things started to heat up again as more U.S. Army divisions moved into the area. The Ardennes salient has been cleaned up and a "big move" was in the offing.

March 2: At long last, the drive has started and we finally received orders to move out. We crossed the Roer River on a temporary bridge; there were many wrecked and half sunken assault boats. We headed through German villages — no civilians left, but much of the detritus of war remained all over the streets. The field hospital had to move away a bit, because the town had not been cleared of mines and booby traps. German prisoners with the unit were barred from the kitchens but enjoyed the Allied army food. Germans were to be treated justly, but firmly, any sign of resistance to be prohibited immediately. We are now close enough to the Front to hear the artillery fire. In Munchen-Gladbach, the devastation was terrible: streets blasted away, many blocks impassible, piles of rubble and tremendous bomb craters everywhere. If this town was just an incidental target, I can't imagine what some of the cities they've really concentrated on must be like.

March 3: We moved into a German insane hospital building outside of Erkelenz replacing a Field Hospital unit. There were still about 80 patients, mostly feeble-minded. We will have three buildings, which is better than being in tents, but there was no electricity or water, and little heat at first. Jack Davis and I walked down the road from the hospital, which is far out in the countryside, into the little village a mile away. Practically the entire village had decamped ahead of the Americans. Apparently the German troops there didn't put up much of a fight because there was comparatively little damage to the village. There were empty morphine syrettes besides little piles of bloody abandoned American and German equipment. The bodies of two American soldiers who had been beaten and shot were in the Field Hospital morgue.

March 6: We are busy in the hospital and restricted to the area because of the fact that there are still several mine fields around here, and there has been a nearby sniping incident. The battle casualties are beginning to fall off as our troops are gaining their objectives. We are annoyed that Monty (Gen. Montgomery), commanding general of the army group, is not letting the Ninth Army keep on going across the Rhine.

March 28: We became the first hospital unit to cross the Rhine with the Ninth Army. Soon they had more Germans than Americans to care for, ill but most not in need of surgery. By then, the Allies were advancing so fast it was hard to keep up. We passed many hundreds of freed allied prisoners trudging along the roads, Poles, Russians, French, Dutch, Belgian and Italian. Some, especially Poles and Russians, were pitiful specimens: emaciated, dirty, pale. The prisoners still had some 60 miles to trudge to a place where they would be fed and get some rest. Met some British who had been in German prison camps, emaciated, wasted, overworked by the Germans. Over 800 British prisoners started the march, only half survived. Americans came to hate the Germans for what they'd done, and doctors found they were the biggest complainers and gripers in their wards. Raised Cain and moaned all the time.

April 16: Hospital headed for the Elbe, a long jump forward, where the 2nd Armored Division took an awful beating when it crossed the river. They were cut off on the other side of the river, and two battalions were pretty much wiped out. Troops that had not yet crossed had to await support of more fire power before crossing.

April 17: We headed off at 7:00 AM in three sections for Wiepke about 22 miles this side of the Elbe and north of Berlin. One section became lost, and the Colonel even went out in a Piper Cub scouting for them. They eventually found us, to our great relief. It was a rough hard trip of about 160 miles and as much dust as we had seen since Africa. We literally ate it. It was bad enough in an open cab of a truck, but the poor fellows up top of the equipment in back were unrecognizable when we finally pulled in. It was particularly bad in one stretch behind a column of tanks. I had never seen such a concentration of ack-ack along a road as there was on this one. The Luftwaffe had been strafing it with regularity. We understand the probable reason for this is the capture of one of our gas columns. Whatever the reason, the Luftwaffe has been out in more strength in this area than at any time since the Ardennes offensive.

There are a large pocket of Germans running around loose who have cut the main road. There are many small pockets of bypassed Germans about. We noticed there are many light armored patrols out on the roads, and a couple of generals' cars passed by. We are in tents again but we arrived so late that the rest of the hospital will go up tomorrow morning and we open for business at 1500 hours.

German Atrocities

April 18: 1945: This afternoon I saw a sight calculated to curdle the blood of Attila himself. It was in a town called Gardelegan, captured by the 102nd division four days ago. A group of about 1,000 assorted POWs and political prisoners, mainly Poles and Russians had started a long march from Germany with Hannover as its destination. They had five potatoes per man per day, and about 600 survived this far. They were in the charge of a Gestapo man, some SS soldiers, and some Wehrmacht non-coms. The Germans decided to murder the prisoners. They were forced into a large stone barn whose floor had been covered with two feet of straw soaked in oil. There were four large doors but no windows. All the doors were covered by guards with weapons, and then incendiary grenades were thrown in. Any attempt to escape was shot down by the guards at the doors. The

Germans were trying to bury the evidence of this horror, but Allied troops came too soon. So several hundred of the burnt bodies, some still smoldering, remained; Americans captured some of the German guards, and the Gestapo man in charge. This scene was 'the ultimate in horror.' General Simpson of the 9th Army told all who saw it to write home, name the town, and describe exactly what they saw, so all will know. A powerful argument against fraternization.

By April 21, 1945 the Russians were only 18 miles from the center of Berlin, and separated from the Allies by only 45 miles. On May 3, news came that Hitler was dead, and peace feelers had been put out by the Germans. Word came that Mussolini had been captured and shot and the Russians had taken Berlin. Suddenly, the hospital was overrun by German wounded or sick. V-E Day arrived May 9, 1945. Aware of the war in the Pacific, the unit had a fairly quiet celebration. Many Americans were able to go home, but essential personnel such as surgeons and others would probably go to the Pacific Theater.

Now with time available for sightseeing. Hyde visited Buchenwald and was horrified by what he saw there, as were his fellow officers.

June 5, 1945: We finally pulled into Weimar a bit worse for wear and found the camp about five miles out of town with the aid of a Russian and Yugoslav who had been incarcerated there. I can't imagine anyone escaping from the place what with tremendous electrified barbed wire fences, several hundred trigger-happy SS guards, and a bunch of ferocious guard dogs plus its location in the middle of hostile country. We were escorted by an intelligent 19-year-old Polish boy who had been liberated after three years of internment in Buchenwald and other camps. He was recuperating from starvation but still far from recovered, despite a month of nutritious American diet. Typical fare was half a loaf of bread and a little watery soup a day for each man. His heinous offense had been that of being a student.

We saw the crematory with its battery of furnaces and its basement room where the SS guards were accustomed to garrote and hang their victims. The barracks were largely windowless wooden sheds about 85 ft. by 25 ft. and in them 1200 men prisoners slept on bare boards with about 12 inches to the man. The hospital with a 900 patient census was even smaller. There was an average of 60 deaths a day in the hospital alone. And Buchenwald is not supposed to be as bad as Dachau or a whole string of camps in Poland!

Epilogue

Dr. Hyde was granted a week's leave in England. On the flight over Germany, he observed the vast devastation of the country, referring to it as "a mess." On Aug. 15, 1945, World War II finally ended. Before returning to the States, Hyde had an opportunity to visit Hitler's "Eagle's Nest" in the Bavarian mountains. Hitler's retreat had a gorgeous view in all directions, but the formerly beautiful interior of the villa had suffered severe damage from Allied bombing. On September 17, 1945 the officers of Hyde's medical unit were flown to Paris en route to home. They flew out of Orly Airport, but first changed their money to "good old American dollar bills." On September 21, 1945 after a stop in Newfoundland, they flew on to Washington, D.C., arriving some 31 hours after leaving Paris. Dr. Hyde's 33-month tour of overseas duty with the Army Medical Corps was over.

Ed Hyde practiced family medicine in Northfield, Vermont for 40 years. In the early years health care involved "house calls" that led him, with his familiar black bag and four-wheel drive, over the outlying hills, in all weather, often at night, for a fee of $4.00. Norwich University conferred Doctor of Humanities on him in 1983. He founded the medical clinic at Mad River Glen ski area, spent each Saturday there for 25 years treating ski injuries, and was an Honorary National Ski Patrol member.

A NURSE'S FIRST JOB:
EXPANDING ROLES

★

Barbara Madden, RN

M Y FIRST JOB AFTER GRADUATING from the nursing school of
a large teaching hospital was in 1942. Rather than joining an
armed service, as did many of my classmates, I returned home as my
mother was in the late stages of a chronic illness. With a keen interest in pediatric orthopedics, I was fortunate that there was a Shriners
Hospital in my home town.

This hospital had a Medical Director who was there about three
half-days a week, and otherwise available by phone. The full-time staff
included eight registered nurses and a variety of nursing assistants,
kitchen, laundry, cleaning and maintenance help. We comprised a small
team of dedicated workers. The children came from all over New England and stayed as many months as necessary for their treatments. At
first, I had the joy and satisfaction of daily care of the children, but soon
was assigned to do whatever was needed — covering the night supervisor's time off (this included preparing supper for the night staff);

writing notes to any family unable to visit their siblings; accompanying a child to a specialist's office in the city (this might include a treat for the child, e.g., their first escalator ride); assisting with cast changes; and filling in for the OR nurse when she took time off. I was 10 years junior to the other nurses so I had recent experience with some of the newer procedures. In one surgery, I held retractors carefully positioned by the surgeon as there was no other physician available to assist in the operation. In this my first nursing position, I had many new learning experiences.

A year passed rapidly and when I returned from my first vacation, I was informed that in two week's time Cadet Student Nurses from the General Hospital Nursing School were beginning an affiliation, and I would be responsible for overseeing the program. Me — a nurse with one year of graduate experience, none involving teaching. I had two weeks to plan the curriculum, purchase reference material, plan classes. No physician would be available to teach so I would be the only instructor. Typically, in nursing schools at that time, a physician would lecture on treatment for a condition, such as congenital club feet, dislocated hips, or spinal bifida, and a nursing instructor would follow up with Nursing Care for each type of patient. A few of these Cadet Nurse Students were within a year of my age, in fact one in the first group, had been a neighbor. Fortunately, I realized lecturing would not provide the best learning experience, so I assigned the students required reading to prepare for the next upcoming topic; we held good discussions as a result. There were eight students per group so this seminar method of instruction worked reasonably well. With each new group, the student RNs must have benefitted from my growing knowledge and increasing confidence.

This experience actually colored my entire professional life. I loved teaching but wanted to learn how to teach better. Following the death of my mother, I took courses in Orthopedic Nursing at Teachers' College, Columbia University. I left Shriners Hospital with a broad range of experience that would not have been possible during peacetime — increased maturity and a clearer vision of my future in nursing. I feel that no child was less well off because of the things I did even though many duties and activities were outside the scope of my preparation in nurses' training.

Brought up in Springfield, Massachusetts, Barbara graduated from Boston Children's Hospital nursing school and spent the war years at Shriners Hospital. She earned graduate degrees from Teachers College of Columbia University and the University of North Carolina, and was an administrator at Boston University Hospital and a rehabilitation hospital in California. She is known for teaching nursing care of polio patients and rehabilitation, including a documentary film that received an award at the International Film Festival in Cannes. After retirement she established rehabilitation programs in Iran and South Africa.

A Doctor Looks Back

★

James McKay, MD
U.S. Army Medical Corps

As an adolescent I wished to be proficient in European languages and undertook two periods of study in Germany. Following high school, I lived with a German family in Frankfurt for five
months in 1935, and as a modern languages major at Princeton spent
my junior year in Munich in 1937-1938. This enabled me not only to
become fluent in German, but also to experience first-hand the growing threat of war, the rise of Hitler, and the malignant influence of
the Nazis on Germany and the peoples of Europe. I also spent time
in France to improve my proficiency gained in eight years of taking
French courses. These experiences proved useful to me during World
War II and provided me with a unique perspective, practical as well as
political, on European culture.

Germany invaded Poland on September 1, 1939 about two weeks
before I entered Harvard Medical School. This fulfilled predictions
of many of my friends and pub acquaintances in Germany who had

foreseen the imminency of a second world war. Convinced of impending U.S. involvement, I signed up around the end of 1940 as an officer in the Army Medical Corps Reserve, about a year before the Japanese attacked Pearl Harbor December 7, 1941. I finished Harvard Medical School in March 1943, and was married on May 30, 1943. After completing an accelerated internship in pediatrics at Babies' Hospital of Columbia-Presbyterian Hospital in New York on December 31, 1943, I went on active duty at Carlisle Barracks, Pennsylvania, February 25, 1944.

My indoctrination into Army ways involved a six-week course in military basics at the Medical Field Service School at Carlisle and six weeks at LaGarde General Hospital in New Orleans. I was then assigned as Battalion Surgeon to the 275th Engineer Combat Battalion, 75th Infantry Division at Camp Breckenridge, Kentucky.

In military lingo, all doctors are called surgeons, and a battalion surgeon is the primary care doctor for a battalion (500-600 soldiers) that is involved in frontline fighting or supporting combat troops. An engineer combat battalion does things like building bridges, laying or clearing mine fields, building or clearing defenses such as booms and barbed-wire fences, all of which are often carried out in advance of infantry units and often under enemy fire. As the battalion surgeon, I dealt most often with everyday medical and psychiatric conditions (frostbite, sinusitis, dysentery, respiratory infections, malingering, combat fatigue) rather than with the treatment of battle wounds and injuries. Emergency procedures such as arresting bleeding, providing an airway, treating shock and pain, were carried out prior to transporting wounded to the Field Hospital for definitive treatment.

By late summer 1944, the 75th Division completed training, I was promoted to the rank of Captain, and we restlessly awaited orders for overseas deployment, which arrived in November (a classic example of Army "Hurry up and wait"). We sailed for Europe on the Cunard liner *Aquitania*. All aboard were part of the75th Division, except for a group of field-grade and senior officers who kept very much to themselves and were said to be headquarters staff of the 15th Army, a new unit designated to reinforce troops in Europe. Later, we learned that the

15th Army was a ruse to fool the German High Command into think-ing we had more troops in Europe than was really the case. After five or six days of zig-zagging in a convoy to avoid torpedoes, we landed at Greenock, Scotland and proceeded to the Cardigan area of Wales, where the 275th was quartered in the village of Velindre. A few weeks later, we boarded landing craft in Southampton, England bound for France. The weather was bad, so the crossing of the English Channel and up the Seine River to Rouen, France took three or four days. The landing craft only had rations on board for a 24-hour crossing, and the Navy officers and crew "bitched" volubly about the shortage of food and its low quality. On the other hand, we Army characters found the food the best we had had for weeks (or would experience for the next six months).

Our first night on European soil we pitched tents on an apple farm between Rouen and Le Havre. The weather was cold, rainy, and muddy, so our detachment dental officer, a friendly fellow, left to see if our host farmer had any apple cider for sale. He returned with a bottle of calvados, which he mostly consumed over the evening, not realizing that calvados is a distillate of apple brandy of higher proof than Ameri-can whiskey or brandy. Needless to say, he had a monstrous hangover, which left him suffering and unfit for duty for several days.

Initiation into Combat

The next day, we headed north in a motor convoy, ostensibly as reserve troops for an expected Allied push into Germany. On arrival in a small village near Maastricht, Holland, we learned of an unexpected German attack, which became the Battle of the Bulge. As our convoy parked along the street awaiting orders, we encountered our first taste of enemy fire, when a German fighter plane strafed us making two passes. My detachment spent that night in a nice house whose occupants informed us that we were welcome either to spend the night in comfortable beds in their house or in the safety of "the caves." We were puzzled as to what they meant until they explained that the obvious prosperity of the town was due to the local mushroom industry, which raised mushrooms within a system of interlocking caves under the town and its environs. Numerous entries and exits proved very handy for hiding and escaping from the Germans. They led us down to the cellar through a camouflaged door into the cave system, proceeding to show us beds of growing mushrooms, packing and shipping rooms, sleeping quarters, and an expertly concealed exit opening onto a vacant field. We thanked them for the tour, but chose to spend the night in the comfortable beds of their house.

From then on until war's end, the 75th Division and its various units were shifted from place to place under different commands, depending on the need for reinforcements. My battalion aid station was generally situated near battalion headquarters with its own attached living quarters and half a mile or so behind the active fighting. However, during the Battle of the Bulge and the Battle of the Colmar Pocket, battle lines constantly shifted, and intermittently we were cut off or surrounded, usually at night.

After the "mushroom" experience, we moved into Belgium, where people were friendly and hospitable, like the Dutch. While higher command was deciding where to send us, we lived for several days on a country farm where our aid station was set up in the kitchen, with living quarters in a connecting hay mow, a set-up we often employed in rural settings. From there, we were ordered to an inn and farm complex along a fog-enshrouded river. On arrival, we were ordered to dig foxholes on a hillside behind the inn because enemy artillery fire was expected. The detachment first sergeant and I began immediately to dig our holes, but the rest of the men just stood around and laughed at us for digging foxholes in such an apparently peaceful setting. The sergeant and I had barely finished when a German artillery barrage began, the shells hitting the top of the hill above us. Of course, we jumped into our foxholes, while the rest of the detachment had to throw themselves on the ground as their sole protection. When the barrage ended, the laughers immediately became frantic foxhole-diggers. When they finished, the diggers deputized one of their members to apologize to me for their disobedience. He did so by saying: "Captain, from now on, when you tell us to dig, we dig!" From then until my transfer to a general hospital in September, 1945, my orders were obeyed promptly and without question.

Battle of the Bulge

We remained at the farm-inn for several days, and we began to see battle fatigue from the physical strain and emotional tension of combat, combined with the associated lack of sleep and personal hygiene. As a method of handling the problem without sending afflicted soldiers back to the rear echelon for psychiatric care (which meant loss of a soldier's services to his unit for a week or more, or sometimes permanently), I developed a form of "mini" R & R (military leave for rest and recuperation), hoping to avoid their dropping out of their units, as well as loss of self respect and that of their comrades-in-arms. This involved assigning the affected soldier to "temporary duty" in the medical detachment, a haircut done personally by me (having a Captain and a Doctor as one's personal barber seemed a particularly good morale-booster, especially for enlisted men), a shave (skillfully done by the medical detachment's podiatrist), a warm bath or shower, a hot meal, and an undisturbed night of rest on a dry cot under warm blankets. The period of sleep usually lasted from 12 to 20 hours, and after a second meal, the soldier was generally ready and eager to return. If not, he was kept on duty in the medical detachment for a few more days when, almost invariably, he was ready to rejoin his unit.

Leaving the farm-inn in mid-December, we moved about from bivouac to bivouac as the weather changed from overcast and foggy, which protected us from being strafed or bombed by the occasional German plane passing overhead, to cold and snowy. Nighttime patrols by the Germans occasionally awakened us when they were fired on. On one occasion several hours after the gunfire had stopped, we heard rustling sounds in the dark around our aid-station tents. A couple of my men sneaked out cautiously to see what was going on. They returned in about 20 minutes, very upset, to say they had seen American GIs cutting off fingers of dead soldiers, both German and American, to steal wedding rings. This was our introduction to some of the brutality of war.

During the next few days, as the weather turned much colder, we started to receive wounded at the aid station. I recall the shock of seeing my first battle wound, a shrapnel wound of the shoulder that had laid bare the scapula and muscles of the back — on Christmas Eve. That same night, one of our company officers was brought in raving mad. He had broken under the stress of having been ordered to send some of his men into almost certain death — for the third time that day.

Christmas 1944 dawned bright and clear. The first of a series of 1,000-plane American bombing raids on German supply lines and factories in the German Ruhr droned overhead. Wave on wave of bombers flew unfalteringly into heavy anti-aircraft fire (or "ack-ack," as we called it), with numerous planes shot down within view, yet flights continued unwaveringly. Prior to that raid, we "regular" soldiers had been scornful and derisive about the spoiled "fly-boys" and their soft "rear-echelon" life we had perceived. Seeing that raid and the bravery of the "fly-boys" who conducted it, totally reversed our opinion. Respect and admiration replaced derision. It still brings tears to my eyes whenever I think of that raid and those brave airmen. The effect of these Christmas bombing raids were apparent almost immediately, as our forces started to press the enemy back, and we became less apprehensive about being overrun during the night.

I next recall we set up the aid station in a deserted farmhouse at the edge of the Belgian village of Grandmenil, where we stayed put for a week or so. From the farmhouse we could look eastward and see a stream forming the line between the Germans and the Americans about half a mile away. The first few days there, we were totally immobilized by an epidemic of dysentery which spread through our troops like wildfire. At first, we were scared stiff that the Germans would use the occasion to attack us, but learned that they suffered the same problem. The aid station was very busy during this period, especially our "restroom", a six-foot trench in an empty woodshed behind the house with a relatively thin log suspended over it to sit on. This could support three or four soldiers at a time, but an overweight customer plopped down abruptly and broke it, spilling him into the half-filled trench below. Needless to say, we not only replaced the log but also put up a sign warning users to "Please Sit with Care!"

I remember another incident while our aid station was at Grandmenil. One afternoon one of our company commanders, who was widely known in our battalion as a blowhard, paid the aid station an unwelcome visit, apparently to give us a hard time about being "rear-echelon" soldiers. While he was there, we heard a German artillery shell coming in. These were common occurrences and we had learned to tell by the sound which shells would land close to us and which well beyond us. One sounded as if it might land close by, so we all hit the dirt, while he sat and laughed at us for being such "sissies"; then, the shells landed about 40 or so yards from us. When the shelling ceased, we got up off the floor, and he continued to mock us, although obviously shaken by the proximity of the explosions. About 10 minutes later, we heard more shells coming. Experience told us they would land far beyond us. However, the noise terrified our mocker, who hit the floor while we sat there and laughed him out of the aid station.

The battalion began conducting prolonged nighttime operations in very cold weather. The upper echelons of command had not foreseen either the bitter weather or the paucity of heat and shelter any better than they had foreseen the German offensive. As a result, we were not only ill equipped going into battle, without adequate cold-weather clothing, blankets, footwear, or sources of heat, but the equipment never arrived until the Battle of the Bulge was essentially over. Many patients during this period suffered from sinusitis and frostbite, to the latter of which I also fell victim from extended cold exposure during night operations.

Shortly before moving out of Grandmenil, we learned the tide of battle had turned, and our troops were advancing eastward into territory held by the enemy. That evening, a Belgian civilian from the next village about a mile away showed up at the aid station to confirm that the Germans had evacuated the village and asked help for his wife who was in labor. After establishing that the village's doctor was busy with another delivery and the man's wife seemed to be in real trouble, I collected whatever relevant instruments I could in the aid station, and accompanied him through a light snowfall to his house. I discovered she really was in difficulty, which proved relatively easy to correct by pushing the baby's head back up into the mother's uterus and then turning it to a more favorable position to exit her pelvis, a maneuver I had learned as a medical student intern at the Florence Crittenden Home for unmarried mothers in Boston. Shortly after the delivery, the village doctor and another villager arrived, informing me that the Germans had unexpectedly pushed back into the village and to skedaddle back to the relative safety of my aid station. I skedaddled.

Next, our aid station moved to the town of Vielsalm as the division advanced. There, we set up in a town building that was airtight and comfortably heated with our potbellied stove, and also offered the luxury of two functioning 60-watt electric light bulbs for the first time in about a month. What a boon this was! We remained in Vielsalm in relative ease as the Battle of the Bulge wound down. Some of my aid men even went to Paris for a weekend of R & R, and our long-awaited winter clothing and extra blankets finally arrived, too late for the Bulge but just in time for bivouacking in the snowy forests around Colmar.

The Colmar Pocket

Our sojourn in Vielsalm was rudely interrupted the end of January, 1945 by orders shifting the 75th Division to Colmar in the Vosges Mountains of France, where the enemy had established a salient just north of Patton's advance. My unit, the 275th Combat Engineers, was completely motorized, so we moved by convoy, with the city of Nancy in France as our first day's destination. Late in the afternoon, our vehicles somehow became separated from the rest of the Battalion and became lost as dusk fell over a deserted, snowy landscape. We were uncertain as to whether it was in American or German hands. Finally, we spotted a large, lighted tent in a field about 100 yards off to our right. We stopped our vehicles, and I went on foot through the snow-covered field to see what it was and who was in it. Fortunately, it turned out to be an American regimental command post, whose occupants informed me that we were indeed on the road to Nancy, that it seemed to be, at least temporarily, in American hands, and that other motorized units of the 75th Division had passed through an hour or so earlier. As we were talking, a haggard-looking infantry squad leader came in to say that they had just taken some Germans prisoner. He wanted to know what they should do with them. He was told that his squad should deliver them immediately to a prisoner assembly area about three miles away, and return for further orders. He saluted and left. About five minutes later, as I was discussing the route to Nancy with the officers in the tent, we heard a burst of rifle fire. A few minutes later the squad leader reported back as I was about to leave, saying they had "disposed" of the prisoners, and asking "Could they return to their unit now?" The regimental officers acquiesced.

We proceeded on, arriving around one AM at the Nancy Opera House where we were to spend the night on bare floors with the rest of the battalion. We found the Opera House to be almost divinely comfortable since it was dry, heated, well-lighted, and boasted indoor plumbing. The next day we drove through more snow, arriving late that night at our bivouac site in a forest near Colmar, only to be ordered to dig foxholes immediately because the forest was under threat of artillery and/or mortar fire. Our resentment about digging foxholes was considerably mollified when we found that after we had managed to dig through the deep snow and the few inches of frozen dirt under it, the digging became easier. When we lay down in the foxholes about four feet below ground, we no longer felt uncomfortably cold. We remained for several days in our forested bivouac about 100 yards off a forest road, along which both American and German troops roamed with equal frequency. Finally, we moved the aid station to a building in a village closer to Colmar and across the street from a bar frequented at night by off-duty Allied soldiers. One night, one of my aid men ran back to the aid station to report that a soldier in our battalion had just shot and killed an Algerian soldier with little if any provocation. It turned out that the American was unpopular with his own comrades because of his frequent flares of violence. He was dragged away by the MPs, and we were given to understand (without details) that he was severely disciplined.

During the Colmar Pocket conflict, we noted that our English and French comrades (except for the French Tank Corps) would "hole up" at dusk and leave the fighting at night almost entirely to us and the Germans, which fostered a sort of comradeship with the latter. It was even rumored that while the Germans and we were night-fighting in the cold, many French and English officers were "shacking up" with local mistresses in their headquarters town of Colmar.

We reached the Rhine the first week of February and enjoyed a few days respite. I still recall a starlit evening, watching the movie "Casablanca" while sitting in a roofless barn in a village along the Rhine. I also remember coming back to our aid station after the movie to find the corporal left on duty there strumming his "geetar" and singing dolefully about his Appalachian home in the West Virginia hills.

The day before moving to our next assignment, the officers of the 275th Combat Engineer Battalion were assembled for presentation of a Unit Commendation by our new division commander, Major General Ray E. Porter, for our service during the Battle of the Bulge. As part of the ceremony, we were reviewed by General Porter, who walked slowly along the line of officers standing at attention, inspecting each officer's posture and uniform approvingly until he came to me. He had noted something wrong about the way I had positioned my ribbons or insignia. He drew a deep breath preparatory to raking me over the coals, suddenly took a second look, noticing my medical corps insignia, resignedly let out his breath, said "Oh, God, you're a *Doc!*" in a disgusted tone, and moved on with his inspection.

The next day, we headed north to a Dutch village near Eindthoven, where we were to relieve a British engineer battalion engaged in rebuilding roads and bridges. My detachment was quartered in the home of a Dutch family whose 14-year-old retarded daughter lived behind a door behind our aid station. She drove us batty by repeatedly singing "Lili Marlene" all day long in a haunting, eerie, soprano voice.

I also remember a meeting between the senior officers of the 75th and those of the British battalion we were relieving. The British commander pointed out on a map the location of various jobs that we were to take over, saying: "We have about 100 laborers working on this big bridge *hee-ah*, 25 on each of these three little bridges *they-ah*, 200 or so on each of the roads *hee-ah*," and so forth. When he finished, our CO (commanding officer) asked how and where he could possibly muster so much manpower. The British officer replied: "Well, it's *sawt* of a lend-lease proposition with the Dutch, you *know-oh* — they *wohrk* on *ow-ah* roads and we live in *they-ah* houses."

We remained in Holland for around 10 days rebuilding roads and bridges, and then moved south into Germany for R & R before crossing the Rhine into the German Ruhr industrial area. We spent two to three weeks quartered in a comfortable duplex house in a small city, either Krefeld or Muenchen-Gladbach. While there, my detachment had the opportunity of going to an afternoon USO concert featuring Lily Pons (in a clinging, strapless evening dress) with Andre Kostelanitz and Orchestra. On return to Battalion Headquarters, the Adjutant, who checked us in individually, asked a corporal in the detachment (noted for his graphic descriptions) how he had liked the concert and Lily Pons' singing? The corporal replied: "Geez, Lieutenant, it was great! What a Baz-o-o-o-m!"

On another occasion, a corporal came into the aid station with a satisfied smile on his face after going out for a walk to get some fresh air. I asked him what had cheered him up. He replied that he had accosted several well-dressed civilians on the street and asked if they were German. Each had replied that he was "Dutch", so the corporal had "beaten them up" for lying. I pointed out that they had probably said "Deutsch", the German word for "German", rather than "Dutch." He replied: "You're probably right, Captain, it did sound sort of funny — but they deserved it anyway!"

The Rhine Crossing

After our R & R was over, the 275th Engineer Combat Battalion was deployed to a deserted village 200-300 hundred yards from the west bank of the Rhine. Soon after arrival, we were visited by a colonel from Division Headquarters who met with the Battalion's senior officers to discuss our mission. We sat in the living room of a house looking down over the river. He told us that our mission was to lay a boom, or weir, across the river in order to deflect floating mines that the enemy might dispatch down river to destroy a bridge being built 20-30 miles north of us. As he finished, several German planes roared overhead, and suddenly we were sitting unscathed in a room without a roof, a bizarre event unexplained to this day.

Since movement along the bank of the river was subject to enemy mortar fire, and it was necessary to reconnoiter for possible sites for the boom to be placed, our CO decided that initial reconnoitering be carried out by my medical detachment because, he reasoned, not carrying arms and wearing our Red Cross armbands, we would be immune from enemy fire. Our first reconnoiter identified the remains of a German aid station that had been hit by artillery or mortar fire. I found their record-keeping methods of interest, being obviously less encumbered by administrative "red tape" than ours. Next, we rummaged through a building suspected of being a munitions factory. It turned out to be an abandoned cigar factory, from which the men in the party who were smokers "liberated" a number of boxes of what, they said, were excellent cigars. We then started back from the riverside when I heard a mortar shell coming and yelled, "Hit the dirt!" The sergeant just ahead of me, in an effort to protect his cigars, was a little slow in responding, and I saw his head give a little jerk just as the shell landed near him. When the shelling stopped after a few minutes, I yelled for everyone to scatter and head back to our aid station. All did so, except for the sergeant, who lay on the ground with blood seeping through his fingers as he held his hands over his face, while he moaned that his left cheek had been shot off. I asked him to remove his hands so I could assess the damage. All I could see was blood oozing out of a small hole in his cheek just under his left eye. Otherwise, he appeared undamaged. After he was reassured, we made our way back to the aid station where a mirror showed him that his face was all there, even though it felt as if it weren't. He remained on active duty, the wound healed, sensation gradually returned to his cheek, and six months later only a tiny scar on his cheek and a small shell fragment in his left maxillary sinus on x-ray remained to remind him of his narrow escape, along with his Purple Heart.

Our Colonel, undaunted by this setback to his theory of the protective power of Red Cross armbands, sent me out the next night with a couple of company officers and their sergeants to scout out some as yet unexplored buildings on the river bank. After dark, we set off with flashlights and were investigating what appeared to be a stash of various building materials when another mortar barrage struck. Fortunately, we had identified covered foxholes with narrow entrances nearby and quickly jumped into them. When the barrage ended, we waited a while before deciding it was safe to continue. The others climbed out of their foxholes and again began looking around with their flashlights. However, when I tried to exit, my canteen kept catching on the under-edge of the foxhole cover. Finally, I dropped back down to remove my canteen and belt. As I began to climb out of the narrow hole for a second time, I heard the squeal of another shell coming, and dropped quickly back into the foxhole. The shell landed and exploded just beside the hole and about a foot in front of where my abdomen would have been had I not dropped back in the foxhole. It was the most terrifying moment of the war for me, and I stayed shaking in the foxhole until my companions came looking for me after the second barrage had ceased. They had all escaped injury by jumping into large sections of concrete culvert lying on the ground near them when they heard the shell coming that almost got me.

The 275th continued constructing the boom, and the Germans, assuming all the activity meant the American attack would come from our sector, began shifting troops and artillery on the east bank of the Rhine opposite us. This left relatively unopposed the area where the attack across the Rhine was actually launched. Tactically, this was a great help to our side, but it also made things more difficult for us because of the increased surveillance and artillery fire, in addition to the mortar fusillades. Most construction activity shifted from daylight to nighttime hours. I made several nocturnal forays across the river with engineers to construct the east-bank anchor site, all to little avail because the boom broke shortly after we installed it. The only actual construction casualty was the almost surgically neat amputation of the lower leg of an engineer from whiplash of a wire cable that broke while he was standing nearby.

The afternoon before the Battalion moved across the Rhine, I crossed the river by motorboat to help interrogate a newly-captured SS colonel who spoke little or no English. I found him to be an extremely defiant and recalcitrant subject for interrogation. First, he objected to being interrogated by anyone below his rank, followed by a harangue on what he would do after Germany had won the war to anyone who had interrogated him inappropriately. Just then, the first wave of one of the 4,000 strong American bomber raids on Berlin passed unopposed over us in the clear late-afternoon sky. We all looked up, and I asked him how he could speak of a German victory while watching a sight like that? In answer, he spat forcefully and angrily shouted, "Propaganda!" We finally gave up on him.

As he was led away, one of the enlisted men who brought another Engineer officer, my first sergeant, and me over the Rhine, spotted a horse with a halter but no saddle, wandering around loose. He was an enthusiastic horseman, and immediately wanted to catch and ride the horse bareback. Because we were in an area we had been warned was infested with mines, his officer gave him a direct order not to do so, and to accompany the rest of our group back to the boat. He responded by catching the horse, vaulting onto its bare back, and whooped and galloped across a neighboring field. He and the horse had reached the middle of the field when a mine exploded under them, killing the horse and leaving him on the ground crying for help in the middle of what we all now recognized as a mine field. I ordered a couple of the men to go down to the boat and bring up a stretcher I had noted on the way across the river. They did so, while I asked for volunteers to go into the field with me to carry him out. We had all been trained in recognizing and disarming mines, but only my first sergeant volunteered. Dusk was falling rapidly and there was no time to waste, so we entered the field, cautiously avoiding mines and tripwires. We finally reached the soldier, finding him painfully but not mortally wounded, loaded him on the stretcher, and carried him out even more fearfully and cautiously because of the increasing darkness. The boat trip back to the aid station was uneventful, but I was so angry with him for disobeying the direct order of his officer and, as a result, risking the lives of fellow soldiers, that before sending him to the hospital for treatment I labeled his wounds as "NLD" (not in line of duty). This meant he would not receive a Purple Heart. It still rankles me that the major in charge of the hospital ward reversed my decision. The major's not indefensible reasoning was that the soldier should not be disqualified from receiving a medal because the incident never would have happened had he not been in a war under combat conditions.

Partly due to the diversion occasioned by Battalion activities, the main crossing of the Rhine 20 or 30 miles downriver was largely unopposed, and our Division followed a few days later. Our units were plagued for the first few days by the loss of two or three soldiers to sniper fire in each town we passed through. This stopped suddenly and completely after (it was rumored) Brigadier General Mickle, our Assistant Division Commander, ordered that from then on, each entry of a town was to be preceded by a heavily armored Signal Corps vehicle, which was to blare out on its loud speaker a warning that any house from which sniper fire issued would be surrounded, set on fire, and every living man, woman, child or animal who emerged killed. This was said to have happened only once before our Division's losses from sniper fire abruptly ceased, albeit at the cost of six or seven possibly innocent lives. There was general agreement within the Division that General Mickle had made a (for us) good decision.

As we proceeded town by town through the Ruhr, our Battalion executive officer, whose responsibility it was to find billets for its members, seemed to find them by ousting laborers from their crowded tenements. I became annoyed with this practice because on our way to these quarters we frequently passed through areas of large houses that looked to me likely to belong to ranking Nazis and/or their sympathizers. I complained to our CO who said, "OK, Doc, from now on you are the billeting officer." This led to many conversations in German between me and those evicted. One of these conversations occurred when an evicted owner ran up to me as we were leaving a billet to thank me effusively in German, in the presence of our Battalion executive officer, for the minimal damage and disorder that my detachment had done to his home. A few days later, I was suspended from duty while a couple of CID (Criminal Investigation Division) investigators questioned my men, and others, as to whether I was a German sympathizer. Thirty-six hours later, I was restored to active duty. My enlisted men, who had friends among the enlisted personnel at Battalion Headquarters, later told me that I had been suspended because the Battalion executive officer suspected that I was in collusion with the enemy.

I have always suspected that this investigation may have dogged me years later at the time of the McCarthy hearings, when I became aware my home telephone was being tapped. Repeatedly, I heard breathing noises that I was sure was neither mine nor that of the person with whom I was speaking. It seemed most noticeable when I was talking with my brother (as I did frequently), who was a naval architect working on atomic submarines in New London, Connecticut at the time. I am not sure whether the person being spied on was me or my brother. In any event, I complained to the FBI office in Burlington. When nothing changed, I angrily called the FBI office in Albany, New York, and the suspected surveillance abruptly stopped.

The advance of the 75th Division into Germany ended in the town of Plettenberg in a pleasant, hilly, forested resort area south of the Ruhr, encircled by about 30 German military hospitals. Each of the Division's medical officers, with two exceptions, was assigned to oversee the operation of one or two of these hospitals. The two exceptions were the only doctors in the Division who spoke German well (a typical example of military "efficiency"). The two German-speaking doctors were me and the Division Surgeon, who hosted a bridge foursome meeting two or three times weekly and consisted of him (a full colonel), my CO (a major who had replaced my original CO, a lieutenant colonel), the Division Psychiatrist (a major), and me (a mere captain).

In Plettenberg I helped commandeer housing for Battalion Headquarters, as well as for my own detachment. For Battalion Headquarters and its staff, we chose the largest and finest house on the north edge of town, the area that had been assigned to the 275th Engineer Combat Battalion. It was occupied only by the owners, their severely psychiatrically handicapped adult daughter, and her live-in nurse. Her father did his best to dissuade us from taking over the house, on the grounds that his daughter really needed to live there in order to receive electric-shock treatments, for which her room was well equipped. We finally reached a compromise: the family would move to a relative's house nearby and the daughter could return for treatments.

The 75th Division remained in Plettenberg, essentially on R & R, for several weeks. I went on leave to Brussels for five days. When I learned there was a tennis club in Brussels, I found my way there, looking for a match. I was quickly paired with a young Belgian, who became a life-long friend. He and I spent V-E Day in downtown Brussels, joining in the deliriously happy celebration, surpassed only by that of V-J Day in London when, coincidentally, I was there, playing tennis at Wimbledon.

A Summer of Tennis

After V-E Day, the 75th Division was transferred to Chalons-sur-Marne in the Champagne area of France awaiting redeployment to the Pacific Theater. Life in Chalons turned out to be a pleasant experience, except for missing my bride. The Battalion Headquarters, Dispensary, and Officer's Quarters were all located in a quaint old hotel on the main street of the town. On a "walk-around" after our arrival, I passed a group of tennis courts and saw a young man playing there who appeared to be a suitable opponent for me, so I waited until he was finished and asked if I could interest him in playing. We immediately hit it off, and he agreed, even though it meant he would have to supply the balls and racket for me.

Some days later, Brigadier General Mickle, the 75th Division's Assistant Commander walked by the tennis court where Louis and I were playing. He stopped and watched for a while, then called me over to courtside and asked if I were a soldier in the 75th. Trembling inside because I was out of uniform, I replied that I was. He said I looked as if I had played a lot of tennis. I replied in the affirmative, and he then asked if I had ever taught tennis. I told him I had spent two summer vacations in medical school as a teaching tennis professional. He then asked for my name, rank, and unit, and said: "You'll be hearing from me." The following morning I and my CO (who was not happy with it at all) received orders from Division Headquarters assigning me to temporary duty, with the mission of developing and equipping a Division tennis team. The order gave me authority to requisition a jeep and driver, authority to requisition equipment from stores in Paris, and blanket authority to use any officers' mess or quarters in France or Belgium, etc. At the same time the Division was notified that a tennis team was being formed, and any tennis-playing officer or enlisted man interested in trying out should report to me. If selected, he would be assigned to temporary duty as a team member. About 20 soldiers applied for the six-member team, which ended up comprising a lieutenant from an infantry battalion in the No. 1 slot, and four enlisted men and me taking the remaining spots.

We soon learned that the best part of our job was traveling around to compete with teams from other divisions, as well as local French and Belgian teams. The culmination was a Corps tournament in Auxerre, France, just as other Corps stationed in Great Britain and Western Europe were doing. The winners and runner-ups of the Corps singles and doubles tournaments became eligible to compete in a GI Championship tournament to be held at the All-England Lawn Tennis Club at Wimbledon, England, in August. The only members of the 75th Division team to make it to Wimbledon were my doubles partner, the infantry lieutenant, and me as runners-up, to Major General Maxwell Taylor, who at that time in his distinguished career commanded the 101st Airborne Division, and his doubles partner, a major.

Our Corps team for the Wimbledon Tournament was coached at the Roland Garros courts in Paris, where one afternoon our practice session was interrupted by loudspeakers announcing the dropping of the first atom bomb on Hiroshima on August 6, 1945. Two days later, the second atom bomb hit Nagasaki and unconditional surrender of Japan followed. This gave us a tremendous boost because we had been waiting for weeks in fear and trepidation of being deployed directly to the Pacific at summer's end.

The tennis team was flown across the Channel just in time to join the delirious celebration of V-J Day in London August 14, 1945. I remember being housed in the outskirts of London, and because public transportation was shut down, my doubles partner and I walked about three miles that evening with officers from the 82nd Airborne Division to reach Trafalgar Square and Piccadilly Circus, the heart of the celebration. On the way, we were spotted by several groups of girls shouting, "Oh, I've *nevah* kissed an *Amer-r-rican!*" which was followed by prompt correction of the deficiency. My chief remembrances of Piccadilly included seeing a woman in a mink coat come out onto the porte-cochere over the entrance to one of the hotels, prance around to cheers, drop her coat to reveal that she was wearing nothing underneath, and then pose nude to thunderous applause from the appreciative crowd.

I do not recall whether my partner and I played in the doubles at Wimbledon, but we both lost in the first round of singles. I do remember warming up with my opponent, realizing (as he did) that he was a much better player than I. Deciding to throw caution to the winds, I hit every ball as hard as I could in hope that this strategy might work if he had a bad day. It was fine for the first three games, which I won quickly, without losing a point. Then, my opponent got serious and quickly ran off a string of 12 games to win 6-3, 6-0, thus putting an early end to my budding Wimbledon career. After Wimbledon, the 75th Division tennis team played a few local matches, and enjoyed one last trip to Brussels where we played my V-E Day friends before resuming our regular duty assignments.

Dispensary Duty in Rheims

Shortly after returning to the 275th Engineers I was transferred to a (military) General Hospital in the outskirts of Rheims (known to GIs as "Reems") as the 75th Division began its post-war demobilization. That duty lasted only a few weeks before a group of enlisted medics and I were trucked to a dispensary located in a former city school building in central Rheims on a Sunday morning, only to find the dispensary staff we were to replace packed and ready to leave, taking their truck and two ambulances with them for transport. Just as we completed the paperwork transferring the dispensary and its contents to me, it suddenly occurred to me that I needed to know: a) who was my immediate superior, b) what our responsibilities were, and c) how and where to get my now hungry men fed. The answers of the dispensary's commanding officer were: a) he didn't know, b) he wasn't sure, and c) go to the Rheims Headquarters office three blocks away to get mess cards for my men, but I'd better hurry because they close Sundays at noon. He then drove off.

It was 11:35 AM, so my sergeant and I high-tailed it to Headquarters. There, the master sergeant in charge said we needed a "buck-slip" to get the mess cards. I asked him: "What's a buck-slip?" He explained that it was a procedure used to cut red tape when requisitioning resources within the command, and that all I needed to do was fill one out, get it initialed by my commanding officer, and bring it to the source of supply — in this case, to him. I asked where I could get a buck-slip, and he pulled one out of a drawer and handed it to me. I took it over to a table out of his sight to fill it out. When I came to the section labeled "Initials of Commanding Officer," I was stumped until I figured out that a case could be made for me being my own commanding officer, so I initialed it, albeit as illegibly as possible, and presented it to the clerk in the office. He looked at it briefly and issued the mess cards. As my sergeant and I left, I was suddenly struck with an idea, went back in, and asked the clerk for another buck slip. The next morning I used the second buck-slip to requisition a book of 100 buck-slips from the Quartermaster's office, and we were in business!

By the end of the week we had two ambulances and a truck (with drivers), needed medical supplies and other equipment, and mess cards for two different messes for the men and three for me. A few days later, the Headquarters Surgeon, a full colonel, arrived unannounced from his office two doors down the street, identified himself as my immediate superior, and said he was there to inspect the dispensary. I showed him around with considerable trepidation, but ended up with his approval. As he was leaving, I thought that it might be a good idea to inform him about my buck-slip shenanigans, which I did. He looked at me, said, "Everything looks fine to me, Captain. Carry on!" saluted, and left.

As ours turned out to be the only military dispensary in Rheims, it was very busy, serving not only the numerous Headquarters personnel (I never did learn just what headquarters it was) and other personnel assigned to it, as well as those passing through USO Headquarters for Continental Europe located about a block away, and not to mention the fact that Rheims was the Saturday-night-leave town for some 150,000 troops lodged in a camp about 20 miles away awaiting return to the U.S. for discharge.

Saturday nights were our busiest, with a steady stream of patients with cuts, bruises, and broken bones from fights and vehicle accidents. Suturing cuts was so common on Saturday evenings that we set up an assembly line for handling them. Early in the evening, nine school chairs with broad writing arms were set in a semi-circle. A "medic" would triage patients needing stitches and seat them in the order of arrival, beginning at the left end of the row. In rotation, another "medic" would clean the wound or wounds, a second would assemble appropriate materials for stitching on the broad arm of the chair, I would suture, a third medic would bandage, and a fourth would arrange for transportation back to his unit, if necessary. The assembly line was usually in full swing from seven PM until midnight.

I also made house calls on ill USO performers in their rooms or dormitories a block away. I still remember my first house call. The dispensary dentist and I attended the evening performance of a USO troupe and were impressed with how exceptionally attractive, and well-coiffed the girls were. An hour after the performance, a request came for a house call for a member of this troupe. I went over to their dormitory and was shocked to find both it and them a personal and environmental mess.

One day, a pretty little "mademoiselle" tripped into the dispensary, identified herself as a civilian employee of one of the offices of the command, and presented me with a letter from her (French) doctor asking if I would administer her a series of six Vitamin B-12 shots which he had prescribed for her anemia. I telephoned him to verify the order. He explained that he did not have any sterile syringes with which to administer the shots intra-muscularly into her gluteus maximae, and would appreciate my doing so, since she was a command employee. I agreed to the favor, and she produced six sterile vials, each containing 10 cc of clear fluid that she brought in her handbag from a French pharmacy. I administered the first shot in the privacy of my office, and gave her weekly appointments for the remainder. Each week thereafter for six weeks, she would trip in for her shot, greet me with an engaging: "Bonjour, mon Docteur," enter my office, drop her panties, receive the shot in her gluteus maximus, and then depart with a cheery: "Adieu, mon Docteur!" Needless to say, following each visit there was a lot of playful banter directed at me by my men.

After several months of duty at this dispensary, I was transferred on January 1, 1946 to Continental Base Section Headquarters in Bad Nauheim, Germany where I was given the job of organizing and operating a large family dispensary, in essence a small community hospital, to provide primary medical care for the headquarters personnel and their families.

By June, 1946 my name finally came up for return to the U.S. and discharge from the army. There was a wait of several weeks in Bremen for a transport ship. It finally came in the form of an empty former "Victory" cargo ship, which rode so high in the water that almost all of its occupants were seasick for most of the two-week voyage home. I remember standing on the top deck to get some air toward the end of the voyage and looking down at the wooden railing on which was carved: "Kilroy puked here. Dern near died, too!" Kilroy was the prototypic GI (Government Issue) soldier, created by an army cartoonist, whose name became legend. The inscription "Kilroy Was Here" was carved or written almost anywhere in Europe where there was space for it.

We sailed into New York Harbor on a sunny summer morning past the Statue of Liberty (with much cheering and tears), disembarked, and entrained for Fort Dix and discharge. For me, the final irony of the military system came at my discharge physical examination the next day, when the Army doctors wanted to delay my eagerly anticipated discharge in order to put me in a military hospital for an estimated two weeks of testing to find the cause of a blood pressure reading of

100/60, which was below normal by Army standards. I explained to no avail that I had had known labile blood pressure since my medical school days. Finally, they agreed to discharge me if I would sign a waiver absolving the Army of responsibility for my *hypotension*, which I did and was discharged. The irony was that on joining the Army four or five years earlier, in order to be accepted I had to sign a waiver absolving the Army of responsibility for my *hypertension* because of an isolated blood-pressure reading of 150/100.

Epilogue

I left the Army with a profoundly cynical view of human character, behavior, claims, perceptions, and religions, which persists to this day. On the plus side, this has enabled me to be relatively objective, even about human frailty, which has helped me as a physician. Another plus of my Army career has been that it taught me how to command, which has been a big help in achieving and holding leadership positions. Because of its inherent autocracy and severity, commanding has also had its negative side, especially for my family.

Born in Manhattan, Jim grew up in New Jersey and attended Princeton University and Harvard Medical School. Studying in Germany before the war, he later served in the European theater as an Army Medical Officer. He was Chairman, Department of Pediatrics, University of Vermont College of Medicine for over 30 years and Co-Editor of a leading textbook of pediatrics. He lived with his wife and four children in Williston, Vermont before becoming a Wake Robin resident.

Wartime

in

Europe

Torpedoed at Sea

★

Miriam Almeleh

WHILE WE WERE WAITING IN THE VILLAGE of Rouses' Point at the Canadian-U.S. border, my young cousin, Judith, age 8, made a friend from the village. She ran to where we were all waiting on public benches by Lake Champlain, crying her heart out. Her new friend had asked Judith where her home was, and Judith replied that she didn't have a home, and the girl called her a liar. Poor little Judith was quite right but how could my aunt (her mother) comfort her — at that moment we indeed had no country, and no place to call home. That is what it meant to be stateless, in this nation-state world, a terribly scary situation to be in.

This story refers to the wanderings of my family from the time we fled Germany in 1933, fearful of the gathering clouds that then threatened Jews in Germany. I was born in Frankfurt, Germany, and was 18 years old at the time described in this story. My family consisted of my mother Lilly Goldschmidt, my two sisters Eva and Ruth (my name was Ellen at that time), and my father Moritz, who had actually divorced my mother before we fled. He helped to settle us in Hove, England when we arrived there in 1933, and then left us and moved to Palestine. We had seven comparatively normal years in England where my sisters and I received good schooling. I was in the midst of nursing school training when, in 1940, we decided to leave England. By then, we had moved from Hove to London where we faced the German bombings, the English anti-aircraft barrages, nightly trips to air raid shelters, and the threatened Blitzkrieg and impending invasion. It was all terribly frightening and proved too much for us.

Departing for China via Canada

So the family packed for the trip to North America. It was illegal to take tender, money, jewelry, or valuables of any kind out of England during the war. We hid valuables such as my mother's two diamond rings in the bottom of cold cream jars. We folded fine materials to look like evening gowns to which we "sewed" straps and artificial flowers for decoration. One evening a young man came to our house. I peeked in to see him working at the kitchen table. He and my mother were going over the wooden base of our Royal typewriter case with a plane, building a false bottom. Afterward, the typewriter was enormously heavy to lift, and of course, I being the biggest and strongest was given the job of carrying it everywhere I went. I lugged it to the train, to the ship, and everywhere on the ship — to and from meals, and even to the bathroom. With great seriousness Mother had cautioned me that I must keep it in my possession at all times. Much later I learned that a sheet of platinum (which accounted for its weight) had been inserted and hidden in the base. While otherwise law-abiding people, we hid these valuables as our only security in an unknown future.

We had been able to book passage on the *Antonia,* a Cunard Line ship and sister ship of the *Athena,* which had recently been bombed and sunk. We were to cross Canada in a sealed train and then take the ship *Empress of Asia* across the Pacific to the international colony in Shanghai. All I knew about Shanghai was that it was in China and I doubt that the family knew much more than I. I have since learned that the refugees lived in Shanghai in abject misery, though perhaps, since we were not poor, we might have fared a bit better.

The only documents we had as we left England were our Nansen Passes (identity cards issued by the League of Nations to stateless refugees) and a landing permit for Shanghai, but no visa for Shanghai. The Nansen Passes were stamped, "Valid for the single journey and only for embarkation by a vessel sailing for Shanghai via Canada from a port in the United Kingdom on 25 July 1940." We had no passports, merely our British "Certificates of Identity."

My mother, my two sisters, and I were joined at the boat by members of our extended family — two aunts, one uncle, five more children, and a nasty little Rehpincher dog. Boarding the *Antonia*, we had to turn over our British Certificates, a booklet the size of a passport, and the identity papers we had been issued as friendly aliens in England, stating that our deportment was flawless (or at least nothing negative was entered in them). I can still clearly see in my mind, the officer sitting at this long table on the ship's deck, taking all the booklets from us and everyone else in line, stamping them and leaving them in a pile beside him to his left, at the end of the long table. As soon as the official was finished with the four of us, and we had walked away from the table so the next person could be processed, my mother said to me in a pleading (scared?) voice I'd never heard her use before, "See if you can get our booklets back, it's the only identifying paper we have in the world." A rush of fear welled up inside me, wanting to steal them from right under the nose of that officer, and Lord knows what would happen, were I caught. I just stood there, and other people in line behind us came and gave up their booklets, which were piled on top of ours. After standing there for what seemed an eternity, I told my mother I couldn't do it and she said: "Well then leave it," in a crestfallen voice that made me feel that I had failed terribly.

The Sea Voyage

We waited on board the *Antonia* for two days in the harbor of Liverpool, seeing the masts of many a sunken ship in the harbor sticking up out of the sea all around us. While awaiting a convoy to be formed, or so we were told, we watched as the sailors on board painted a huge red cross on the top deck of our ship, signifying a neutral carrier. We had 350 children on board who were being evacuated from the war zone — the German bombers were expected to respect that. What we did not know of course, but the Germans evidently did, was that we also carried a cargo of gold. Nice, don't you think, putting aboard hundreds of children to camouflage all that gold?

Though we waited two days in Liverpool Harbor, we never got into a convoy, but a destroyer finally arrived and accompanied us north until it turned back at the northern end of the Irish Channel. The sea was so rough that Ruth and I were almost the only people on board who made an appearance at supper. It was all rather new and exciting, and we had great fun choosing anything we desired from the ample menu.

The next morning I got up from my bunk and fainted. My mother had the ship's surgeon called. He came to our cabin and said I was suffering a form of seasickness and suggested I go up on deck and get some fresh air. I did. It was a raw, drizzly day. I was walking around, licking a forefinger periodically to determine the wind direction because if I were to throw up, I didn't want it back in my face. Suddenly I saw something big, dark, wet and smooth jump out of the water, perhaps 50 feet from the ship, describe a flat arc, then dive down and disappear again. Having little or no experience of marine life, I wanted to run down and tell my mother I had seen a whale, when there was a concussive impact that knocked me into sitting position — I can best describe it as feeling like standing on a floor of loose boards when somebody dropped a heavy keg of beer right behind me. I picked myself up and wanted to go below, still not suspecting anything, still wanting to report on my "whale."

The purser (second in command of the ship) had all the glass doors of the round dining room closed except one, the only one through which I could get inside. The purser stood by this door with a sailor in whites and said, "Please don't tell anyone what you've seen, we are telling the passengers that we have sent a depth charge against a submarine." I asked in all innocence, "What *did* we see?" and he looked at me but didn't answer. Actually, of course, we had been attacked by a German U-boat. The first torpedo missed (that's what I had seen) and the second one hit, making a hole in the ship, but I hadn't the slightest inkling of that. The crew had to pump water from the hole we had sustained, until we landed, but none of the passengers knew anything about it. Meanwhile the ship zigzagged north toward the shores of Greenland to avoid the U-boat. We then turned west and eventually southward through the straits of Belle Isle to Quebec where we were let off, instead of getting to our planned destination of Montreal. The *Antonia* then went on to dry dock in Halifax, Nova Scotia, to get the torpedo damage repaired.

Canadian Stopover

We were supposed to have landed in Montreal and were to go straight into the sealed train that would take us refugees directly to the *Empress of Asia*, the ship on which we had booked passage for Shanghai. We had missed the train because the *Antonia* had been torpedoed and we had lost time on our detour to the north. We were put on a train for Montreal, and because the Cunard Line was responsible for us all the way to Montreal, we were served a free dinner in the train's dining car. Once in Montreal we took rooms in the Berkeley Hotel, and meanwhile we had learned that the *Empress of Asia* had been bombed and sunk in Shanghai harbor and half the passengers had drowned. So, what to do?

My mother and her sister Rosi somehow managed to attend a dinner dance to meet up with the American consul. There had even been some talk of our crossing the Canadian/U.S. border illegally, but evidently the risk that we'd be caught and deported back to Germany was too great. Then there was talk of our going to Nicaragua, but my mother didn't feel safe going there with three young daughters, so I believe they then decided on Mexico, and made arrangements for visitor visas for us to be able to transit the United States on the way. There was much conversation over the phone with my uncle Jakob Michael in New York, who helped with the planning.

With all the things the adults were doing, we were finally issued (i.e., they bought) Polish passports to travel with — either for the U.S. or Mexico. I guess those countries would not accept our Nansen passes. Somebody must have made money on the deal because none of us had ever been to Poland, let alone acquired Polish citizenship. Since it was a matter of life and death, the Polish visas must have cost a pretty penny; possibly, we owed thanks to my uncle Jakob.

There was some talk that one of my aunts charmed the Canadian immigration officer — no one would say how far she went — but we got permission to stay in Canada a while longer. Now, looking back many years later, I can barely imagine the horrors the adults went through, what ends people might go to if they were desperate, and yes, they were desperate — we could have been shipped back to Germany at any moment! There was even talk (and my mother warned me never, never to tell anyone at the time) of considering whether some or all of us might cross the border illegally.

One day in Montreal we were invited to the home of a friend of Uncle Jakob's. We sat in what can only be described as a beautiful and grand estate among some old trees with their enormous trunks and refreshing shade. I recall sitting there and letting the feeling of quiet relaxation wash over me. It was almost like an "it's all right" feeling in those horrendously uncertain days when one couldn't question the adults because they were nervous and uncertain too, probably afraid to reveal their inner thoughts and plans to us children for fear we might talk.

Eventually, when the family had obtained visas to Mexico, the required vaccination, and permission to stay as visitors in the U.S. for a few weeks, the 13 of us and Barry, the dog, took the train from Montreal to the U.S./Canada border at Rouses' Point. Unfortunately, the American border guards felt it was unlikely that such a large party would be coming into the U.S. "for a short visit before continuing on to Mexico" as we had claimed. They made all of us get out of the train, with the dog and all our worldly belongings (trunks). There we stood on the railroad platform in a dinky little town on the border between two countries, one of which we had hoped to enter, at least temporarily.

There were interrogations, and it was there that little eight-year-old cousin Judith sobbed out the sad words that I have used to introduce this story: "We have no home."

Safe Harbor in America

Finally, after a 12-hour wait, the authorities permitted us to board an express train with all our belongings. The train was air conditioned but I couldn't sleep. As daylight came, I watched in fascination as the hills on the far side of the Hudson River rolled into view through the fog, and vanished again into fog as we passed them. Uncle Jakob and Aunt Erna Michael met us at Grand Central Station in New York, and their chauffeur drove us out to White Plains to stay at my uncle's estate in Scarsdale. The eight of us refugee children and the Michael's three children had a good time.

We stayed several weeks in Scarsdale and finally made our way to Mexico City where we remained for seven months. I was able to resume my nurse's training despite having been seriously ill with hepatitis. We had to obtain German passports with a big red "J" on them to return to the U.S. It was very disturbing to see the German officials at the German Consulate with their Nazi swastika arm bands. However, we were finally safe, and able to move to New York.

Thus ended the long hegira of the Goldschmidt family — in 1933, from Germany to England; in June 1940, from Canada to Mexico via the U.S.; and finally, in February, 1941, from Mexico to the U.S. and home at last to New York City. This all transpired before the United States entered World War II.

Born in Frankfurt, Germany to a family of orthodox Jews, Miriam emigrated prior to World War II with her family, first to England, then to the United States following a brief interlude in Mexico. A registered nurse from Mt. Sinai Hospital, she worked two years in Israel, before settling in Bridgewater, New Jersey where she raised a son and two daughters. After earning a BS in sociology and a Masters in Social Work, she became Executive Director of a family service agency.

Paris under German Occupation

★

Paul A. Bailly

THE LAST BOX I OPENED UP after arriving at Wake Robin in the fall of 2007 was full of miscellaneous old family papers. The biggest surprise was a bunch of French ration coupons for food and clothing dated October 1949, the final month of nearly 10 years of rationing in France. Ten months before the start of rationing, when Hitler's armies gathered to invade Poland in late August, 1939, my family was preparing to return to our Paris residence from vacation at a Brittany beach. France's imminent declaration of war and call for general military mobilization changed my father's plans.

He was on a train to Paris on September 1, 1939 reporting for duty at Air Force HQ at the intelligence message decoding center. During World War I, he had served four years in an observation balloon unit above the front lines. In the 1930s, as a reservist, he had spent many evenings and weekends learning encrypting and decoding skills in preparation for the inevitable conflict with the perennial Teutonic invaders. By the first week of September 1939, only mothers and their children were at the beaches, while the men had left to serve their country. Popular wisdom was that young children should be removed from large urban centers, coastal areas, and frontier zones, all potential targets of German bombings.

Life in the Early War Years

In mid-September my mother and her three sons, Jean age 17, Pierre age 14, and I age 12, departed from Brittany in the family automobile. My mother had never driven so after a few driving lessons, oldest son Jean obtained his temporary driver's permit and off we went. After some initial engine stalling in the countryside, he acquired adequate skills and drove us safely to Paris. There Pierre and I picked up some winter clothes and took a train to Auxerre, a small town in northern Burgundy where we stayed with wonderful cousins until June 1940. In Auxerre, we joined a Boy Scout troop, and when not in school, we pulled a cart through the streets to collect old and unused metallic objects to be melted down for the war effort. We accumulated large heaps of scrap metals, which were stored adjacent to the railroad freight station. Ironically, in 1947 those heaps were still there, never used.

Curiously, from September 1939 to May 1940 the war between the Germans and the Franco-British alliance was fought with little intensity and events were largely at a standstill. The front lines in northern and northeastern France remained static, and battles were only intermittent. It was referred to as the "Drole de Guerre" (Funny War). A friend of my father, at the front, wrote that farmers sometimes continued working their fields between the lines while artillery fire was being exchanged overhead. They sold their milk to both sides. By February 1940, after decoders of younger ages had been trained, my father was sent home because he was 45 years old and had three minor children. He was needed in the business he had founded after his Army discharge in 1918.

The German Blitzkrieg

In the first days of June 1940 tank battalions, part of the German blitzkrieg, invaded northern France, meeting only token opposition by skirting northward through the low countries (Belgium and Holland) and avoiding the allegedly "impregnable" Maginot Line of fortifications separating French territory from Germany. At lightning speed, the enemy overwhelmed more than half of France. This sudden and unexpected thrust aroused, both in farmers and city dwellers of northern France, a latent secular fear of the foreign invaders. Within days, hundreds of thousands of panic-stricken families started moving southward with whatever belongings they could take in automobiles, buggies, horse drawn farming carts, handcarts, etc. Many fleeing in their vehicles exhausted their fuel supply and were unable to refuel. Abandoning their cars, they started walking, often joined by French soldiers retreating en masse to avoid being taken prisoner. When the news of the armistice that had been struck between France and Germany reached these endless migrant crowds on the roadways, they turned around and slowly returned to their homes. This episode became known as "L'Exode." Some were away from home for only a few days, others for several weeks.

During this migration, my parents and my maternal grandmother left Paris in our family car, picked up my two brothers and me along the way and joined "L'Exode." German fighter planes sporadically strafed these human columns if retreating soldiers were spied among them. Consequently, my father avoided main roadways and followed only small country roads. We reached La Rochelle on the Atlantic coast where cousins welcomed us. We saw for the first time, with awed dread, young and athletic German soldiers jumping out of their tanks and running stark naked across the beach to go swimming in the ocean while paying no attention whatsoever to the handful of shocked onlookers. After spending two days with our cousins, my father, having found sufficient gasoline and learning of the armistice, decided to drive us all back to Paris and return to our apartment. We were some of the first to be back in the deserted capital. Many Germans arriving in trucks and command-cars were already moving into requisitioned hotels, buildings, and apartments.

Life under the German Occupation

By mid-June, we learned the main terms of the Armistice. France was to be governed by a French Government, not by a German Military Government as was the case for Belgium, Holland, and the Central European countries invaded by Hitler. The northern half of France, the Eastern front, and the Atlantic coastal areas would be a zone occupied and controlled by German armies. A southern zone of France would be "free" and non-occupied. A Demarcation Line with numerous checkpoints would separate the two zones. All travel between the zones would require permits from French and German authorities. An important condition of the Armistice was that the French Navy ships in Mediterranean and West African ports and the French armies stationed in French territories in North and West Africa would remain under the authority of the French Government, which was to be located in Vichy.

When the Americans and Allies landed in North Africa in 1942, these French troops and what was left of the French Navy promptly rallied to the Allied cause. Consequently, the German armies then immediately crossed the Demarcation Line and occupied all of France, thus gaining access to ports on the Mediterranean. The Demarcation Line, however, remained an infamous obstacle to travel. All the checkpoints continued to be staffed and guarded by Germans and travel permits were still required.

German occupation of France lasted four years, a sad, hungry, and painful period for most of the French populace. My father kept his business going as best he could. Private automobiles were not allowed. In Paris, the subway was the only public transportation. Many Parisians rode bicycles. Passenger trains within the occupied zone were infrequent. Occupation plans were well laid. Within days of the invasion, the occupiers started confiscating more than half of French agricultural production and about half of non-agriculture products for shipment to

Germany, thus creating shortages and the need for rationing, and also sparking a fast growing black market.

One item that saw considerable increase in production and supply was tobacco. Although French smokers were largely adult men, during the occupation tobacco rations were issued to all men and women 18 years and older whether they smoked or not, so a pack of cigarettes became the standard unit of black market transactions — four packs of cigarettes for a pound of margarine, eight for a pound of butter, etc. Was this the result of a "one size fits all" bureaucratic planning or a clever scheme to induce the hungry population to expend efforts to reduce their food shortage by participating in the black market? In my family, only Jean, my oldest brother, smoked, so we had the two tobacco rations of my parents to supplement our food rations. My brother Pierre and I used much of our non-school time bicycling off to exchange cigarettes for food in different parts of Paris.

Standing in lines (queues in French) at food and dairy product shops and at clothing stores was necessary if one wanted a chance to exchange ration coupons for something to eat or wear. I recall many mornings arriving at six AM at the door of a milk shop so as to be one of the first in line when doors opened at seven AM, then rushing home with ½ liter of unpasteurized low fat milk that my mother boiled immediately to preserve it. Many people in line went home empty handed.

Coal was the main raw material for heating Paris apartments and buildings. I remember vividly the winter of 1941 with its record cold temperatures and the dire shortage of coal. My maternal grandmother told me that on some frigid winter days, she stayed for hours in the Underground because stations and trains were warmer than her small suburban apartment, which she could heat only for a few hours a day with her coal ration. My family did not have enough coal to effectively run our central heating furnace in our five-room apartment so all rooms were left unheated except one. After my brothers and I had returned from school, Mother had returned from "queuing" for some food, and my father had arrived home after work (but before curfew), we heated only one small room where we all sat as close as possible to a little four-legged, blue enameled coal stove venting into an old fireplace. Most of the time, we did our home work and ate dinner with our gloves on. Then together, we listened to the regular French language radio program of the BBC, our only contact with the free world and the only reliable news available about the war involving the many fronts of WWII. The censored French newspapers, magazines, and radio only emphasized the achievements of the Reich and Allied defeats. During the BBC transmission, there were always German electronic detection trucks in the streets trying to spot apartments receiving the "verboten" emission. When they suspected an illegal reception, they sent French policemen to arrest the oldest male and confiscate the radio set.

German Oppression

If a German soldier was killed in Paris by French insurgents, who were generally members of the Resistance, the Germans announced the following day that hostages would be shot in reprisal. The number of hostages varied with the military rank and the numbers of Germans killed; on average it was about five people for each German. Hostages were selected among men recently arrested for cause, as well as men randomly arrested in public places. The subway stations, which were usually crowded, were sites commonly chosen to round up hostages.

The Germans outlawed all youth groups considered to be military in organizational structure, and therefore, a potential source of future insurgents. The Boy Scouts were strictly "verboten." However with the encouragement of our parents, my brothers and I remained very active in the Boy Scouts, which functioned as it had before the war, but without uniforms. We would meet and go camping dressed like all other boys of our ages. Camping a few times a year for a week or two was a real break from life in the large "occupied" city. We scouts traveled by train somewhere to the countryside where few occupiers were stationed. We obtained food from farmers who sold us eggs, flour, vegetables, fruits, and meat without food coupons.

Luckily, we never ran into any trouble while camping. However, one of our group leaders, a close friend of my brother Jean, did not appear at our weekly meetings in Paris for a month. We later learned from his father that he had been arrested in the Pyrenees Mountains while assisting downed Allied pilots to return to England through Spain. He spent two years in the Buchenwald concentration camp before being liberated by Patton's Third Army. My brother Jean, who spoke English well, served as an interpreter after Paris was liberated and joined a military team that freed the Buchenwald inmates. He found his scouting friend there, alive but thin as a rail.

Forced Labor

During the occupation my brother Jean was the only person in our family to be directly affected by the Germans' requirement that young Frenchmen work in France or Germany in armament factories or related industries. Given the choice to be sent to work in a plant in Germany or to work in a coal mine in France, he opted to become a coal miner in northern France for two years. The Franco-German government agency, which recruited French citizens to support the German war effort, was called the STO (Compulsory Work Service) and the young "recruits" were euphemistically labeled "designated volunteers." There were about 600,000 such "volunteers" in Germany during the war. Many of the 1.5 million French prisoners of war taken to Germany after June 1940 also worked there in armament plants or in agricultural production. At one time there were more than two million Frenchmen forced to work in Germany, replacing the German soldiers serving in the armies of the Reich. The factories and agricultural fields of France were similarly short of manpower, yet France was forced to contribute much to the war effort in Germany.

In May 1944 my brother Pierre, after his first year in an agriculture school, was working as an intern and field hand in a farm 250 km. south of Paris. He wrote that if I could manage to join him, I could work as a field hand in the same farm, which could use additional manpower. Food was growing scarcer in Paris, and the widely rumored imminent landings of Allied armies somewhere in France portended more turmoil. It seemed evident that the Germans would not leave French soil without a hard fight. My parents decided I should join Pierre since food would not be scarce on a farm. The trains were practically all requisitioned for German transport, so I planned to bicycle to that farm when my school year was over at the end of June.

Liberation of France by the Allies

On June 6, 1944 I was in literature class, writing an exam. I recall we had one hour to write an essay on Lenin's statement, "Steam concentrates, but electricity disperses." The professor was an avowed communist who had often vaunted the importance of his party to the future of France. We were half way through the exam when loud noises and vociferous shouting and singing of the Marseillaise erupted in the corridors of the school. A young man wearing a Resistance arm-band suddenly entered our classroom and announced that Americans had landed in Normandy, and that the Ministry of Education had instructed all schools to close immediately and to send all professors and students home. Pandemonium ensued. We jumped on our desks singing the national anthem and tore up our exam papers. The professor left the room ahead of his students. That evening, the BBC gave a sobering account of the immensity and difficulty of the landings. A few days later we learned of the toll of casualties on the beaches in Normandy and the heroism of our liberators.

Not Yet the War's End

Early one morning in mid-June I left Paris on my bike. By six PM I was within 25 km. of my farm destination located a few miles south of the Demarcation Line. At a cafe where I had stopped for a glass of wine, a man told me that on the direct paved road the checkpoints at the Demarcation Line were all manned and crossing permits were required. I did not have a permit. He suggested a longer dirt road with an unmanned checkpoint. I set out on the dirt road in a steady rain. After about 10 km. I could see ahead a tricolor sentry-box with a control barrier but no sign of life. I kept pedaling, passing the sentry box and a barrier gate in the driving rain. Suddenly, I heard a loud order in German to halt and looked back. I spied about 10 meters distant a German soldier without a helmet, walking out of his shelter with rifle pointed. I yelled back in French and in German that I was going to a farm nearby. The sentry, looking old and tired, slowly lowered his gun and waved me off. I promptly departed but will never forget this close encounter.

Epilogue

I had studied German at school for four years, but without any conversational exercises, knew only enough to speak short sentences. The only use of the language, which I had practiced with Pierre during the occupation years, was to give directions to German foot soldiers in Paris when they were seeking directions, like the way to the railroad station. He and I would purposely send them in the wrong direction. We did not tell our dad about this practice until after the liberation, because it could have caused them great concern.

Paris was liberated by Allied forces in late August 1944. Following my summer at the farm, I returned to Paris in September. My parents had already resumed the tradition of inviting friends for lunch on Sundays. They asked me each Sunday morning to walk around our neighborhood and approach American soldiers enjoying R&R. We invited them to join us for lunch at our home. After they deciphered my badly accented English, our liberators readily accepted with a great show of appreciation. My family expressed our gratitude for their sacrifices, and the GIs enjoyed a much-welcomed change from the usual K Rations.

Born in 1926, Paul grew up in Paris and spent the war years under German occupation. After the war he attended university in France and did graduate work at Stanford, earning his PhD in geology. He returned to France for obligatory military service in 1952, serving in Algeria. Subsequently, he worked for U.S. companies in mineral exploration and mine development.

A Child's Memories of the
War in Britain

★

Caroline Fay

MY FIRST MEMORY, when I was four years old, was rushing into the drawing room and my parents cautioning, "Shhh." It was September 3, 1939. They were sitting on either side of the fireplace listening intently to the radio — Germany had invaded Poland, and Britain was declaring war. I don't remember anything unusual happening during the first few months of the war. Fathers of my friends were being called up, and one of my uncles joined the RAF at the age of 17. My father and his two brothers, who were civil engineers, were not called up, nor was my mother's brother, an uncle of mine who owned and operated several farms.

The Early Wartime Years

My brother was born at home in March 1940. For some unknown reason I recall that my father was in the Isle of Islay at the time (he was very rarely at home and we didn't know his whereabouts most of the time). At this time, we still had two maids, a nanny, and a full time gardener. We had a very big garden — lawns, flower beds, trees, a greenhouse, large vegetable garden and orchard. My mother kept chickens, rabbits for food (my pet rabbits were off limits), and geese on the tennis lawn to keep the grass short — the rest had to be cut with a push mower. Luckily the gardener, Morris, was too old to be called up. He cycled 10 miles each way to work every day.

At age five, I was sent to the local school over four miles away. I often had to travel by bicycle, as petrol was rationed. I remember falling off on one occasion and being picked up by a kindly old lady. My father accompanied me to school when he was at home. The following year I had to leave school because I contracted "double pneumonia" and nearly died. My parents ate their meals in my room and despite the blackout, there was always a fire blazing. Thanks to sulfa drugs, which were new, I recovered and was then sent away to a weekly boarding school. Just after my illness our nanny was called up (I am still in touch with her). Another was hired, and as quickly fired, because she proceeded to steal my mother's precious silk stockings. The maids were able to continue to work for us because they were too young for conscription.

Of course we didn't take holidays. Our big excitement would be visiting my grandparents who lived 30 miles away and owned several farms. They had a petrol allowance (pink petrol) so we could drive out into the country to see them. For most of the kind of farm work done by tractors today, they used cart horses. The farm work was done by Italian prisoners of war who were conscripted to take the place of his farm laborers. The POWs were very kind to me and enjoyed being on the farm well away from the war.

My grandmother had a full-time gardener whom I called Tinkerbelle (really Tinker). I helped him churn butter every Monday on the wooden table in the scullery and then shaped it with butter paddles. The mulberry tree in their extensive garden provided leaves for my pet silk worms. There was lots of activity when a pig was to be slaughtered. The hams were hung from the ceiling in the maids' sitting room, and every part of the pig was used for food.

All the beaches had been mined because the invasion was expected to happen on the coast off Norfolk near where we lived. Because there were no swimming pools to enjoy, my mother would pull out an old tin bath, fill it with water, and my brother and I would splash around in that to cool off. Food and clothing were rationed. My mother cut up her grey flannel blazer to make shorts for my brother, and I remember the ends of my shoes being cut off so there was room for my toes. We were more fortunate than most people because we had vegetables and fruit from the garden and chickens, eggs, rabbits and geese for our table. In return for getting corn for our animals, we had to donate a certain number of eggs a week to the war effort. Any leftover eggs were preserved in waterglass, the beans were salted in large crocks, and the apples were kept in one of the garages on wire shelves. Our milk and bread were delivered by pony and cart. It was a great thrill when the milkman allowed me to drive the cart down the lane.

Preparations for the Normandy Invasion

My parents often invited airmen to our house when they had a free day. We soon learned not to ask where so-and-so was. If that person was missing, the expression used was, "he bought it last night." I recall standing by the back gate and watching a "dog fight" overhead. A German plane was shot down one night, and the enemy airmen who parachuted down were so scared they hid in a haystack, only to emerge the next morning with their hands in the air. One night I was awakened by a huge explosion. The big bang was a bomb load that a German bomber unloaded as it was being chased by our fighters. The bombs landed about 100 yards up the road. My parents were on duty in the next village and had left my two young aunts in charge. They had put my brother and me in the bed under the stairs, as it was the safest place in the house. I recall how much the bed shook because the two of them were so nervous. Despite our windows being taped and shuttered, all the windows blew in on that side of the house. My parents were driving home and at first thought that it was our house that had been struck.

We found many pieces of shrapnel in the garden. I still feel a chill if I wake up at night and hear a single plane flying overhead. We were in the line between where the "doodle bugs" (V-1 rockets) were launched on the continent and the city of London. We learned that if we heard the engine stop, that V-1 rocket was starting to descend. I still hate the sound of a siren.

My sister Victoria was born on June 6, 1944. My father telephoned my boarding school to inform me about her birth while planes were flying overhead. He was one of the few who knew that D-Day was pending because he was part of the team of engineers that designed and oversaw the construction of the so-called Mulberry Harbour. This portable dock facility was being fabricated from parts manufactured all over Britain and towed across the Channel for the landings in Normandy. There were often convoys of U.S. troops going past our house. One day I picked a bouquet of my mother's flowers, squeezed through the hedge, and presented them to the passing Americans. They gave me chewing gum in return.

The War's End

Certain things I had never seen before. Early in 1945 my parents took me by train down to Devonshire to look at the new boarding school they were sending me to. I remember seeing all the barrage balloons flying over London. The first time I saw fireworks was when we went into King's Lynn on May 8, 1945 to celebrate V-E Day. All the church bells were tolling, a novel sound for me because during the war, the bells were only to be rung in the event of invasion.

Although the war had ended, rationing remained in effect for more than two years. At that time, my sister was registered as a vegetarian, which permitted my family to purchase nuts and peanut butter. Because of the many post-war privations families bore, even the cost of my school uniforms presented some difficulties at times. The fare at school left much to be desired. Few candies were available. When my uncle returned from North Africa, he brought some bananas back with him. My brother, four years old, remarked, "What is this funny shaped pear!"

Epilogue

I remember being slightly ashamed that my father was not in the military service during the war. He was only a member of the Home Guard, which was formed in 1941 to defend Great Britain in the event of an invasion. He was away from home for long stretches, but we never knew where he went. Only after the war did we learn that he was often dropped into occupied Holland to get in touch with friends who were members of the underground (his company was Dutch). He never really talked about this except for one episode when the Dutch took over a German Officer's Mess after surrender and discovered a magnificent Steinway piano. My father who was a brilliant pianist was not allowed by his Dutch friends to stop playing it until his fingers were blistered. My father was decorated by Queen Juliana of the Netherlands for his work to help the Dutch resistance. His award was

Father, Robert Douglas (circle), British Home Guard

the equivalent of a knighthood in England. I have his medal, and my brother the letter from the Queen allowing him (my father) to accept the honour but stating he could not use the title in Great Britain.

The following is a message to the British people from Prime Minister Winston Churchill that demonstrates to American readers just how desperate was the plight of our nation and the very real fear of an impending invasion by Hitler's forces:

A MESSAGE FROM THE PRIME MINISTER

If invasion comes, everyone — young or old, men and women — will be eager to play their part worthily. By far the greater part of the country will not be immediately involved. Even along our coasts, the greater part will remain unaffected. But where the enemy lands, or tries to land, there will be more violent fighting. Not only will there be the battles when the enemy tries to come ashore, but afterwards there will fall upon his lodgments very heavy British counter-attacks, and all the time the lodgments will be under the heaviest attack by British bombers. The fewer civilians or non-combatants in these areas, the better — apart from essential workers who must remain. So if you are advised by authorities to leave the place where you live, it is your duty to go elsewhere when you are told to leave. When the attack begins, it will be too late to go; and, unless you receive definite instructions to move, your duty will be to stay where you are. You will have to get into the safest place you can find, and stay there until the battle is over. For all of you then the order and the duty will be: "STAND FIRM."

This also applies to people inland if any considerable number of parachutists or air-borne troops are landed in their neighborhood. Above all they must not cumber the roads. Like their fellow-countrymen on the coasts, they must "STAND FIRM." The Home Guard, supported by strong mobile columns wherever the enemy's numbers require it, will immediately come to grips with the invaders, and there is little doubt will soon destroy them.

Throughout the rest of the country where there is no fighting going on, and no close cannon fire or rifle fire can be heard, everyone will govern his conduct by the second great order and duty, namely, "CARRY ON." It may easily be some weeks before the invader has been totally destroyed, that is to say, killed or captured to the last man who has landed on our shores. Meanwhile, all work must be continued to the utmost, and no time lost. The following notes have been prepared to tell everyone in rather more detail what to do, and they should be carefully studied. Each man and woman should think out a clear plan of personal action in accordance with the general scheme.

— Winston Churchill, Prime Minister

Born in England, Caroline attended boarding and finishing schools where she studied music and learned to speak French, then went on to secretarial college. After the war, she was married in Montreal, had three children, and became a single mother. She moved with her second husband to Charlotte, Vermont.

Fleeing Turkey

★

Eleanor Gardner

You could not find a more beautiful spot in this world to spend the summer than the shores of the Bosporus just outside Istanbul, Turkey. Stretching from the Black Sea to the Sea of Marmora, it is busy all year long with the passage of cruise ships, tankers, sailboats, and countless little fishing boats. Near the ancient towers of Roumeli Hissar, our home overlooked this timeless waterway.

Early in the summer of 1939 my father died, my older sister was married and departed with her new husband for the United States, and my younger sister left to join her fiancé. Mother and I settled down to enjoy the restful summer life on the campus of Robert College.

The last peaceful days of August were suddenly shattered by an urgent announcement from the American Embassy saying that everyone not intending to remain permanently should get out immediately. That meant us. We gave our grand piano to a friend, arranged for the college to take over our furniture and packed up the few family treasures we wished to take with us.

In a couple of days we were aboard the Orient Express bound for Paris. The Embassy there hustled us over to London where the next morning in the lobby of the hotel, the ticker tape flashed the news that Hitler had invaded Poland. Racing to help all the Americans trying to flee Europe, the Embassy arranged passage for us on a Swedish ship in Liverpool that would be flying a neutral flag.

We spent the next ten days zig-zagging the North Atlantic, dodging U-boats and icebergs. We finally arrived safely in New York Harbor and were able to get in touch with our families with the news, "Here we are, come get us."

Born in New York City, Eleanor has lived in Turkey, Cambodia, Pittsfield and Sudbury, Massachusetts. She graduated from Middlebury and did graduate study at Boston University for teaching children with learning disabilities. She and her husband Frank (deceased 2007) both have World War II memoirs appearing in this volume. .

A World War II Odyssey

★

Tad Kowalski

CERTAIN LIFE EVENTS remain with us forever. For me, these included the years leading up to World War II when I was in high school and living in Kutno, a town in central Poland about 60 miles west of the capital, Warsaw. Ominous clouds gathered on the western border of Poland. Most of Europe seemed oblivious to Germany's rearmament, which was prohibited by the Treaty of Versailles, yet Hitler had designs to dominate all of Europe, as he said in *Mein Kampf.* The Austrian Anschluss, acquisition of Saarbrucken and Sudetenland, and occupation of Czechoslovakia all transpired without a shot fired. These events took place with the tacit agreement of England and France as affirmed by Prime Minister Chamberlain proclaiming "peace in our time" after his infamous Munich meeting with Hitler.

To accomplish his objectives, Hitler needed to defeat both France and England in the west and Russia in the east. To avoid fighting on two fronts, he negotiated a non-aggression pact with Russia containing a secret article for the two countries to attack and divide up Poland, thereby freeing Germany to attack France and Great Britain to the west.

The Polish government began defense preparations. It appealed to Western powers for assurances they would open a western front if Germany attacked, but the Chamberlain government was pressuring Poland not to provoke Germany, so defense preparations had to be surreptitious. Because of a large ethnic German population in western Poland, the country began surveillance for Nazi sympathizers. There were rumors on both sides of the border of spies being captured.

Life in our high school was variously affected. Boy Scouts was converted to a quasi-military organization of 14-18 year olds. We were unarmed, but received training in map reading, camouflage, aircraft spotting, etc. We marched in formation to patriotic rallies and assisted with auxiliary duties to relieve soldiers for military duty.

While in 1938 everyday life was not materially affected, by dawn of 1939 the nation's mood changed as the populace sensed the inevitability of war. The border between Germany and Poland witnessed increasing "incidents." Pictures of alleged dead German and Polish soldiers appeared in newspapers, and Germany lodged complaints with the Polish government about mistreatment of the German populace in border regions.

By August 1939, when Hitler signed the non-aggression pact with Stalin, preparations became urgent. The Polish Navy was sent on an "official" visit to France and Great Britain to avoid its being trapped in the Baltic Sea. The government ordered partial mobilization of the armed forces, but incredibly, did not disperse the air forces, which were later caught on the ground and destroyed by the Luftwaffen.

Mobilization

First, we boys reported to military barracks on the outskirts of Kutno where we were assigned light office duties for a few hours daily, which we treated as a lark. However, as the gravity of the situation grew over the summer, we worked six hours a day. We were fed a real soldier's lunch of surprisingly good quality and quantity, including delicious rye bread baked by army cooks. Thoughts of these barracks meals came to mind in France again when I was served my first soldier's meal that was equally fine and included a carafe of *vin ordinaire*.

We dug air raid trenches in town. I was assigned to the mobilization office where we told farmers to bring their horses for cavalry use. We gave each farmer a receipt and promised government reimbursement after the war. The government also requisitioned cars, motorcycles and bicycles. I got to keep my bicycle because of my duties at the collections office. Only after the blitzkrieg did Polish and Western generals realize that they had been laying plans for the previous war. They had learned nothing from the Spanish civil war where the German army perfected techniques of modern warfare. So the German panzers rolled over our horse cavalry and foot soldiers at blitzkrieg speed.

As September approached, we attended many nationalistic rallies. We would gather at school, usually after supper, then as a group march to the main square in front of town hall where the citizenry gathered. Our Latin teacher, a veteran from the 1918 liberation of Poland who had marched from Italy with Polish forces under the command of General Pilsudski, was a firebrand. He stood on the town hall balcony, delivering a patriotic speech that moved the crowd to respond with shouts of "Fight Germany till we enter Berlin!" and such slogans. The populace was oblivious to the realities of the overwhelming strength of the German armed forces.

Perhaps the most ominous move by Germany was dispatching their powerful battleship *Gneisenau* to Gdansk (Danzig) on an "official visit." The battleship was anchored in the middle of the harbor, and with its 16-inch guns and heavy armor was in complete control of the city. The Polish Government was helpless because Gdansk was a "free city" and according to international law, ships could visit freely.

September 1, 1939

The day World War II erupted, I was to take an entrance exam for senior high school. That morning, Friday, September 1, I awoke early, aroused by commotion coming from the direction of the rail yards south of town. We heard explosions and high flying aircraft. I arrived at school for the 8:00 AM exam and sat at a desk. We got our exam papers and began answering questions. About 15 minutes later, the school director entered the classroom and told us to stop writing, hand in our papers, and quickly go home. He stressed not to stop on the way and to walk as close to the buildings as possible. This sounded strange, but he gave no reason, just told us to listen to the radio.

Military music played on all radio stations. At noon, Chopin's "Marche Militaire" came on, and then the President addressed the Citizens of Poland:

> Early this morning Germany's armed forces crossed the Polish border on a wide front and are advancing into the interior of our country. Earlier on the Luftwaffen carried out extensive raids on selected targets, especially our military airports, railroads, and centers of communication. Our armed forces are resisting this unprovoked invasion, and the Polish Government is appealing to our Western Allies for help in accordance with the treaties that are in effect.

The President urged that citizens resist and not abandon hope. Then, more martial music played, often interrupted by strange announcements, for example: "B7, D15, W35" or "B6, D16, W33." We came to realize that our armed forces had divided the country into small quadrants on the maps, and these announcements gave positions of German planes operating over Polish territory. In our naiveté, we thought, "Now that we know where the German planes are, they will not get back to Germany. Our air force will shoot them down."

As days passed, we noticed disturbing events and signs of distress. We saw Polish soldiers marching eastward away from the front. German planes began low flying missions, unafraid of ground fire. Radio announcements were no longer optimistic. I had a radio that could receive long, medium, and short wave stations so was able to pick up the radio station in Schenectady, New York. Since my parents had lived in the U.S. prior to World War I and could speak English, they translated real war news, which was not encouraging. The advance of the German army into Polish territory was astonishingly swift. Polish forces were pushed back into the interior in disorganized groups. A defense line was prepared around the capital Warsaw in central Poland.

There were sporadic reports of heroic resistance. A widely circulated episode involved defense of the Westerplatte peninsula around Gdansk where the German battleship *Gneisenau* began shelling coastal areas. When the Westerplatte defenders were forced to capitulate, eight of our soldiers in desperation elected to commit suicide rather than surrender. They shot one another on the beach in such a way that their bodies formed the word "Nie" (No, in Polish). Polish and German cameramen took pictures of the fallen bodies, published by both sides.

Kutno under German Domination

Meanwhile in Kutno, my town about 150 miles east of the prewar boundary, we saw increasing numbers of Polish army units moving eastward towards the capital. Mixed with them were thousands of refugees trying to escape the invaders. It amazed me to see refugees trekking east in horse drawn carts, buses, cars, and motorcycles, and I thought of the many receipts I issued that summer for horses and motor vehicles. The refugees streaming by were of all ages and physical condition, and needed food and shelter. The town inhabitants at first feared being overrun by lawlessness, but the police enforced order and we witnessed no problems. In fact, most of the police force remained on duty until the German security forces, including the dreaded Gestapo, took over. Even the local jail remained secure, and no convicts managed to escape.

In the middle of September the German army overran our town. When refugees ceased passing through, the days and nights became eerily quiet. German planes started flying almost at tree top level since the machine guns located on grain silos on the outskirts of town had been removed. German Junker bombers were easy to spot because their twin engines ran at slightly differing revolutions, producing a characteristic throbbing sound. Once they started flying low, we stopped running for the trenches. We spied German army units passing by with tanks and artillery. To my surprise, advancing troops were all motorized, with no soldiers on foot or cavalry. In fact, the Germans collected and shipped our horses back to Germany for farmers. After the front line troops passed through, the rear echelons occupied our town along with the dreaded Gestapo. While the German army was outfitted in a pleasing blue-gray color, the Gestapo wore forbidding black uniforms or dark suits with black trench coats and wide brim hats. It seemed strange for the clandestine Gestapo to be dressed so conspicuously. A German civilian administration was established, retaining lower level Polish personnel. Posters appeared all over town proclaiming sets of rules and regulations, printed in German and Polish. These notices all displayed an eagle holding a swastika in its talons.

One of the first posters demanded we turn in all guns and ammunition to authorities under penalty of death. Another required all Jews to wear a yellow Star of David on outer clothing and to give way to approaching Germans. A later notice required all radios to be handed in, but I did not comply immediately and learned that a Polish Government-in-Exile had been established in France where Polish armed forces were assembling. A Polish Navy, consisting of four destroyers, two submarines, and the passenger ship *M/S Batory*, began to operate out of England.

Western Poland was overrun by the latter half of September, and the battle for Warsaw was joined, bombing leveling large areas of the city. Kutno was in the flight path of the bombers, so we had a grandstand view of the low-flying planes with their distinctive engine sound. The defenders fought bravely but succumbed to the highly mechanized German forces and heavy bombardment. At this point, Russia, backed by a secret clause in the Molotov-von Ribbentrop pact, invaded Poland from the east, capturing many Polish troops. Polish army units were instructed to retreat southeast toward the Hungarian and Rumanian borders and cross into these neutral countries. A race between the retreating army units and Russian forces began. With Russian intervention, the war in Poland rapidly drew to a close. There was mass capture of trapped forces on both fronts. The Russians sent captured soldiers to the vast expanses of the Siberian sub-continent, the Germans to POW camps in Germany.

Luckily, a substantial number of army soldiers and almost the entire air force personnel of Poland managed to cross the border into Hungary and Rumania before the Russians blocked escape routes. Then, Polish soldiers were spirited away to France to join the expatriate Polish Army, Air Force, and Navy. Thus, history repeated itself. In World War I, Polish armed units were organized in Italy. After the 1918 Treaty of Versailles creating a free Poland, these forces marched to Poland under the leadership of General Pilsudski. The renowned pianist Ignace Paderewski returned to become the first president of newly-liberated Poland.

Life was increasingly oppressive in Kutno. Almost daily, a new restriction was imposed. The populace was advised to move into villages where food was more easily distributed. An endless (it seemed) trek of prisoners of war marched westward through town towards Germany. Many escaped as prisoners were led through the narrow streets. Escapees needed civilian clothing to avoid recapture. The civilian population willingly aided these Polish soldiers. I spotted an older friend from high school called up to serve in the Polish cavalry as he was marching through town with hundreds of other soldiers. I alerted my parents, and we quickly managed to get him out of the line and bring him to our house where he changed into civilian clothes and returned home about 20 miles away. Later, he joined our group of three who escaped from Poland to Hungary in December 1939.

There was a distinct difference in behavior of the first wave of German soldiers passing through Kutno, the frontline troops, and the army of occupation. The former were only interested in fighting the retreating Polish army while the latter were more unruly and concentrated on subjugating the population without bothering with the niceties of international law. They would break into houses looking for valuables or liquor, beat up people with or without provocation, and maintain order through sheer terror. Under occupation, there were incidents when a German soldier would disappear and later be found killed. Immediately, soldiers would close off the area, arrest 20 to 40 passersby, line them up in the street, and execute them on the spot. No attempt was made at separating children, old people, or invalids. The terror was deliberate, and it worked. A third group of occupiers were the Gestapo.

Their role was to suppress any signs of resistance to the occupation by any method. They were unrestrained by laws or conventions. Their appearance in black uniforms with the skull and crossbones insignia instilled fear and foreboding. Gestapo operations have been well documented, but reading about them is not the same as living under the day-to-day terror of their presence.

Almost immediately after collapse of organized armed opposition, the Polish underground resistance movement formed. The Armia Krajowa (Polish Underground Army) was divided into two sections. One consisted of uniformed army units operating deep within the forests of eastern and southern Poland. The second were thousands of three-person units in mufti in the cities. These three-person units (troikas) were organized such that each member knew the other two members of the unit, and just one other person of another unit. This limited exposure of clandestine cells in case of discovery by the Gestapo. The armed resistance in Poland was directed initially from Paris, and then London after France capitulated in June 1940. A Commander of the home front in Poland was appointed to coordinate long range British aircraft parachuting in personnel, guns, and ammunition. This organization was extremely effective throughout the war, suffering relatively few losses. The general in charge of the underground forces was finally captured in 1945 and executed.

A spectacular achievement of the underground army occurred when an experimental V-2 rocket launched from Peenemunde went astray, landing in a river in Poland. This resulted in a feverish race between German soldiers and the Polish Underground to find and retrieve the rocket. The Underground got there first, dismantled the rocket, and managed to put it aboard a returning British supply plane. The British government, sensing the danger posed by this new weapon, dispatched RAF bombers to try to destroy the Peenemunde research facilities.

German Annexation of Polish Territory

Poland was divided into three regions by the two powers. Russia occupied eastern Poland and started shipping the educated populace to

Siberia and captured soldiers to Asia. About 20,000 Polish officers were taken into the Katyn woods and summarily executed. People of Ukrainian origin were forcibly relocated to the Ukraine.

Germany annexed western Poland, so Kutno became part of Germany. A German-administered zone was created for the remainder of Poland, with a German governor located in Krakow (Cracow). By the end of September, life began to settle down. The food supply system was restored, although substantial amounts of food were shipped to Germany, creating some scarcities. Germans established a monetary system with the German mark substituted for Polish zlotys. An interesting phenomenon, also common following the liberation of Europe in 1945, was using cigarettes as valued currency. One could buy most anything with cigarettes, the amount dependent on the scarcity of the item. People, it seems, were willing to forego food for days but could not do without nicotine for even a couple of days.

Initially, the school system was re-established by the local civil administration. I began to attend class in November. After one week, however, the high school was closed by the Germans. The stated reason was that "Polish and other non-Nordic races were destined to be subservient races, therefore did not need education beyond being able to read and write." This hit me very hard, and I immediately began to think what to do next, discussing possibilities with my parents. We were aware of the creation of the Polish government in France and of the thousands of Poles who managed to reach France when the fighting ceased. I had another thought: if I could reach the United States, where most of our relatives now resided, perhaps I could continue my studies. And thus, thoughts of reaching France, and ultimately the U.S., were born.

Life in occupied Poland grew worse by the day as the Germans consolidated their grip on the country. The Polish populace was organizing more effective resistance. Both sides were claiming more successes, but there were also failures. The Gestapo with its ruthless methods lacking legal constraints and their infamous concentration camps was feared so much that Polish underground members were trained in many methods of suicide, if captured. Although the underground fighters relied on the network of "cells of three," the Gestapo countered by infiltrating one informer into several of the cells, thus exposing multiple group members. One such case occurred while I was still at home. It involved a classmate of mine who, for reasons I never found out, decided to cooperate with the Germans. He managed to expose about a dozen underground cells. In early morning raids, the Gestapo arrested over 300 people and shipped them to a concentration camp in Germany. We never heard from them again. When the Underground discovered this betrayal, they managed to capture the betrayer and held a clandestine trial. After conviction he was shot by firing squad. Surprisingly, the Germans on finding his body did not summarily execute a number of Poles in retribution as they normally did when a German soldier was killed.

Once my high school closed, I planned my escape to France. I linked up with two friends who shared thoughts of fleeing Poland. The three of us began planning in earnest, and by mid-December 1939 were ready to embark on our adventure.

Beginning of an Odyssey

As a young lad when Poland was overrun, I sought permission of my parents to flee my homeland, now under German domination, for Paris. Decisive factors were closure of Polish high schools and universities by our occupiers and relegation of non-German races to roles as serfs. Two friends and I laid plans for escape to Hungary, still neutral. Using hidden radios we picked up western news broadcasts reporting formation of the Polish Government-in-Exile in France, which became our destination. Often, I have reflected on my fate if I had stayed in occupied Poland — ending up in a concentration camp, killed as a randomly selected hostage, or joining the partisan underground army?

Escape required passage through several countries without passports, visas, money, or any idea of conditions we might encounter. Our plan was to cross the Carpathian Mountains separating Poland from Slovakia and Hungary in the south. We chose wintertime, as waiting for summer would allow time for the Germans to organize border patrols to block escape routes through the mountains. Between Poland and our destination in France lay the hostile territories of Germany, Austria, and Italy, all parts of the German-Italian Axis. Deteriorating conditions at home and growing excitement for the adventure made us eager to leave. For me, going alone was out of the question, I needed companions.

Prior to World War I, my parents emigrated separately to America where they met and married. After the war, they decided to return to Poland and start life anew in a place roughly halfway between where they grew up, selecting the town of Kutno. While in the U.S., they had befriended another Polish couple also wishing to return, who elected to purchase a farm about 20 miles from Kutno. My parents became owners of a specialty food store in Kutno. Both couples embarked on new lives in central Poland. One couple soon had a baby boy — me.

For many years the two families prospered. I spent many summers on our friends' farm and enjoyed the companionship of their children. Their eldest boy was conscripted into the Polish army prior to 1939 and captured by the Germans. After his escape, it did not take long for this boy and me to decide to flee together. We co-opted a high school friend, the oldest of us three, to join our odyssey.

The Escape Route

Travel within the country was controlled, so we needed passes to board a train. The chosen escape route was through the Ukrainian village that my mother came from in the mountains of southern Poland near a pass leading into Slovakia. Her relatives still lived there, giving us an excuse to visit and approach the border. The German army was still busy consolidating its occupation of towns and countryside in central Poland and had relegated guarding the southern border to local Polish police.

Time was of the essence. Our chosen route led from Kutno to Warsaw where we were to join up with a fourth friend from school. He wanted to be included in our adventure over the objections of his parents. Then, we would proceed to Cracow, change trains, and go on to Sanok near my mother's village of Posada Jasliska. Preparations were hasty to minimize chances of someone learning of our escape plans. Mother gave us a U.S. five-dollar gold piece still in its gift box (a present of visiting American cousins), Polish zlotys for train tickets, food for travel, and a box of tea (later a barter item). I stashed a book of logarithmic tables in my pocket at the last minute — I wasn't sure why — along with extra clothing.

So, one morning in December 1939 we three set forth on our fateful journey. Farewells were brief and casual, as though to return in a few days. Changing trains in Warsaw, we met the fourth member of our group, but at the last moment he elected to remain in Poland. Eventually, he joined the Polish underground army instead. In Cracow, the three of us spent time between trains touring the famous Merchants' Square. We finally reached Sanok in early evening and made the rest of the journey on foot.

My relatives welcomed us warmly, and after supper all went to bed. Next morning after breakfast, the local police called us in for interrogation. They separated us to compare our individual responses. Having prepared for this eventuality, we recounted similar stories. We said my family was deciding whether to move back to the family village, which was not in the part of Poland annexed by Germany, and where food might be more available. We said my parents would not allow me to travel alone because of my age, so the two older boys accompanied me. As this seemed plausible, the police did not arrest us. However, they did send the older two boys off to the Sanok police station while allowing me, as the youngest, to remain free. The police were pretty certain what was really going on, but they handled the situation delicately, as there was already a Gestapo office in the village overseeing local police.

At this point, the situation became critical since for me to cross the mountains alone was out of the question. I spent the day with my relatives considering the alternatives, all involving returning home. But early in the evening, a cousin arrived with welcome news that the two boys being taken to the station in Sanok were back in the village in hiding, and after dark we were reunited. What had occurred was that the policeman putting them on the train told them to jump out the other side of the carriage and make their way back to our village. The policeman also had alerted our cousins in the village about this, so as the boys approached, they were sequestered in a safe house. The future began to look brighter.

Crossing into Slovakia

It turned out that the safe house was one used by smugglers when crossing back and forth from Slovakia. A party of smugglers in the house that evening decided to sleep after the day's trip and return the following night. It was unsafe for us boys to wait another day in the village so we decided to cross the border that night. We got a guide across the mountains — a young cousin who offered to lead us. However, he had to return to the village before sunrise to avoid the police. This meant that he would be able to lead us only to a point where lights of the Slovakian town would be visible ahead in the distance.

The most prudent way into the border town was not to carry luggage or bundles in order to appear local. That meant carrying everything on one's person. So, we piled on two pairs of underwear, trousers, and sweaters, etc. and slung extra boots over our shoulders. We set forth at a brisk pace in spite of the deep snow. The night was bright under a full moon. Still, we had difficulty maintaining a straight path while traversing the mountains because of ridges and ravines. Lacking a compass, the trick was to line oneself up with a tree or rock on top of the next hill and head off in that direction. But down in hollows the marker would be obscured, so a knowledgeable guide was essential. We kept mostly to wooded areas, avoiding exposed, moonlit fields. After about two hours, silhouettes loomed ahead and we jumped into woods, but it turned out to be women smugglers shouldering large bundles. The remainder of the journey proved uneventful, and our little group arrived on a hill overlooking the lights of Medzilaborce in Slovakia. With warm thanks, we bid goodbye to our guide who returned homeward.

As it was only five AM and streets were empty, it seemed risky to walk into town, so we elected to wait a couple of hours. We were tired from the excitement of the previous days and the strenuous night, so without much forethought we lay down under a tree in deep snow and slept. I recalled this brief slumber long afterward because my exposed ear rested in the snow and part of my earlobe froze; eventually I lost it. Once people began moving in town, the three of us descended and mixed in with the crowds.

The train for the Hungarian border was not due until afternoon. To get off the streets we decided to rent a hotel room, but to do so required local currency. The eldest of us exchanged my five-dollar gold piece; then, I proceeded to the railway station to buy tickets. I feared my inability to speak Slovakian would alert the ticket clerk so I asked for tickets in German. After paying for the tickets and hotel, little money was left for lunch. In the village we sauntered separately but kept within view of each other. We finally boarded the crowded train to Snina, reaching the town on the Slovakian-Hungarian border without incident.

As it was still quite light, we located a small, empty coffee shop on a side street. The owner seemed friendly, and since Polish and Slovakian languages are similar, we were able to communicate. The owner realized immediately what we were up to. We needed a place off the street to await darkness before attempting to cross into Hungary. By now, we were quite hungry but had little money. This was where the small package of tea proved useful. The owner was more than pleased to provide sandwiches and hot soup in exchange for the tea.

Around five PM, we decided that the eldest of us should walk along the road leading to Hungary to scout the approach to the border. The other two waited in the coffee shop, but when our friend failed to return by eight PM, we figured something must have gone wrong and decided to proceed by ourselves. Obviously, going along the main road was inadvisable so the two of us cut through fields to the east where the border ran north-south. The moon was rising in the east by then, and we walked in that direction over some hills. Following the moon seemed to be the way to keep walking east. We had forgotten how quickly the moon moves across the sky. As a result, after about five hours we were nearly back to our starting point. By then, tired and cold, we threw caution to the winds and chose a fixed path that led us to a railway bridge over a swift-running river. Crossing proved to be dangerous because the bridge lacked a roadbed and we could see the river between the railroad ties. To make matters worse, the wooden ties were very icy so we had to use great care crossing in the darkness.

Internment in Hungary

Traversing the bridge safely, we spotted lights across a stream and footbridge leading to a village. Exhausted, we crossed, only to find two soldiers waiting for us. The soldiers asked, "Lengel?" This did not sound like Slovakian or German so we relaxed a little and let the soldiers lead us to the village. Later, we found that "Lengel" means Polish in Hungarian. Finally, we arrived at a house and were shown a room with two mattresses on a dirt floor. In no time, we were asleep.

The next morning, we were awakened early. After breakfast of bread and milk, the soldiers loaded us on a truck along with about 20 other escapees who had crossed the border that night, not an unusual number we learned. The truck brought us to the nearby village of Csop, where we were lodged on a pig farm. Accommodations had been created for escapees by displacing pigs. After showering, we were examined for flea bites and lice. Those with infestations were issued new clothes and their old ones burned. Fortunately, we passed inspection, and I kept my clothes and spare pair of boots.

Life on the farm settled into a routine. The wake-up call was to squealing and grunts of more than 2,000 pigs. We refugees got breakfast after the pigs were fed. We learned we would be transferred soon to a special camp with better amenities and food. The two of us wanted to find out the fate of our friend who disappeared after leaving the coffee shop in Snina to scout the border. We asked others if they had any idea what happens to those apprehended by the Slovakian police. Nobody knew, but most thought that they would be sent back to Poland, i.e., turned over to the Germans. As we were about to leave the pig farm, a truck arrived, and wonder of wonders, our friend was aboard so we were reunited with much hugging and some tears.

En route to the new camp, our lost companion related his story. It seems that the border crossing was newly created after German conquest of Czechoslovakia. The country was divided into three regions: Czechs were incorporated into Germany, Slovaks were placed under control of a Nazi sympathizer priest (like the notorious Quisling of Norway), and the Bessarabian region where we remained under Hungarian control. The new border crossing still lacked a proper guardhouse and barrier. Our friend walked right into the border post without noticing it and was held by the police until 6:00 PM when they closed the post and went back to Snina. It seems if we had only waited another hour, we could have walked along the highway into Hungary without any problem. He was held at the police station for many days, being fingerprinted and interrogated, but not mistreated. Then, one evening his cell was left unlocked. Since nobody was around and it was after 6:00 PM, he just walked out of the station and strolled along the road into Hungary.

The new camp on the outskirts of the town of Nyiregyhaza was quite a step up. It had been a summer camp for government employees, and now was winterized with wood stoves and proved quite comfortable. The Hungarian army under a young Army captain administered the camp. A Polish commandant selected by the refugees set the daily routine. Accommodations were barrack style with double bunk beds. Three meals of typical Hungarian dishes of good quality were served daily. One issue that soon surfaced was serving "pepper" soup for breakfast, a real throat and stomach burner! The refugees' organization complained to the kitchen staff to no avail, perhaps due to the language barrier, so we organized a strike and boycotted breakfast. After a few days, the commandant was informed, and the next day milk was offered in place of soup. A fringe benefit of the strike was that the commandant began making regular rounds and communicated in German directly with refugee leaders and complainers.

Life was orderly but monotonous. News from the outside came mainly from new arrivals that brought facts and rumors, the one indistinguishable from the other. There were no Polish newspapers or radio broadcasts. To relieve the tedium we were allowed to visit nearby towns. We were given a little pocket money to buy chocolate, tooth paste, and so on. The nearby hills produced Tokay wines of wide repute. Evenings, we could visit local taverns where there always was a Gypsy band with violins, cimbaloms, and button style accordions. Everyone would order warm spiced Tokay wine to while away the time and listen to melancholy Gypsy music.

Relations between the camp commandant and the refugees grew increasingly warm, so one of us, a noted artist, secretly carved a chess set and presented it to the commandant with a flourish in a ceremony ending with warm spice wine for all. Every so often, families in neighboring villages would invite refugees to their homes for supper to spend an evening together. It took a lot of arm waving and non-verbal gestures to carry on conversation. Photographs, maps, and books aided the dialogue. On one such visit I produced the book of logarithmic tables I had brought from Poland. Our host that evening was a Latin teacher, so much lively finger pointing at Latin words in the text ensued. At last, I understood why I chose to carry this volume across the border.

The population of the camp was mixed, consisting of policemen, soldiers, teachers, laborers, artists, farmers, and others, but lacked women even though this was the sole refugee camp. Apparently, women faced less danger at home than did men, who were conscripted into forced labor. There were nightly arrivals of Poles crossing the border. However, the camp census remained stable, as refugees were also fleeing to the Polish Consulate in Budapest. This fact probably did not escape notice of the commandant, but we assumed he received a daily allowance based on camp numbers. If he failed to promptly report missing refugees, the amount budgeted would be larger and he could siphon off funds for other purposes.

Flight to the Polish Consulate

We boys started to plan the next step in our efforts to reach France. During these unsettled times, the Hungarian government allowed the Polish Consulate to operate without official sanction in Budapest. Once a Polish citizen reached the consulate, he would receive identity papers and not be sent back to internment. The consulate then assisted refugees to reach France.

To get to the consulate meant somehow obtaining money for a rail ticket. One must leave camp while avoiding camp guards, reach the railroad station, buy a ticket, and get on the right train. Then, in Budapest, one had to find the consulate without being intercepted by police. All this had to be accomplished without speaking Hungarian. Since Hungary was part of the Austro-Hungarian Empire prior to World War I, most older individuals did speak or understand some German, which was an aid to Poles.

My two older companions were to leave first, since they were of military age and would immediately join the expatriate Polish army in France. Pooling our resources, we had just enough to purchase two train tickets so the two set off, promising to send for me as soon as possible. Being left alone in the camp was difficult at first, but I forged new friendships and time passed quickly. Eventually, a letter arrived from my friends informing me that passage to France was quite easy.

The main obstacle was getting to the Polish consulate in Budapest, and they advised haste. Rumors were circulating that the Germans planned to attack Russia, using an invasion route through Hungary. Without delay I checked with our Polish camp commandant about scheduling my escape. It was a rule that the numbers of individuals fleeing the camp at any one time should not be excessive, so as to avoid embarrassing the camp commandant.

My problem was obtaining money for train fare. Luckily, I still had an extra pair of boots and sold the better pair to secure funds. Getting out of camp was no problem, as evenings refugees could go into town. At the station I waited for others to arrive so as not to be conspicuous in the empty waiting room. Purchasing the ticket turned out to be easy. All I needed was to say "Budapest," and of course, pay. When the train arrived, I understood the word Budapest over the PA system, but the departure platform was unclear. As I approached the door to the platform, I spotted soldiers checking the identity of passengers. Fearing I would be caught and sent back to camp, I decided to stroll out of the station along the railroad tracks, then double back. Luckily, this deception worked, and I arrived at the platform just as the train was departing.

It was hard to find a seat, but eventually, I sat down next to a man wearing the uniform of a railroad employee. The six-hour trip was long, it was late, and I feigned sleep to avoid conversation. When a vendor came through the carriage offering sandwiches and refreshments, thirst forced me to ask for a drink in German without problem. The man next to me must have taken notice of my use of German, but he showed no apparent interest.

All went smoothly until the train arrived in Budapest, and passengers started leaving. At this point, the rail employee tugged my sleeve and indicated to follow him, so of course I did. The man proceeded directly to the passenger exit where I saw soldiers checking identification. At the exit the man showed his ID and we walked out together. Out of earshot outside, he quietly asked in German, "Address?" I immediately showed him the consulate address. We walked together for a time. When the man spotted a young Hungarian soldier, he spoke to him, showing him the consulate address. The soldier nodded agreement, and I had only a moment to thank the man for his kindness before he went on his way.

The soldier and I walked for over half an hour, finally arriving at the door of the Polish consulate. The soldier gestured towards the building, and again I had only a brief moment to thank him before he disappeared. It was four AM and the doors to the building were locked. The temperature was below freezing, and there was always the possibility of a police patrol intercepting me so I rang the doorbell. After some time, the door opened and a man addressed me in Polish as if he anticipated who would be ringing the bell at that hour. He said that the consulate opened at eight AM so I should stretch out on the boiler room floor and wait. At eight AM, I proceeded upstairs and with my birth certificate and high school photo identity card was quickly processed. So, one segment of my life ended and other began.

I have often thought about this entire episode, how a complete stranger noticed a boy in need of help and came to his aid without thought of recompense. Where is he now, this Good Samaritan? Did he ever consider this act might have determined the boy's entire future? And what about the young soldier who went out of his way on a cold night to lead a stranger to an address of little consequence to him? Did he realize how this kindness would affect the life of another human being? What if I had not been helped by these total strangers, and instead been picked up by police and sent back to internment camp? What then?

Escape to the West

The consulate had no problem issuing me a local permit. Since I was not of military age, I was sent to a Polish high school in Balaton Zamardi on the shores of Lake Balaton south of Budapest and resumed my education. The school was located in a Hungarian technical school in this summer resort town. I was now confronted with reaching France before the impending German takeover of Hungary.

A surprise awaited me on arrival. The school principal was a former teacher of mathematics from my Kutno high school. How unlikely an occurrence? The school curriculum comprised whatever subjects our existing teachers could offer. They too had escaped but chose not to continue on to join Polish forces in France. We lacked textbooks in Polish, which precluded self study. The extremely cold winter kept us mostly indoors, although a few boys had brought winter clothing, and there was lots of borrowing and scrounging. The main attraction outside was observing commercial fisherman who cut holes to drag fish nets underneath the ice.

News of the war was not encouraging. Encountering little opposition, Hitler continued to expand the Third Reich. Indications were that the Eastern European bloc of countries would succumb to German occupation. The only bright spot at the time was defeat of the Russian invasion of Finland. I hungered for education, and prospects of a well staffed high school in Paris propelled me onward. Fortunately, the principal, a family friend, understood my desire and placed phone calls to the Polish consulate in Budapest informing them I was coming. He gave me a letter stating that the school administration did not object to my proceeding on to France. This was "another crossroad" in my life aided by the efforts of a kind human being.

The consulate proved extremely helpful. I was granted a Polish passport and given accommodations in a Polish hostel. In two days, I had the necessary visas (Hungarian exit visa, Yugoslavian and Italian transit visas, French entry visa). All this had to be done without attracting undue attention, because international law forbade neutral countries from issuing visas to nationals of countries at war. Since the Polish Government-in-Exile in France was technically at war with Germany, the Hungarian government had to walk a fine line and deny visas to Polish nationals of military age (18-50 years). I had no problem because my age was well documented, but others often were met with questioning glances by border guards when they travelled as a 17-year-old but looked 30.

Before departure I had a toothache so the consulate obtained an evening appointment with a local dentist. After supper I searched for the address, which took some time to locate in a darkened building. Luckily, the dentist spoke German so I was able to convey my complaint. While discussing possible treatment, he poked around in my mouth, which was quite stiff from exposure to the cold night air. Before I knew it he had my tooth in his hand. I had not felt a thing.

For the journey to France the consulate organized four groups of five and assigned each group to depart in separate carriages using two different Budapest rail stations. Scheduled to leave March 20, 1940, we assembled at the consulate the previous evening. We were to travel on the famous Orient Express due to arrive from Istanbul at two AM, taking us through Zagreb, Yugoslavia, and on to Venice and Milan. We would then transfer to a local train going through Turin and cross into France at Modane.

Each group had an assigned leader, but we traveled separately in the streets. The night was bitterly cold, and when I noticed a movie theater, I bought a ticket with my remaining Hungarian coins. So, I saw "Snow White and the Seven Dwarfs" without understanding either the English or Hungarian subtitles. When the theater closed around eleven, I walked a while to keep warm because the suburban station I was assigned to opened only one hour before train time. As soon as it opened, I found a warm corner in the empty waiting room and dozed off. Luckily, the stationmaster woke me up and led me outside into the fresh air. The room heated by a coal-fired stove was poorly ventilated. What I thought was restful sleep risked becoming carbon monoxide-induced slumber. Soon, others arrived and my leader handed me my passport, a bag of sandwiches, and five U.S. dollars for the trip.

Having embarked at the last station in Budapest, I found all seats occupied so I settled down on a hard trunk, spending two days and nights sitting on it. Sleep was impossible as I had to stand to allow people to pass by every few minutes. After going through passport control at the Yugoslavian border, people came aboard offering to change money into local currency at black market rates. Throughout the trip I changed my five U.S. dollars into Yugoslavian dinars, Italian lira, and French francs. To my amazement, thanks to the black market, I ended up in France with more than the five U.S. dollars I started with, despite purchasing coffee and fruit on the way. Enterprising vendors sold us drinks and snacks at the stations, and when the train pulled away would shout to give them the spoon and return the glass at the next station. They were well organized.

Although Mussolini's Italy was allied with Germany, we had no trouble traveling to France. Once there, we were housed on an army base where we showered, were fed breakfast, and slept. I still recall the warm welcome we received that day, as well as the first banana I ever ate and the soldier's fare of a carafe of *vin ordinaire* each mealtime, including breakfast. Soon, I was sent to the Polish high school in Paris to continue my "Ardua ad Educatio" with the hope my odyssey was over, but this was not to be.

Parisian Life in Wartime

I arrived in Paris in April 1940. Still too young for the army, I attended a Polish high school in the Sorbonne area on the "left bank." The school was housed in a vacant building called Lycee Fenelon where we took classes and meals. We slept in nearby dormitories belonging to the Lycee St. Louis, a prestigious French College. We were chaperoned by our teachers, since according to them we had to be protected from the

"French influence" — whatever that meant. The school building had a small courtyard that was unpleasantly hot in the summer of 1940. A pass was required to venture into the city and we tried many dodges to sneak out. Students with relatives in Paris were allowed to visit them, so many of us "acquired" relatives.

Located on Rive Gauche, our school was in a neighborhood not lacking in attractions. Paris was enchanting to our eyes and we roamed the city, but without money could not use public transportation and went about on foot. We explored the Quay d'Orsay, Garden of the Louvre (the museum was too expensive), Place de la Concorde, Arc de Triomphe, and the Eiffel Tower. A favorite haunt to while away time was Chanteclair, a music store where one could listen to classical music. One could sit down in front of a machine upstairs, put on earphones, and dial a number from a directory identifying the desired music. Downstairs, the operator placed the requested record on the gramophone. I spent many satisfying hours listening to symphonies there, instead of sweltering in the school courtyard.

As we did not speak French, we interacted little with Parisians but sensed an almost surreal wartime atmosphere. There was no rationing, no blackouts, no food shortages. Paris was indeed the "City of Lights." However, one morning we awoke to sounds of explosions from the suburbs. We learned that German planes had bombed the Renault factories, and German armed forces had crossed the border into Belgium, Holland, and France. Our summer bliss was shattered. Just as the previous September in Poland, blitzkrieg tactics decimated the French and British forces, which could not withstand the German panzers. Soon we saw pictures of refugees, this time fleeing westward. The German army was rapidly approaching Paris. Our school director was ordered to evacuate the school.

Flight to the Coast

With the help of our priest we were invited by a French church school to a summer camp near Biarritz, which we reached by train and truck. Whenever we saw girls along the way, being boisterous youths we cheered, waved, and whistled at them. The priest escorting us did not interfere, and on one occasion actually joined in when an older woman passed by. He explained his behavior, stating "we priests are allowed to employ housekeepers over 40 years of age, so I can wave to women past that age. Of course, some priests employ two 20-year olds to comply with this age restriction." We hoped he might accompany us to England, but unluckily, he chose to remain in France.

Our stay in Biarritz was short-lived. The German army was racing along the coast to cut off escape routes to England. After only a few days we awakened early, boarded trucks, and hastened to St. Jean de Luz, the French port near the Spanish border. We dared not cross into Franco's Spain where we would be interned and most likely turned over to German authorities. With flames visible in the towns just to our north, we awaited tenders on the beach to take us aboard the *Arrandora Star*, one of the ships Britain diverted from mid-Atlantic to rescue fleeing refugees. Just as I caught the rope ladder slung over the ship's side, someone yelled, "Lift your legs!" Luckily, I did and avoided by only inches having my legs crushed as the waves dashed the tender against the ship.

We sailed westward into the Atlantic, then north of Ireland to avoid prowling German U-boats. On its next voyage, the *Arrandora Star* would be sunk en route to Canada with Italian POWs aboard. We disembarked at Liverpool and continued to London by train. Our reception in England was remarkable. The British people and government officials could not have been more hospitable. At first, we were housed in a vacant hospital complex in the Chelsea district of central London where we were issued toiletries, clothing, and pocket money to use in the small camp store.

Wartime London

Our Polish high school from Paris was re-established in a London University College dormitory in Ealing Broadway west of downtown London. It was a pleasant suburb with lots of greenery and grassy lawns typical of England. The English staff welcomed us and provided our first meal. I recall the table set out in the style of landed gentry, not for a bunch of teenage refugees recently saved from Hitler's clutches. Each place setting had a cube of butter, cup of sugar, and bottle of Heinz salad cream. With healthy appetites, we started piling butter on our bread when someone at the head table announced, "The butter, sugar and mayonnaise at your place are your rations for the week." Immediately, all knives began scraping off butter. Severe food rationing continued in Great Britain until 1954.

From then on, meals quite delicious to our taste were prepared by Polish women. We had only the complement of teachers who accompanied us from France, consequently there were no physics or chemistry classes, only religion, English, mathematics, and philosophy. School life proved to be dull without sports or library facilities. Air raids and aerial dogfights over London provided the only excitement. Daytime raids continued until mid-September when the German Luftwaffe came in massive force. A monumental battle ensued all that weekend. Losses were high on both sides. Then, Germany started running out of trained pilots and sent bombers only at night to strategic targets. Except for the area of the London dockyards, the civilian population was spared. However, when British bombers later staged a provocative raid on Berlin, Hitler was so enraged he ordered indiscriminate bombing of civilian areas. This change of strategy actually may have saved the British war industry and quite possibly Great Britain from defeat.

With little pocket money, we could not afford the Underground to central London where blackouts dimmed the lights of Piccadilly Circus and Leicester Square. We missed the excitement of the metropolis so when called to clean up bombed areas in Central London, we all volunteered. By late September, night bombers hit the financial and newspaper districts near St. Paul's Cathedral, areas only populated during daytime hours. Small incendiary bombs had started hundreds of roof top fires that might have been avoided by tossing bombs off rooftops or smothering the fires with sand. The government then promulgated a Fire Watchers law requiring all buildings unoccupied at night to have someone standing guard.

That autumn we were called to help clean up bomb damage to the British Museum. We rescued many exhibits and stored them away. When the museum was hit again, we again cleaned up the damage, but when a third call came a few days later, we felt "what's the use?" Luckily, the museum was spared further damage. The effect of these almost nightly air raids was the opposite of what one might expect. Instead of discouraging the populace with thoughts of surrender, the constant danger only enhanced their resolve to stand up to the Jerries and support the armed forces. The behavior of the Royal Family and leadership of the government led by Churchill elicited a remarkable response from the British people. The King's refusal at the suggestion of the government to move to Canada with his family produced a swell of affection. Frequent visits by George VI, the Queen, and the young princesses to bombed-out areas of London added intensely to the bond between the Royal Family and the public.

One October evening just before six PM, I was resting on my bed and looking out the open window. I heard the drone of bombers and the characteristic whistle of a bomb. Before I could hide under the bed I saw a flash in the garden about 50 feet from the window, followed by a muffled explosion. It all took place in probably 30 seconds. The question at dinner was, "Did the bomb explode?" We had to find out. The hole in the soft soil was about two feet wide. General opinion was that an unexploded bomb (UXB) was buried deep beneath the garden. On the other hand, I was sure it had exploded as I had clearly seen the flash and heard the explosion. To decide who was right, we did what any young and foolish boys would do — we threw rocks into the hole. Nothing happened. Soon Fire Wardens came to inspect the damage, checking from a prudent distance of a couple hundred feet away. They decided to evacuate our school to a vacant building two blocks away situated just over the wall from our garden. Since our "UXB" did not obstruct vital traffic, we were at the bottom of the list for a bomb disposal squad to investigate. Fire wardens established a post 300 yards up the street from our school and closed it to motor and pedestrian traffic.

Life in an abandoned house without heat or hot water while sleeping on hardwood floors did not suit us. We could view our former comfortable bedrooms beyond the garden wall. Before long we started climbing over the wall at night to sleep in our cozy beds. We took showers and turned on radios. That was a mistake. Lights and music in the evacuated building attracted the wardens, who found a house full of boys having a ball with a presumed unexploded bomb nearby. So back we went to Spartan living. But this episode pushed our bomb to the top of the list. A disposal unit arrived and started gingerly digging around the bomb crater. Soon, they uncovered a large crater underneath where the bomb actually had exploded. If they had just believed my story, we could have stayed home instead of roughing it for more than two weeks.

School life again became routine. Christmas was approaching. It was a melancholy time with those we loved still in Poland, no family gatherings or gifts around the Christmas tree, only worries about the outcome of the war. Nightly bombings continued. Again, while everyone was in the dining room, we heard the whistle of a bomb. An explosion shook our building. We ran out and looked down the corridor to discover half our building was missing. We had received a direct hit on the end of the house where we slept, but of course we had all been in the dining room. The Ministry of Education decided that "two bombs too many" required our evacuation from London. They chose a spot in the middle of Scotland. Our new home was a fabulous castle-like hunting lodge named Dunalastair House.

Life in Scotland

So we moved from a metropolis to the middle of nowhere. Our only neighbors were a flock of sheep across a stream on the slopes of Schiehallion Mountain. For diversion, we could climb the mountain or hike to the tiny village of Kinloch Ranoch, three miles round trip. What culture shock. Soon snow fell and the mountain and the foothills were covered with beautiful white stuff. Silence pervaded after London's noisy traffic, aircraft racket, and bomb explosions, but it provided a nice change, and finally we could concentrate on studies. We were located just short of 57th latitude, as far north as the middle of Hudson Bay.

This gave us our famous "white nights," cloudless nights with a full moon when we could read books at midnight.

One such night we heard the characteristic engine sound of Junker bombers and saw their silhouettes high in the sky. A few hours later, they returned flying eastward. Next day, the radio news reported that Glasgow shipyards had been bombed the previous night by the Luftwaffen flying out of occupied Norway. As it turned out, it was raining that night and the wet highway running parallel to the Clyde River a few miles north of Glasgow reflected the rays of the moon so that the pilots mistook the road for the river. Houses on both sides of the highway were destroyed with substantial civilian casualties, but the vital shipyards were spared. As far as the German Air Force knew, however, they had bombed the shipyards. This was the only instance Glasgow was bombed. I became aware of war news reports categorizing one of two types of casualties: civilian, "good," or military and industrial, "bad." World War II was the first war in which civilian populations were on the front lines.

Glasgow University

On May 15, 1941 I graduated from high school and was recommended by the Polish Navy for admittance to Glasgow University to study naval architecture. The Navy was already laying plans for post-war operations in free Poland. The war news got brighter once the threat of invasion from across the Channel receded and Hitler attacked Russia.

Life at the University was tough at first. Language difficulties grew, what with understanding the Scottish brogue and scientific terminology. Students in my classes did not resemble the stereotype of dour Scotsmen found in literature. They were full of spirit, enjoyed life, and would play tricks on our professors — and anybody else. Some of their hi-jinks merit recounting.

In the first year we had a Dr. Green, an assistant to the famous Lord Kelvin, recalled from retirement during the war as lecturer in Natural Philosophy (since the days of Newton, Glasgow's term for Physics). His lectures always began with "let us take a point and call it P" and finished with at least a dozen points on the blackboard, all called P, so we dubbed him "Dr. P-Green." Whenever we tried to ask questions, he would say, "Ask me during the break." Since we had a long trek to the next class, we explained we did not have time for questions then. His reply was, "Come see me at my home after the classes." That was a big mistake. We organized a list of students to ask the same simple question. Precisely at 11 PM, the first student on the list rang the bell at the professor's home. Next on the list rang five minutes later, and this went on until two AM. Questions were answered during class time after that.

One of Glasgow's streetcar lines terminated outside the university's main gate. Most times, a streetcar would be sitting there awaiting scheduled departure. The streetcars were double-deckers with a door at each end at the top of the stairway. The motorman and ticket collector would sit in the upper deck with closed doors to keep warm while awaiting departure. After an exam, some engineering students decided to unwind. They descended on the waiting streetcar and locked the doors to the upper deck, trapping the men inside. Then, one of the electrical engineering students activated the controls, and with the rest of us on board, proceeded to drive the streetcar downtown. In town, all the students departed, leaving the trapped employees to be rescued.

The buildings at the university had a central bell tower with two quadrangles. During the war each quadrangle had a huge metal container filled with water as backup for fighting fires started by a bomb. The university was on top of a hill overlooking a park with a large pond where ducks thrived. During exams one morning, arriving students and staff were startled to see several dozen ducks swimming in the reservoirs. During the night students had transferred sleeping ducks to the quad's water containers.

Since my finances were shaky, I sought a job to supplement my income. The law requiring a watch in empty buildings also applied to Glasgow. A building in central Glasgow advertised for a firewatcher and I applied. Two people had to be on the premises from six PM until seven AM to watch for firebombs. Since there were no more air raids in Glasgow, I spent many quiet nights in that city. We had a nice room with two beds (we were allowed to sleep if there were no raids), a teakettle, some biscuits, and a small bottle of whiskey that were always left in the room.

The building belonged to a whiskey distillery located in the Scottish highlands. Bonded distilled whiskey was brought to the building and stored in huge vertical wooden casks with spigots near the bottom. Each morning, in the presence of a Customs Agent raw whiskey was drawn from the cask, then the spigot sealed by the Agent until the next morning when the process was repeated. The owner paid duty to the government for the amount of whiskey withdrawn daily. The raw whiskey was a clear liquid with the consistency of glycerin. They diluted it to 80-proof strength for bottling with water from a Scottish lake, then added burnt sugar to produce the requisite color.

United States entry into the war after Pearl Harbor brought a complete change of outlook about outcome of the conflict among the British populace. No longer did we wonder how the war would end, only when. Of course, there were to be many anxious moments ahead, but the final outcome was no longer in doubt.

Royal Naval College, Greenwich, England

In April 1944 I graduated from Glasgow University in Naval Architecture. The war was progressing well for the Allies. The Polish Government-in-Exile located in London was planning its return to Poland. There was need for trained personnel to start modern industries after the years of German occupation. Rebuilding naval facilities was required to modernize the Navy on return to Gdynia, the Polish naval base on the Baltic Sea.

The Polish Navy in England solicited my interest in working in postwar Poland and taking the three-year course in warship design offered at the Royal Naval College in Greenwich on the south banks of the Thames east of London. As I wished to pursue higher academic degrees, I readily agreed. After passing an entrance examination in July 1944, I began studies at this exclusive College, which strictly adhered to British naval tradition. My class included a Norwegian, Greek, and Canadian student as well as 18 British naval officers.

Sir Christopher Wren, famous for rebuilding London after the devastating fire of 1666, designed the Royal Naval College as a naval hospital for injured and retired seamen, similar to the accommodation for the Army's Chelsea Pensioners, which still exists. In 1873 the Royal Naval College relocated from Portsmouth to this complex at the north end of Greenwich Park. Quadrangles housed offices, classrooms, and living quarters referred to in naval tradition as "cabins." During the war WRENS served as stewards, cleaned, made beds, polished shoes, and so on. The Painted Hall provided an impressive setting for assemblies, conferences, and balls, and in 1939 became the dining facility of the College. We dined at long wooden tables running the full length of the hall. Navy cooks produced savoury, five-course meals, and each fall King George VI supplied venison from his hunting estates to be enjoyed.

The "piece de resistance" of life at the Royal College was Mess Night on Thursdays when we dressed for the occasion. Officers were in so-called "Mess Undress" and we civilians in dinner jackets. The welcoming Marine Band and the stewards wore uniforms from the days of Nelson, and lighting was supplied by candelabra. Dinners were unfailingly superb, and ended with the traditional "passing of the port," everyone in turn charging his glass from a bottle proceeding up and down the table with replenishment by stewards, as needed. The Admiral would then raise his glass and toast "To the King." We remained seated for the toast — it seems that the Navy was granted this privilege by the King in the days of wooden vessels because of the restricted headroom in ship wardrooms.

Several events marked my Greenwich days. After Nelson's death, his body was viewed in the Painted Hall in his coffin placed on a wooden table. The table is now in a passageway beneath the chapel, and tradition calls for every new student to lie down on it, which I did. Near war's end, the Germans fired V-2 rockets at London that flew over Greenwich, and one struck a nearby Woolworth store crowded with customers. Windows trembled, yet our professor continued lecturing without interruption, despite about 200 casualties. The "good thing" about V-2 rockets was that they were supersonic, so if you heard it you were safe. Sounds were heard in reverse order, first the explosion, then the more distant propulsion noise.

The UN held its first plenary session in London in 1946 near Parliament. A memorable event was a United Nations gala dinner hosted by the British government in the Painted Hall. Delegates dined in mess dinner tradition. We students witnessed the affair from the Upper Hall. Prime Minister Clement Atlee presided, and afterwards, diners retired to the Wardroom where we mixed with delegates. British Foreign Secretary Ernest Bevin told risqué jokes, and the memorable evening ended in early morning.

Epilogue

In April 1947 I completed courses at the College. The Western Allies allowed Stalin to take over Poland and install a communist government. The wartime Polish government in exile, which had sponsored me at the Royal Naval College, was unable to return to Poland. I then decided to seek more Western longitudes.

Born in Kutno, Tad as a 16-year old high school student escaped from Poland, fleeing to France, then Great Britain as the conflict spread. During wartime, he attended the University of Glasgow and Royal Naval College in Greenwich, England. After the war, he emigrated to Canada and the United States and now resides with his wife Claire at Wake Robin. After the war, Tad learned that his father had fought in the Polish Underground. He was caught by the Germans and sent to Mauthausen–Gusen, a concentration camp in Austria where he died, they said, of influenza. Happily, Tad brought his mother to live in Canada where she lived to be 99.

French War Bride

★

Martha Schultz

IN 1939, I WAS A TEENAGER when the Germans invaded France. We lived in Calais on the English Channel at the time. There was heavy bombardment the night the German army reached the city. We all ran to the bakery shop across the street to hide, as we did not know what to expect. By morning, we could see a German soldier pacing back and forth, though we could only see his boots through the little basement window. We were afraid to go outside, but after waiting some time, we decided to risk it. Fortunately, the soldier was friendly, handing out candy to the children. Despite kind behavior by this soldier in our first encounter, a level of concern pervaded our lives for four long years.

Starting in 1942, the Americans began bombing the railroad quite close to our place. Almost nightly, I recall running down to the kitchen and crouching under the table; that was the only protection we had. Often they missed their target, and the bombs landed near us. One American bomber was downed right next door to us.

In 1944 the Allies landed in Normandy and liberated northern France, including the port city of Calais. While I was living and working in Lille, one of my girl friends and I attended an event at the local dance hall. An American soldier invited me to dance. He was assigned to driving a truck for the U.S. Army in the Lille area after having seen action in the Battle of the Vosges in Belgium. We later married, and I vividly recall the day in 1945 when we drove in a jeep to Belgium to buy a wedding ring. All the way back to France we sang the American song: "You are my sunshine, my only sunshine."

After our marriage we lived in France for about four months until my husband was recalled to the U.S. and discharged from the Army. Two months later in 1946, I was able to join him in the U.S. I was one of some 500 war brides who boarded a large ship at Le Havre to meet their husbands stateside. On the voyage many of the girls were seasick, especially those who were expecting babies. On arrival a number of them had to be carried from the port on stretchers and taken to the hospital for treatment.

My husband met me in New York and we drove to Bethlehem, Pennsylvania where we built a house the following year and lived in it for over 50 years. My family believed I would come back to France, but I remained in the United States. My husband died in 2000 at the age of 90, and I moved to Vermont to be near my daughter who lives in Waterbury, Vermont.

Born in Bethune, France, Martha lived in Calais and Lille where she was employed in sales. She met and married her GI husband in France in 1945. They settled in Bethlehem, Pennsylvania where they raised three children, and she pursued her lifelong avocations of sewing and gardening.

ESCAPE FROM GERMANY

★

Renate Wilkins

SOMETIME IN 1938, BEFORE "KRISTALLNACHT," a night reign of terror on the Jewish population of Germany, our relatives in the United States urged my mother to make plans to leave Germany. They had information that we did not get in Berlin about how serious the situation was for people like us with Jewish backgrounds. Because my father was a superior court judge with a pension, my parents decided to make plans for her, my brothers and me to leave for England, where we had close friends, with plans to go on to the U.S. as soon as possible. However, after "Kristallnacht" in November of that year they decided that my father should not stay either. So, appropriate plans were made. However, nothing was easy and so my younger brothers and I were sent on to England in January 1939. Our English friends made arrangements for us to stay with them, and finally my parents were able to join us in May. My mother worked as domestic help, and my father went to Manchester to stay with his sister there. We three children attended school while we were there.

On September 1, 1939, a Sunday morning, we were in church when the sirens began to blast, announcing the start of World War II. Hitler had invaded Poland. It was one of the eeriest sounds I had ever heard. I was 15 years old and very upset. Hitler's actions seemed a bad omen for our being able to leave for the U.S.

Almost immediately, complete blackout regulations were imposed, so one literally could hardly see anything outside at night. Nothing much happened in England for a number of months and to our amazement, we were able to embark from Southampton on a refugee ship in late December. Again, blackout regulations were strictly enforced on the ship; even smoking outside on deck was prohibited. Except for some fairly rough seas at times, we experienced no problems during the voyage and arrived in New York City on December 27, 1939, one of the coldest days of the season. My mother's brother met us and drove us through Central Park. His car was a convertible and when the top came down, we could hardly believe what we saw — the sky line of New York on a crystal clear night.

We stayed with my uncle and his wife in their New York apartment until early January when my mother's sister and her husband came to pick me up and take me back with them to Black Mountain College in North Carolina. My youngest brother was to stay with the uncle in New York and start school there, and my other brother stayed in England with our friends to finish school there. This plan made it possible for my parents to try to get their feet on the ground and figure out how to make a living in this brand new country, starting with nothing. At this point my father was already 65 years old, so that my mother, who was much younger, would have to be the wage earner for the family.

Josef and Anni Albers were on the faculty at Black Mountain College and were to become noted artists before long. I lived with them and first finished high school in the Town of Black Mountain, then started college in the fall of 1940. On December 7, 1941 I was in my study at college, listening to the New York Philharmonic when the radio program was interrupted by the announcement of the bombing of Pearl Harbor and a state of war between Japan and the United States. It was a stunning moment for me. My thought was, "Here we go again!"

Some of the men I knew at college registered as conscientious objectors, but quite a few faculty members were drafted. Some of my close friends lost fiancés and, of course, we heard of tragedies all around us. Except for these events, I considered myself very fortunate since we lost no one in my immediate family. I left Black Mountain College in 1943 and moved to Cambridge, Massachusetts, where I worked for the American Friends Service Committee and eventually finished college at Boston University. Of course, there too the war was always on our minds until it finally ended in 1945.

Born in Germany, fleeing to England, and arriving in the United States at age 15, Renate attended Black Mountain College in North Carolina and graduated from Boston University. She pursued an academic career leading to the position of Dean of Students at Mount Holyoke College.

The
Home
Front

Memorable Meetings

★

Anne August

IN WORLD WAR II I SERVED AS SECRETARY to the Financial Advisor of British Imperial Censorship in the Western Hemisphere. This office screened war information from outposts in Bermuda, Trinidad, and other offshore locations in the Caribbean.

In the summer of 1941 war appeared imminent. I was enrolled in a business course, taking Gregg shorthand, typing (on an electric typewriter), and related subjects, such as double-entry bookkeeping. Shorthand became my "thing" because I became proficient at taking dictation close to conversational speed. An English friend of my father's in banking came to the city searching for a place to locate a New York office of the British censorship bureau and to serve as a liaison between London and Washington. Previously, my family had taken in his two young daughters during the London blitz. They lived with us for several years, becoming little sisters to me. The banker now needed a secretary with solid security clearance credentials and sound stenographic skills, so in June 1941 I began work.

One memorable event was my first trip to Canada just after Roosevelt and Churchill had held a summit conference in Quebec City to discuss the war situation in Europe. My boss wanted me to attend to take shorthand, transcribe speeches, and record conference minutes. We travelled by train from New York to Quebec City. A neophyte traveler, I managed to lose a piece of luggage, which was a source of considerable embarrassment as well as an inconvenience. The loss had a profound effect on my wardrobe until it was eventually located. While I remember some of the dignitaries at the meeting, I now recall little of the substance other than intense anxieties expressed by the British over the progress of the war with Hitler.

Another trip was to a highly classified scientific meeting in Miami Beach attended by some 50 chemists and scientists. Two of us were expected to record each day's presentations and to deliver transcriptions of the proceedings the next morning, in addition to offering sociability at the evening gatherings of conferees. Chemical terminology proved very challenging to transcribe since we lacked scientific backgrounds. We did so purely phonetically. Fortunately, the scientists had excellent memories and could usually recognize and correct the text provided to them if given the first syllable of a word, so it all worked out okay.

That trip proved to be fun and sometimes relaxing. I recall the almost daily afternoon thunderstorms in Miami that briefly rolled in during September. One only had to stand in a doorway for a few moments and wait until the storm receded, then proceed on one's way. I got to experience for the first time the wonderful fresh vegetable drinks at the health juice bars, and of course, the fresh Florida citrus fruit. An uncle of mine, a noted artist who resided in Miami, I found out, was contributing to the war effort by designing camouflage colors and images to be used on military equipment.

In 1948, three years after World War II ended I did get to view the devastation wrought on Europe by the war. With friends I motored through Northern France, Belgium, and Holland and got to see the many shrapnel-pocked houses, flattened town squares, and bombed-out cathedrals. I finally could envision, in part, what it must have been like to live under the threat of heavy and often near continual bombardment and to subsist under an occupying force.

May it never happen here.

Since the war, Anne has led a diversified lifestyle — horse woman, skier, anthropologist. She was an innkeeper in Stowe, Vermont, had two husbands, raised pheasants, established a kennel for cocker spaniels and Labradors, traveled extensively, and is an expert gardener.

CONSCIENTIOUS OBJECTOR

★

Thomas Bassett

Tom's experiences during World War II were vastly different from those of most of his peers, but they influenced the rest of his life just as profoundly. He was classified "CO" — Conscientious Objector. After achieving official status as a CO, he was sent to Big Flats, New York, where there was a Forest Service tree farm. The inmates had to weed the tree area. As Company Clerk (like MASH's Radar) he got to know all the camp inmates. They were in general fine men with high ideals. He made lifelong friends there. They were subjected to many insults when they travelled outside the camp, but supported one another in their strongly held beliefs. The camp was run by Quakers, and the experience resulted in Tom's becoming a lifelong and devout Quaker himself.

Born in Burlington, Vermont, Tom Bassett attended Yale, the University of California, and Harvard University where he earned an advanced degree. He taught at several universities and was a librarian at the University of Vermont for 25 years. Tom died in 2001. His wife, Alice Cook Bassett, provided this story.

REMEMBER WHITE MARGARINE

★

Elizabeth Corliss

D URING WORLD WAR II it became the accepted practice to use margarine in place of butter. Butter was scarce and rationed; we had to tear one coupon out of our food ration book in order to buy it. The dairy industry felt threatened by this increased use of margarine, which consumers rarely used before the war, and insisted that it must not look like butter.

So it came white, looking like lard, but with a small packet of yellow coloring enclosed. When the coloring was mixed into the margarine, that made it look more like butter, especially when spread on toast or bread. Mixing in the coloring was a time-consuming and tiring chore. The margarine had to be softened just enough so that the color could be worked in, using many strokes with a big spoon. There was always the danger, however, of softening it so much it would start to melt. Disaster.

My Uncle Bill and his sister Margaret both prided themselves on their cooking skills. I was present when Uncle Bill and his wife came to dinner at my aunt's home one night. Aunt Margaret served creamed onions, usually a pasty white, but this time they had a golden tint. Immediately, Uncle Bill wanted to know her secret, suggesting that perhaps she had loaded them with butter. What she wouldn't reveal to him was that she was coloring the margarine at the same time that she was preparing the onions and thought it would be fun to put just a tiny bit of the yellow coloring into the sauce.

Once my mother had a different experience with margarine coloring — and certainly not planned. She was squeezing the little margarine coloring packet when it suddenly burst and sprayed the kitchen ceiling a bright yellow.

Betty had two brothers in the Army, both of whom served in Europe. During the war she worked in Albany, New York where she lived with her Aunt Margaret's family. In 1944 she moved to Schenectady and served as Director of Christian Education at a Presbyterian Church for 36 years.

A Child in World War II

★

Jacky Duffek

DECEMBER 7, 1941 WAS JUST A WEEK before my 10th birthday. My
clearest memory of that sunny winter day in western Pennsylvania was of my parents standing in our front yard and my mother crying.
Later, we were told that we were going to move to Kansas City, Missouri, where my father would be stationed. Although as the 35-year-
old father of four children and exempt from the draft, he had enlisted
in the army. My image of Kansas City was of dirt streets, buildings
with false fronts, cactuses, cowboys and Indians. My younger sisters
and brother were as excited as I was about this new adventure.

Kansas City turned out to be a perfectly normal city after all, though
much larger than the small Ohio River town we came from. The war
seemed very far away; my father went to work every day in the city, and
came home at night for supper. We had no air raid drills at school, but
we did collect tin foil, mostly off cigarette packs, for "the war effort." Our
allowance was paid to us in red Defense Stamps rather than dimes. It was

fun to stick them into the little books, and tremendously exciting when we had a full book and could redeem it at the bank for a $25 War Bond.

Our father planted a Victory Garden in the back yard. The only thing we much liked from it were the green beans, which were not a huge success, as our Newfoundland dog, looking for a cool place to lie down to escape the Kansas City heat, decided that the bean patch was the ideal place. We thought he could have instead chosen the Swiss chard or the kohlrabi, which we loathed, and left us the beans.

Rationing included meat, butter, and gasoline. Worst was the butter. I hated the taste of margarine, although it was fun to squeeze the plastic bag it came in until the little capsule of yellow dye broke and colored that disgusting white stuff to make it look like butter. What joy! My siblings didn't mind the flavor as much as I did. One of my happiest memories is of a note in my Christmas stocking, reading "Go look in the icebox," where I found a quarter pound of butter with my name on it. I made it last for a long time and shared it with nobody.

Later in the war, my father was stationed in Washington, D.C. We stayed in Kansas City and would go to meet him at the railroad station when he came home for occasional weekends. Because it was extremely hot in the summer, I wore shorts and a halter top. Once, an elderly lady complained to my mother about my "indecent exposure" being inappropriate for the soldiers to see, although as a fat 11-year-old, I did not seem to attract much notice from the servicemen.

I was at summer camp in the Upper Peninsula of Michigan in August, 1945. I was with a group of campers at an isolated mountain lake when we saw distant fireworks lighting up the sky one night, and when we hiked back down to camp two days later, perhaps we were the only people in the United States who did not know that the war had ended two days earlier. There were brilliant northern lights all that August in red and yellow streaks and concentric circles that covered the sky. We always believed the display symbolized the coming of peace.

Born in New York City, Jacky grew up in Pennsylvania and the mid-West. She was a teacher, and after four children, she became an elementary school librarian. Following retirement, she and her husband lived on Cape Cod for over 10 years. Her favorite avocation is painting, which she continues at Wake Robin.

ESSENTIAL MANPOWER

★

Frank Gardner

Pearl Harbor day found me newly married, fresh out of M.I.T. with a ScD degree in physical metallurgy, and in my first permanent job in industry. In the previous two months my wife and I settled into a home near my work, but also only 20 miles from New York City, which we sometimes enjoyed. I worked in Mahwah, New Jersey, in the laboratory of American Brake Shoe and Foundry; it was one of the nation's top experimental foundries.

One Sunday afternoon, it happened to be December seventh, my Uncle Tom and Aunt Ruth Streeter decided to drive over from Morristown to Mahwah to pay us a visit. Unfortunately our words of greeting were words of horror with the news that Pearl Harbor had just been bombed by the Japanese. Understandably, our visit was short as Aunt Ruth, at that time, was a member of the Marine Corps Women's Reserve. Later she became its first director.

At the lab at American Brake Shoe, my first assignment was a magnetic sorting of some 30 different heat-resistant alloys, iron-based, with varying amounts of chromium, nickel and other components. The goal was to achieve the maximum degree of heat resistance with minimum amounts of these very strategic metals which were in short supply. Later, I became a member of a three-man team carrying out extensive investigations with these metals. We tried to develop new specifications for the casting and vise-fabricating of tank turrets, and improving their resistance to shell penetration. A year or two later found me running a high-temperature "creep" lab where we sorted out the best high-temp alloys to be used in rocket and jet engines. These would also have utility in oil refinery construction and gas-cracking units. The goal was to extend the product lifetimes of these components.

Up to now, the lab head had shielded many of his staff from the draft by registering us with the War Manpower Commission, by requesting that we be deferred because of the essential nature of our work on behalf of the war effort. By 1943 I was dissatisfied with my contribution to that effort and started contacting the Office of Field Service in Washington. Their mission was to provide scientists and engineers with opportunities to accompany new military equipment and weaponry overseas. All my initial efforts failed, but I persisted. On one visit my contact said, "Frank, would you be interested in an opening for someone with your background at the University of Chicago?" Work in a domestic lab was not what I was seeking, so I said "No." And that was how close I came to becoming part of the Manhattan Project for development of the atom bomb.

Born in Baltimore, Maryland, Frank grew up in Brookline, Massachusetts and earned a DSc in Metallurgy from Massachusetts Institute of Technology. After working at American Brake Shoe, he held the position of Chief Scientist, Office of Naval Research. He and his wife Eleanor whose memoir also appears in this volume have been lifelong members and active in the Episcopal Church. Frank died in 2007 after completing this memoir.

A Co-Ed's Story

★

Patricia Haufler

IN THE FALL OF 1941 I began my quest for a BA from Middlebury College, Class of '45. The first four months — September to December — were the only "normal" ones I would experience. On Sunday December seventh, I along with other new Kappa Delta pledges was enjoying a welcoming supper in the KD rooms. Shortly thereafter, we learned of the attack on Pearl Harbor. Although we experienced shock at the news, at that moment we had little realization of how the event was to affect the remainder of our college years as well as the remainder of our lives.

Life at "Midd" became more serious. Christmas '41 was the only school vacation of usual length. Thereafter, the holiday breaks in college were foreshortened. Christmas vacation consisted of only a few days before and after Christmas. Thanksgiving break comprised morning classes, followed by Thanksgiving dinner and a free afternoon. No one had permission to go home to celebrate. There was a war on.

In the fall of 1942, those who could afford to do so were asked by the college administration to pursue an accelerated curriculum. Their education would be packed into three semesters per academic year. So we "war kids" were the first to attend regular classes in the summers. I did so for the next two years, allowing me to earn my diploma in October 1944 instead of June 1945. It meant almost non-stop studying from September 1942 until my graduation — 22 continuous months of full-time college courses.

In the fall we were asked to team up and go to the apple orchards to harvest crops. Most of the able-bodied women at Middlebury volunteered for this contribution to the war effort. My roommate and I worked as a team, taking turns picking from high in the tree limbs and passing the fruit to the partner below. I remember some gorgeous days when we were transported in open trucks to Champlain shore orchards. These junkets seemed marvelous adventures.

As the war progressed and days turned into weeks and weeks into months, attendance at daily Chapel shrank as each group of military reservists was called to active duty. It was a sad time, as all those lovely young men left a campus that increasingly felt depleted. At regularly scheduled times we women went downtown to the Red Cross facility to roll bandages. Just as regularly, we took turns going to Porter Hospital to donate blood. I remember one afternoon riding my bike a goodly distance out to the clinic for the drawing. After a short lie-down I pedaled back to campus in time to wait on table in Forest dining hall. It did not occur to me that such a sequence was not sensible until someone noticed my excessive pallor and took a fully-loaded tray from my raised arm and escorted me to a bed.

We coeds did not have to experience an education deprived of male students for long. In my junior year the student body was increased by the influx of Navy V-12s. These young men were privileged to have the opportunity to continue a college education and at the same time prepare for commissioned duty in the Navy upon graduation.

In many ways, having them on campus was similar to having the regularly enrolled male students of former times. But there were differences. One such that had its humorous side was our curfews. In peacetime 1940s Middlebury women were required to sign out in the evenings and return to their dormitories by 10 PM on weeknights, 11:30 on Saturdays, and within 20 minutes following any special events that lasted longer (dances, etc.). However, there were times when the Navy men had an earlier curfew than we, so that instead of being gallantly escorted to our dorm doors, we often found ourselves tearing up the hill to Hepburn or Gifford (men's dorms) to get our dates signed in on time. This was really essential, because while a coed's late return was not looked on kindly, a tardy arrival for the Navy boys had wartime consequences resulting in military disciplinary action.

We co-eds were subject to the same rules imposed on the rest of the nation: gasoline, food, and shoe rationing. We were not as pampered as were those who preceded or came after us. Our education suffered from lack of opportunity for foreign study or travel experiences. I think we were more sensitive to the importance of such opportunities than we might otherwise have been. Contemporary Civilization and History courses taught by Profs who had experienced World War I helped us to understand better what was happening to the world. We were sobered by the deaths of former classmates.

Upon graduation, some of the coeds took jobs that were directly conditioned by the war. I ended up doing copywriting and editing material for General Electric, which was very much involved in supplying essential wartime materials: generators, searchlights, electric motors, and turbo-superchargers, to name a few. At this point I particularly remember writing about the until-then-secret B-29s. I did not come to know my GI husband-to-be until after the war when he returned to his former job at G.E. doing work similar to mine. In November 1947 we married.

After graduating from Middlebury College, Pat raised two sons, taught children with learning disabilities for many years, and then founded a communications consulting firm with her husband whose World War II memoir is also included in this volume.

Uncle Ed and Aunt Jo

★

Sally Johnson

WHEN I WAS A CHILD . . . Uncle Ed was in The War. He was an officer on the aircraft carrier *Lexington*. I still have a postcard of the *Lexington* in a little gold frame on my bookshelf. Aunt Jo was very positive. She had twinkling blue eyes and hair wound into a bun on top of her head. No matter what happened, she always said "Think Victory."

I didn't know my cousins, Joe and Eddie, until the family moved back to Vermont from Hawaii where they were born. (Aunt Jo said "When each one of the boys was born, I was kept flat on my back in that wonderful Naval hospital in Honolulu for a week — *can you imagine — ONE WHOLE WEEK!*")

They all returned in winter — Uncle Ed was crisp in uniform — bringing his family home before he went to sea duty. The boys — slightly older than I — had never seen snow. They rushed out of the car that first day into a real snow storm and were on their hands and knees

294

in the whiteness. I had never met them — but I went over and said — "Look, make a snowball" — and showed them. It didn't take them a minute to catch on. Aunt Jo laughed and laughed. Everyone made snowballs. I threw one at Uncle Ed and it made a big white blotch on his navy blue coat. I thought I shouldn't have done that, but he laughed and threw one at me.

Uncle Ed had found them an apartment on Robinson Parkway — dark and under the eaves. Aunt Jo looked around and said she would brighten it up. She made curtains and slip covers. They got a cat and named it Lisbon because that was where Uncle Ed was first stationed. Eddie made model airplanes of balsa wood and tissue paper. Joe made radios of wires and crystal, with hard plastic earphones. They seemed very warlike.

After a year or two they moved to Washington, D.C. where Uncle Ed came back for shore duty. They had a duplex house where Aunt Jo made blackout curtains and used ration stamps. Uncle Ed was sent to the Pacific where the war raged. The boys were at boarding school on scholarships.

Aunt Jo worried and worried and always said to "Think Victory." She took me to the movies — the news came on — called "The Eyes and Ears of the World"— the only real pictures we ever saw besides *Life* magazine. The camera on the screen whirred and turned its enormous eye to look exactly at you. Navy ships were shown firing huge guns that jumped back after firing. Aunt Jo stood up and took my hand — "Come on Sal, we'll Think Victory outside."

She said she couldn't sleep and went to the Navy Department to ask for a job, to work *hard*. They asked what she could do and she told them she could sew. Can you sew silk? "Oh yes — but that's too nice." It was for parachutes — in a big factory in nearby Maryland. She said she was frightened at first. She said men's lives depended on her skill and care. She worked 12-hour shifts and was advanced to an inspector of other girls' work. She made friends with them and taught them to "Think Victory" too. She slept and slept, she was so tired.

On spring vacation I went to stay with Aunt Jo and the boys in Washington. All their neighbors seemed to be Navy — with star flags in the windows — mothers and kids keeping each other company — asking "Have you heard?" — "I got three letters" — "Do you know where he is?" Everyone talked about The War. One Navy lady had a new baby and her husband was sent to the West Coast — she was to follow by train. Aunt Jo and I took her to the station — Union Station in Washington — we went on the bus. Two Navy wives, a young girl and a baby so tiny all you could see was a blur of pink. To go to Union Station in wartime was a crush of uniforms and girls and old people — many crying, all pushing — all looking for the right track — trying to hear the announcements.

Aunt Jo had been across the country many times — from sea to shining sea — she knew the system and forged ahead with mother and baby. We went into the train — I can't imagine how — and found the berth for them to travel in. It was an upper. "Oh dear— with a baby — how am I to manage with a baby?" The conductor came — hurried Aunt Jo and me away. "Think Victory," Aunt Jo called as we squeezed out into the aisle. I was worried — I'd traveled in an upper berth — my grandfather lifted me up and down. "What will become of them?" I asked. "Don't you worry two minutes about it," Aunt Jo said. "Some nice Naval officer with a lower berth will give them his, before the train leaves the station — they'll be fine — just fine." And they were. But the mother wrote from California that it was an *Army* officer who gave them the lower berth!

Aunt Jo and Uncle Ed were married long before I was born. My Dad tells about being best man at their wedding — in Burlington, Vermont in June — right after Annapolis Naval Academy graduation. Naval ushers — crossed swords — sparkling uniforms. The men were dressing and drinking upstairs on the top floor at Granddad's house. Uncle Ed couldn't find the buttons for his uniform — they were removable for polishing. He panicked — "My God, Bob — I can't be married without my buttons!" (Dad told this so well) "You'll have to go down street to the Army/Navy store and get me six Navy brass buttons." OK — Dad went.

Now Burlington was an Army town — Fort Ethan Allen and all that. The man behind the counter looked everywhere — but not a Navy button in any case or drawer. Dad looked carefully at the Army buttons — "What's the difference?" He asked. "I guess it's eagles and anchors," the man said. He'll never notice — not today. Dad thought and got six eagles. Uncle Ed put them on — they worked perfectly. He said "I do" and walked with Aunt Jo under the swords and didn't say a word about the buttons. "Did he ever notice?" I asked Dad. "You bet he did," Dad said, "afterwards he said to me — 'Don't ever tell her it wasn't legal with all those damned eagles.'"

Aunt Jo knew Uncle Ed was on the *Lexington* and due to be reassigned — but she didn't know when. Then headlines came that the *Lexington* had been sunk. A terrible naval disaster for America — a great triumph for Japan. She still didn't know. Mother went down to Washington to be with her — they were close sisters. I don't know just when the call came — but in the middle of the night, collect from no one knows where — "this is Seaman Smith — Mister Woods said to call this number and say he was all right." You know they always call you Mister in the Navy.

Long after that — I don't know how many years of battles at sea, Aunt Jo and the boys spent the summer at Granddad Howe's camp at Cedar Beach, and Uncle Ed came home from The War. We all went to meet him at the little train station in Charlotte — it was a real station then. He climbed down the train steps in a dusty, rumpled uniform. Aunt Jo and the boys ran to embrace him. Dad held me back, and I heard him say "My God — his hair is white!" It was — like snow.

After the war Sally graduated from college, married, and worked in book publishing. Her current interest is the restoration of old houses in Essex, New York.

WAR THROUGH THE EYES AND EARS OF A CHILD

★

Claire Kowalski

SEVEN DECADES AGO, I WAS A CHILD GROWING UP in Quebec City, Canada, and feeling secure with my parents, despite the Depression and my father's illnesses. We spent summers at my grandmother's home in beautiful lake country in northern Ontario. An early childhood memory is coming out from first grade in 1936 and for the very first time seeing sky writing behind a small airplane. One of my classmates declared as a matter of fact, "That means there is going to be a war." For Canada, World War II began September 3, 1939 and ended on V-J Day, August 14, 1945.

On Friday, September 1, 1939 Mother was preparing for our return to Quebec following vacation. I was beside her as she and a neighbor talked about the Germans marching into a country called Poland and saying that some families there were undergoing separation as children were being sent to safer places. To think of children having to leave their parents was the saddest thing I had ever heard. We arrived in

Quebec early Sunday afternoon. As we got off the train, my father was standing on the platform. He told us that earlier that day Canada had followed Britain's lead and declared war on Germany.

By 1940 we had placed a large map of Europe and the eastern shore of North America on our kitchen wall. Each evening after listening to the six o'clock news, my parents and I would identify the points on the map to which the German army had advanced. One time when a baby sitter was with me, I said I was afraid that the Germans would invade Canada. She took me to the map and pointed to Newfoundland. Then she explained that her brother, who was a soldier, was there and that he would never let the Germans land in Canada. From that moment I felt safe.

Before long, we school children were doing our part by giving our pennies to the Red Cross and collecting and folding tin foil wrappings from cigarettes, chocolate, and food products to be recycled for the war effort. Sometimes, instead of buying ice cream cones or candy, we saved our nickels to buy a 25-cent stamp at school to put in a booklet. When the booklet was finally filled, we proudly exchanged it for a much-prized $5 War Savings Certificate. In school assemblies we often sang "There'll Always Be an England." I don't remember hearing anyone complain about the rationing during the war years.

At the beginning of fourth grade, Farina Schwartzman joined our class. Her family had made their way to Quebec from Romania. Farina was unlike anyone I had ever met and we quickly became friends. Her grandmother, an invalid, could not be left alone. On days that both of Farina's parents had to be at work, either she or her older sister would stay home from school to be with their grandmother. No other child I knew did this. Another refugee in our class, Ishobel Chisolm from Britain, had been sent with her siblings to spend the war years with cousins in Quebec. By sixth grade I was earning ten cents a week to accompany another refugee, Susan, to and from kindergarten. She had been sent to Canada with her young brother and their nanny.

Late in 1940 Canada sent many of its military men to Singapore and Hong Kong. I recall how on a Sunday afternoon Lt. Arnold Wood-side, who until a few months before had worked in the office my father managed, visited us with his parents. They beamed proudly as their son, handsome in uniform, told how his regiment would soon be leaving for Hong Kong where he was looking forward to new experiences in the warm sun. He did not return. I do retain a vivid memory of one Quebecker I met when he came home after spending five years in a Japanese prison camp. His teeth had rotted, his vision deteriorated, and the weight he had gained since his liberation hung on him loosely.

Many enemy prisoners captured in battle in Europe were sent across the Atlantic to be interned in Canada. Three miles from my grandmother's home, a luxurious lakeside holiday lodge had become the main building of a POW camp for German officers. When a prisoner escaped, sirens were sounded in town and throughout the area. This aroused excitement among us children but no real sense of alarm. Chocolate, luxury foods, ice skates and other sports equipment were among the many gifts sent for the prisoners by sympathetic Americans, even after December 1941. The Canadian Home Guard, made up largely of veterans of the First World War, served as prison guards. By the summer of 1944 they oversaw prisoners who had volunteered to construct a lakeside retaining wall, pier, and recreational facilities in town. When walking or bike-riding, I would see these strong, tanned, muscular, and healthy-looking Germans apparently enjoying their physical work.

Near our town was Little Bergen, a training camp for Norwegian airmen who had escaped their country to fight on with the Allies. Each summer there were street dances attended by Home Guards, Norwegian airmen, and local residents. When I was 13, a burly Home Guardsman asked me to dance. My Mother quickly turned on him with a loud, "Indeed you cannot dance with this child!"

In August 1943 the first Quebec Conference was held in the Citadel and Chateau Frontenac within the walls of the old city. Winston Churchill, Franklin Roosevelt, and Canada's prime minister, Mackenzie King met there. Among other decisions, they secretly set the date for D-Day for June 1944. My father remarked that he had seen Churchill drive by in an unescorted car. I also heard that during the conference Roosevelt had so enjoyed the strong, aged cheddar cheese made in Quebec that he had some sent to the White House. Churchill and Roosevelt met for a second Quebec conference in September 1944. That time I was able to observe some of the conference participants sitting in the balcony of the Anglican Cathedral at Sunday morning services. In those days I always sat in the opposite balcony.

The war in Europe ended May 8, 1945. It happened that the weather in Quebec was warm that day and physical education classes were held outside. Our gym teacher had heard the news minutes earlier. She informed us, and then she quickly quieted our jubilation, pointing out that many people would be suffering for a long time yet from war injuries and deprivations. I learned later that her fiancé had not survived the war.

Memory tells me that on August 14, 1945 the radio had alerted us to listen for a special speech by President Truman at seven PM It was anticipated that he would announce the surrender of Japan, and indeed he did. I ran "up street" (as the expression was) to join the celebration in that small Canadian town where I spent so many happy summers.

Time changes those things that remain in the memory, and also the nuances about what is recalled. I do know, however, that during World War II those around me were certain that we were engaged in a necessary war. Each in our own way wholeheartedly supported the war effort. Today, we also live in a time of war. But many of us American citizens feel very differently about the way our country is waging this war than we ever felt during World War II.

A native of Quebec City, Claire is fluent in French and English. She holds a Masters Degree in Social Work and has worked in family and adoption services. She later taught gerontology at the University of Rhode Island, coordinated the Elderhostel program there, and worked with many groups of senior citizens. Claire has traveled extensively and lived abroad with her husband Tad, who also has a chapter in this volume.

THE BRIDE WAS A CAMP FOLLOWER

★

Hildie Lawrence

Hildie and Sidney Lawrence

DESPITE THE WAR CLOUDS that had been rapidly gathering, I went on a six-week European bicycle tour with 17 other students from American colleges in the summer of 1939. We stayed in youth hostels and met many of the German people. Besides the usual sights, we saw lots of army tanks and military vehicles in some towns. One member of our group took a picture of a tank and promptly had to surrender his film to a soldier demanding it be returned. I did get to see Hitler briefly in a parade when another girl and I broke away from our tour group in a neighboring town to go into Munich on our own. Actually, seeing Hitler had less of a lasting effect on me than the feeling I got from interactions with average German citizens. They were obviously living in fear. I sensed it in everything they said or did. On the street (and even in doctors' waiting rooms) the common form of greeting was not "Good morning" but "Heil Hitler!" while raising and extending one's right arm in salute. To call it a police state does not capture the feeling of dread we all sensed in these everyday activities.

We returned to the states on August 22, 1939, less than two weeks before Hitler's troops marched into Poland. The students on the trip following ours were roused from sleep in the Belgian youth hostel where they were being housed and told that their trip was cancelled; they had to take the next ship home.

The ensuing months brought many reports of conquests by Hitler's army. Beyond American convoys for British ships, I was unaware of any help the United States was providing the Allies at that time. Then came December 7, 1941 and Pearl Harbor. Our nation declared war on Japan, soon followed by a declaration of war against the Axis powers of Germany and Italy. At that time, I was working for the Swiss pharmaceutical firm Sandoz. The following day, December eighth, we were not very productive and accomplished little; we were too busy worrying and rehearsing what to do in the event of an air raid.

Neighborhoods were organizing for the war effort, and I volunteered to become an Air-raid Warden. We frequently passed on to all in the neighborhood the instruction, "Turn out the lights." In March, my future husband proposed to me and we agreed to wait until war's end to get married. In April he was called up, and after a short stay at Fort Dix, he called to say he was about to board a train but had not been told its destination. For the first time, I cried at work. Later, he told me he was being sent to an airfield in Louisiana. I had just joined the Aircraft Warning Service, a volunteer organization with secret headquarters in Manhattan. I was not even free to tell my aunt about this, though I was living with her at the time. I worked from four to six hours nightly at AWS, then departed in the morning for my job at the pharmaceutical firm after roughly four hours' sleep.

Wartime Marriage

Sid, my fiancé, was assigned to Operations at Lake Charles Army Air Field, part of the Army Flying Training Command. The airfield was for pilots being taught to fly for the Army Air Force. Sid thought he might be with them for the duration and said we could be married. I agreed and gave my notice to Sandoz. I bought a simple dress and packed my bags. Sid's parents and my aunt accompanied me to the station. After many hugs and tears, I ran to the train gate just a bit too late — it had just left. Somehow I managed to find a plane to New Orleans. Then I caught an overnight train to Lake Charles, where Sid met me at the station. He had found a family for me to stay with, and they welcomed me warmly. It was my first of many such experiences of genuine Southern hospitality. I could not help comparing it with the comparative coolness of New York hospitality.

We were married by a judge at the home of a couple whose parents knew Sid's family and spent a honeymoon week in New Orleans. Then we moved into the home of a kindly doctor's widow. Again, her hospitality proved to be warm and her friendship unstinting; maybe Sid's uniform helped. I worked first in the financial department of a local department store, and finally found a job as a bank president's secretary.

Sid was hearing talk of an imminent move to another location, so I felt I must get a job on the airfield so my job would be more readily transportable. Soldiers in the field didn't know where they were going or even whether housing was available, but I sought — and got — a job as the Executive Officer's secretary. I soon learned the ways of the military. My boss was a colonel, an old West Point grad, who had little patience with the casual ways of the young "flyboys." He let them know it was to be "spit and polish" from then on. He didn't like the way they marched, and he definitely did not like their sloppy salutes. At reveille, the men were awakened by a bugle call but the Colonel decided that wasn't working. He declared that henceforth they would be awakened by both the bugle and a cannon boom.

Next, we were moved on to Victoria, Texas to continue Sid's pilot training. The few civilian employees could not find housing there, so we were put into the Bachelor Officers Quarters and ate in the mess hall. I became the Intelligence Officer's secretary; an enlisted man was assigned as the clerk. We liked our work and intently followed the progress of the Allies in the war. I kept a big map over my desk so I could visualize the battlefronts.

Later, Sid got papers transferring him to a field in West Monroe, Louisiana, where there was no job for me. So I left with Sid and was able to find a job working for the local Chamber of Commerce. We rented a room in town, and when the Army had a few little houses built, we moved into one. The houses were known as Yucca Flats.

Toward the end of 1944 I became pregnant, and when Sid was sent to Houston, Texas, we found a new house just outside Houston. I stopped working. The people next door were also Air Force. Our daughter, Terry, was born in May 1945 in a Houston hospital. My aunt, a nurse, came from New York City to stay with me and the baby. In early July Sid was sent to a field in west Texas before going overseas. We sold the house, and my aunt, the baby, and I boarded the train for New York. The baby was happy and well-behaved. In New York we stayed at my aunt's apartment and looked forward to the daily letters from Sid. We heard and read about the last weeks of the war, from the demise of Hitler in April to the devastation of the atom bombs in August. In November 1945 Sid at last got his discharge and joined us.

Epilogue

A few years later, when our oldest daughter was in fourth grade, we were part of a group of people chosen to entertain the Hiroshima Maidens, survivors of the A-bombs. American surgeons had offered their surgical expertise in treating the badly scarred victims. We invited two of the Maidens to our house, and had our daughter's teacher join us for lunch. The Japanese girls were lovely and we communicated pretty well with a made-up sign language. They made a little cube of cotton fabric, stuffed it, and when it was finished, showed us a game they played with it in Japan. It took dexterity to throw it from one person to another, sometimes under a knee, sometimes under an elbow. We presented each of them an American souvenir, but nothing compared to what their gifts meant to us. What a good feeling — to know that people can be so kind to each other after a terrible war when they were the worst of enemies.

Hildie was born and educated in New York City. A wife and a mother, she taught elementary school in New Jersey for 20 years. She became well acquainted with Vermont by spending many summers here.

Swansea Childhood

★

Robert McEwen

M Y DAD AND I WERE IN THE GRAIN ROOM when we heard the
low approaching rumble of the engines. It grew much louder,
and looking out, we saw the blimp slowly cruising directly toward us.
Low, very low, and as its shadow approached above the chicken yards,
the flock set up a squawking chatter, flying in all directions as if a fox
or skunk had invaded the chicken house. It passed over us like a silver cloud, the crew in the gondola clearly visible, trailing anchor lines
almost touching the trees.

We used to see them almost every day cruising over the bay and up
the river by the Firestone plant and that other factory ringed by barbed
wire and armed guards. We learned later the secret factory made the
newly developed Fathometer which looked for submarines that sometimes brought saboteurs to our shores. The FBI caught a suspicious
looking character looking across the water with binoculars, or so the
story went in whispered secrecy to every kid in our school.

There was a poster in the classroom, "Loose Lips Sink Ships." Outside was a large wire bin to collect aluminum pots and pans donated to the war effort. On Tuesday mornings after pledging allegiance to the flag and prayer, Mrs. Chase would collect our dimes and pennies and pass out war stamps. A full book of stamps worth $18.75 could be exchanged for a $25 war bond (at maturity). Once a week the teachers led us quickly to the basement past the buckets of sand where we lay on the floor with a book over our heads.

In the sky over the Quonset Naval Air Station, fighter planes with snarling engines would engage in dog fights, and on the boys' playground we would cheer. Hidden behind the big geography book we would draw pictures of airplanes. Some kids could tell by the sound of the engines the type and model of an aircraft, or so they claimed.

My parents and relatives did not like President Roosevelt; they always voted Republican. They had lots of WASP prejudices that I had to sort out later. But the war was good, if difficult, for a self- employed chicken farmer. On Fridays, my dad would put on clean clothes and take the '36 Pontiac, loaded with chickens and eggs, rhubarb and asparagus, and whatever other vegetables were in season, to Fall River to deliver door to door on his route. They were glad to see him, for meat was in short supply. As a farmer he received more gas coupons, but tires were a problem. Almost every week he returned with one flat, sometimes two, and with only one spare we could hear the thumping tire and scraping rim coming down the gravel drive. He jacked up the car, patched the tube, tested it in the water tub, and pumped up the tire with a hand pump. There were patches on top of patches.

Chicken feed was frequently scarce. I remember one night driving with him, upper half of the headlights blackened, down between the tracks of a crowded railroad yard, steam hissing and rising from giant locomotives. A man with a flashlight opened the big door of a freight car, and they loaded hundred-pound bags of grain into the Pontiac trunk, on the fenders, the back seat, and the bumpers (Was it black market?).

Joe Piva came in the spring and shoveled the accumulated piles of chicken manure into his truck and used it on his potato field. It was also great for our four long rows of rhubarb. Joe gave us several large burlap bags of potatoes in the fall. While some foods were scarce, we always had lots of chicken, eggs, potatoes, and a big bowl of rhubarb sauce. The milkman delivered two or three one-quart glass milk bottles, three inches of cream rising to the top, on our back porch every other day. Some of the chicken feed came in coarse cotton bags with printed floral patterns. Mother washed and ironed them and sold them to women who used them for sewing clothing. Her Home Circle Groups knitted balaclavas, scarves, and mittens for the soldiers. I was dispatched to gather milkweed pods that were to be used in making life preservers.

When the siren sounded, Dad donned his warden's arm band and hard hat, threw his bag with gas mask and first aid kit over his shoulder, and walked his assigned route with a dimmed flashlight, checking houses for drawn blackout shades. At home I was reading thrilling tales in *Boy's Life*, looking at bloody gory war scenes in *Life*, absorbing self reliance from my well-worn Boy Scout manual, or listening to the Lone Ranger or The Shadow shows on the radio in a darkened room.

Epilogue

I don't particularly recall the war's ending, and I was too young and sheltered to remember the attack on Pearl Harbor. The blackout shades were stacked in a closet for many years; we bought a black and white Dumont television set and a new Nash Rambler; and I started high school. A dozen years later, I pinned on my wings as a U.S. Air Force pilot. After Gloria and I married, I learned from her father, who had emigrated from Germany after World War I and become a U.S. citizen, that he had been picked up in the broad sweep of Germans and Japanese nationals at the start of WW II and interned for investigation at Ellis Island. For two weeks, his wife who spoke only German and some broken English and had three small children did not know what had happened to him.

Born in Fall River, Bob grew up in Swansea, Massachusetts, graduated in civil engineering from the University of New Hampshire, and earned a PhD in Earth Sciences at Cornell. He spent six years as a pilot in the Air Force, and then lived in Fairfax, Virginia while working for the U.S. Geological Survey.

Dinner with FDR

★

Polly Middleton

Polly Middleton and Conyers Read

THE COMMITTEE TO DEFEND AMERICA was an organization in Philadelphia in which my mother and stepfather, Conyers Read, were active. He taught English history at the University of Pennsylvania. He was very concerned about the imminence of war and suggested that we three take a vacation out west before anything developed. We went without leaving an itinerary, and on our return found a message from General William "Wild Bill" Donovan, asking my stepfather to head the British Empire section of the Office of Strategic Services (OSS), the forerunner of the CIA.

We moved immediately to Washington and rented a house decorated with zebras cavorting on the dining room walls. It was there that we entertained Ambassador Bajpai from India and his wife for dinner. My mother had checked what they could eat but all Mrs. Bajpai ate was peas. She had a diamond in her nose, the sight of which caused our maid nearly to drop the soup cups.

I was back at Putney School in Vermont when Mother wrote informing me that they had been invited to the White House for dinner at eight PM on December 6, 1941. My parents arrived promptly five minutes early and sat in the car until eight o'clock. They were served oysters to begin the meal, which Mother couldn't eat. James Roosevelt offered to take them from her until there was a loud call from the head of the table: "Jimmy, pass down the oysters!" Shortly thereafter, an aide came into the room and whispered into President Roosevelt's ear. He immediately left the table and did not return for dinner. It was approximately 8:30 PM in Washington, and 3:30 PM in Hawaii. I can only speculate as to whether a message was sent that had some connection with the Pearl Harbor attack the very next day. My mother, of course, always thought so.

After the war started, E.A. Speiser became head of the Near East section of OSS and Ralph Bunche was called to head the African section. My mother became an officer in the American Women's Voluntary Services, AWVS, headed by Anita Phipps. Mother's roommate at Sweetbriar College was a lieutenant in the Navy, stationed in D.C. When I came home from school in Vermont for holidays, I often attended some of the classes at AWVS and learned (and forgot) among other things how to splint a leg, develop film, perform CPR, and drive a truck. During two winter vacations from college in Vermont, I worked at the Army Map Service in Bethesda, Maryland, the first year in the Maintenance Department where I believed I was resented — until the day when my boss pinched my bottom. I told him I would report him to his superiors, and the attitude of my co-workers to me quickly changed. Since I was on a prolonged vacation from Bennington College (to save heat in Vermont), I didn't have to worry about losing my job as the others did, who may have been harassed, also. The following year I worked the four to midnight shift, learning to read Japanese road maps and signs, which might have been needed by our troops in the event of an invasion of the mainland. Our family moved three times, and I remember the last move on N Street in Georgetown was close enough to the Cabin John trolley that I could walk to it and return home at midnight by moonlight along the Potomac.

Epilogue

Except when I contracted chicken-pox at age 19 (!) followed by an extended leave from college because of the sequelae of encephalitis, the times I lived in D.C. during the war years seemed almost magical to a teenager. I recall many concerts at Watergate, Dumbarton Oaks, and the Library of Congress. There were friends in Virginia and canoeing on the Potomac above the Great Falls. To have come to know the many friends of my parents involved in wartime activities was a privilege, and though most are no longer living, they still live in my memory.

After the war, Polly became a pianist and piano teacher with studios in New York City and Italy. She married composer Robert Middleton, a professor of Music at Vassar College, who also has a World War II story in this volume.

GREENWICH VILLAGE IN WARTIME

★

Ruth Page

IWAS ONE OF FOUR SWARTHMORE WOMEN who had graduated in 1942 and shared an apartment in the Village in New York. Getting a job wasn't difficult with so many men, and some women, away in the Service. One of us was on Life magazine staff, one in Insurance, one in Real Estate, and me a secretary at the so-called Book Publishers Bureau, later re-named the Book Publishers' Assn. Our office was on the 14th floor of a building on the corner of 34th Street and Fifth Avenue, just across from the Empire State Building.

At that time book publishers were friendly with one another, as of necessity they needed to be if they wanted help with wartime problems. The worst of these was the paper shortage. The government was consuming massive amounts to produce the tons of documents needed for wartime instructions, including individual pamphlets for each service-man and woman, plus government-information books for them. This huge demand made paper scarce for commercial book publishers. At the central office, we sent out information to all the publishers about paper availability. Those who needed specific amounts for particular jobs were put in touch with others who had leftovers; and regular releases listed what type and weight of paper was needed by each, and where various types and weights were available as a publisher finished a job and had paper left.

Americans were asked to donate paper to be recycled. To inspire them one or two authors — one of them Mary Roberts Rhinehart — who had hand-written their books for submission to the publishers offered to sacrifice those originals. At least in the case of Ms. Rhinehart, I know John Day publishers refused to let her trash that paper, thinking such manuscripts had real value as they were.

On the 40-something floor of the Empire State Building were the offices of the War Production Board. Book papers came under their jurisdiction, so about once a week I visited them to learn the latest regulation-changes or to get advice. Perhaps they handled other things as well, but I knew nothing of that. All kinds of war production of course had to be managed by the government in Washington. I assume there were similar offices in other cities. The one I visited didn't look big enough to manage the whole country.

I was fortunate in that the Board of Directors of the Publishers' Association met monthly, and when my boss was unable to attend, he sent me. That was a real thrill for a book-minded 21-year-old. Eight or more CEO's of book publishing companies allowed me to take notes at their gatherings. They were all men, and were delightfully friendly; sometimes one would come to our office to talk with the boss, and would have me help track something down, or quickly type up notes for them that they could carry back to their offices. I also arranged their yearly banquets, visiting the best hotels, locating printers for the programs, and once even suggesting a speaker they might need. As a result of this, I always attended the banquets to make sure things went smoothly. (Once I rescued Whitney Darrow, CEO of Scribner's when he got lost in a hotel and couldn't find the exit. I wrote him a rhyme about it the next day, and he responded with his own rhyme. Fat chance of anything that informal happening today, those in the know tell me).

I recall that at one meeting of the publishers' Board of Directors, publisher Robert deGraff, an imposing figure well over six feet tall, stood to talk about the Pocket Books he was producing. He had started earlier, and was discussing his system. He said the idea was to make paper-back books that sold for 25 cents; when others said he'd go broke he said he didn't think so. His company would get a penny from each book sold, and so would the author.

As we all know, the idea of Pocket Books caught on like wildfire, so deGraff's company and the authors throve. Soon other publishers were bringing out cheap paperbacks of their own. Penguin, Dell, and many others have succeeded, and voracious readers are thrilled. We can spend our money on hardcover books we want to keep permanently, and read the rest in paperback, discard them after a time, or give them to other readers.

At that time Greenwich Village was alive with writers, painters, photographers, poets, and of course plenty of secretaries. It was easy to meet and befriend such folks. Across from us on 12th Street between Fifth and Sixth Avenues was an apartment with four Counter-Intelligence agents from Vermont, including Ralph Nading Hill, the expert on side-wheeler ships on Lake Champlain and author of two books about them, plus one book for young people. We called him Zeke because he was tall and rangy, like a guy in the comics named Zeke. He was a man of many talents, played the piano (we always asked for the Twelfth St. Rag) and told hilarious stories, mostly based on Vermont-style humor. The other men there were Proctor Page; Hank Swift, son of the Dean at UVM; and Phil Cullins, father of today's well-known Tom Cullins. So we married two of them — Proc became my husband, and Hank married blonde Betsey Peirce.

Proc and I became engaged just before he went off to war. He was not happy about his assignment: he had been sent to Berlitz Language School for the special six-week course in French, and studied hard. His buddies on the same course went to France, as he wished to do. Instead the Army in its bumbling way sent him to India and kept him there for a year — on a tea plantation. His one experience of getting shot at was when they gave him a new pair of boots to take to a General in

Burma, part of the CBI Theatre (China-Burma-India), handing him a little briefcase to give the general at the same time. He flew "over the hump" in a plane that was delivering food to fighting troops, and Proc was sitting at the rear of the plane where the doors were open for the food-drop. Over a ground-battle, where Japanese were shooting at the plane, they made the drop. Luckily their plane didn't get hit.

On top of that, when Proc delivered the boots he was also asked for the briefcase. He admitted he'd left it at their last stop for re-refueling, so went back for it and luckily it was right where he'd left it. Apparently that was the real reason he'd delivered the boots. Why the dickens they didn't tell him that, we'll never know.

My roommates and I in the Village got to know famous Life photographer Alfred Eisenstadt, brought home to dinner a couple of times by roommate Peggy who worked in the so-called "Party Department" at the magazine, and he had lots of anecdotes to share from his experiences of life at Life. Peggy also befriended well-known photographer Peter, from Look magazine, who lived down on Fourth St. We all enjoyed Peggy's position, because at least once a month Life gave her two tickets to a play or concert to write about, and we took turns using the extra ticket. At other times, we could hear the New York Philharmonic in summer when they played outdoors in Central Park. We climbed to the top seats in the grandstands, spread a blanket, and perched up there to enjoy the music. In those days, Central Park was safe, as were the streets and subways of New York. We traveled freely, alone or together, and never had problems. The worst that ever happened to me was that one night walking home from a movie somebody snatched my lovely Liberty silk scarf off my head and disappeared with it. That was right on Sixth Avenue, and I can't imagine what use the guy made of it. I hope he gave it to his girlfriend.

At that time meat was very scarce; we all had ration books with stamps for meat and for fats, and they were fairly limited rations. That resulted in a lesson to my roommates (I did all the cooking, as all of them had had hired cooks at their homes). When I went to Mr. Fine's Grocery Store on lower Fifth Avenue, I was thrilled to find calf-hearts. Most people didn't know what they were, and shunned them. So I bought a couple of them, sliced them, and sautéed them in a pan with a little oil. My roommates loved them — they were delicious and chewy. I even bought a whole beef heart once and roasted it with lots of onion. It made great gravy, and they liked that, too.

Mr. Fine, like other grocers, had one day a week when women could bring in cans of leftover fats the storekeepers turned in for wartime treatment and re-use. We got a kick out of his sign that was a reminder: "Women May Bring Their Fat Cans in on Tuesdays."

The night after Mary Steeves got engaged, she and I were riding on the top deck of a bus, and talking about it. There were only six other people on the top deck. They heard our happy, no doubt noisy chitchat, and were clearly enjoying it. We all sang "Happy Engagement toYou"! New York was in many ways a very friendly city, though it was true that most people couldn't help much if you got lost. They knew the geography of the city only well enough to learn the subway routes to home, train stations and jobs, along with the shops on Fifth, Madison, and Sixth Avenues.

Among all these folks, servicemen found friends, and eagerly told us of their plans as they headed for Europe. Now and then a guy from college would come by and we'd give him dinner. None of them ever seemed to think they might not make it back. A few of them never did, and even if we'd only known them briefly, we found it heart-breaking.

Ruth Page has been a writer and editor all her working life. She and her husband wrote and produced a small weekly newspaper (The Suburban List) in Vermont for 21 years. The paper won a number of awards from the New England Press Association, including the top award for editorials one year.

Small Bits for the War Effort

★

Elizabeth Pasti

Even my 10-year-old ears recognized that something serious had happened when I listened to the somber tones of my mother and the huckster as they weighed out the produce purchased from the horse-drawn cart that late summer day in 1939; Hitler had invaded Poland. Tense as that made the adults in our household, it was nothing like the shocking news of that December day two years later when Pearl Harbor was attacked, making World War II ours as well as Europe's war. We left the radio on loud enough for all of us to hear as we performed necessary chores — an unusual event in our household. Our usual custom was to put all activities aside and sit quietly listening to the radio for a particular program, and then turn the radio off. Hoping that better news would follow that fearful announcement, we instead learned of the tragic loss of lives, planes, and ships. We kept our ears glued as much as possible to the radio, but better news was not in the offing anytime soon. We listened with alarm to President Roosevelt's address to the nation and the Proclamation of War by Congress the following day.

My parents were not really news junkies; they were busy trying to make ends meet, welcoming a sixth and then a seventh sibling into our economically stressed family. Our family "Victory Garden," a quarter-mile down a steep hill in a community plot, was not very productive and certainly did not elicit much enthusiasm from us children, the principal but desultory laborers, nor did it contribute much to the war effort or to family meals.

I wasn't worried about my father being drafted, as he had lost the vision of one eye in a childhood accident, and my brothers were all younger than I. But I still spent anxious times as I fulfilled a homework assignment for current events class, making a notebook of clippings about the war. I was truly worried that the Germans would be able to do more than send submarines close to the East Coast of the United States. I followed with great anxiety the ebb and flow of the Battle of the Bulge.

What could I do personally to further the war effort? We were making do without, but in our economic stratum we were used to that. My father put the car up on blocks and took the streetcar to work; my mother dealt with ration stamps and went to work on the night shift at a defense plant, which kept her away from home for about 12 hours every day. That put much responsibility on my 13-year old shoulders as the eldest of six children (a seventh baby had died a few days after his birth).

Still, I wanted to do something that directly helped the war effort, so I and several of my high school classmates volunteered to be airplane spotters at a local (Baltimore) airfield. We diligently studied the silhouettes of the various enemy planes in the Airplane Spotters' Guide, and felt very important as we spent Saturdays eagerly scanning the skies, half hoping to see something exciting and scared to death that we would. Two years later, in spite of my intense shyness, I signed up to be a USO (United Services Organization) hostess, and did spend one evening at the canteen before my parents insisted that hostessing was totally inappropriate for a 15-year-old.

We were still fighting the Japanese at the time I finished high school. I had seen my Civics teacher cry at the announcement of the death of President Roosevelt in the spring of 1945, the first time I'd seen a grown man cry. My high school boy friend enlisted in the Navy as soon as he graduated that June. He was visiting my family in August that summer, eagerly awaiting the date he was to report to the Great Lakes Naval Training Station. He was slightly deflated when the Japanese surrendered, and even more so when, right after he got to Great Lakes, he broke out with measles and was hospitalized. It just wasn't the heroic military service he had fantasized. Of course, spending weekends gleaning bits of corn (I spent my last year of high school in Urbana, Illinois) left by farm machinery wasn't heroic either, but we were eager to participate in any way we might to support the war effort.

Three years after war's end my husband George and I lived in London, England for nearly two years. The aftermath of the war in Britain was eye-opening to me, more so than to George, who had served in the Pacific during later stages of the war, and following the surrender of Japan, was able to observe the privations experienced by the Japanese. Food in England was still severely rationed, unlike the modest food shortages and rationing Americans had experienced during the war. Whole sections of London had been blitzed to rubble. There was remaining bitterness over how wealthy the American soldiers had seemed. We overheard two women in the bread queue commenting about our flaunting our American wealth because we bought two loaves of bread at once. The house in a working class neighborhood where we rented a room was broken into twice in four months. It seemed clear to me that America had been fortunate in many ways. And seeing the still fresh scars of war-suffering in London enhanced my feelings that there must be better ways to resolve conflicts than inflicting such terrible suffering. I would still like to believe that.

Elizabeth married a college professor, raised a family of five, and at the age of 50 years became a college administrator in Plattsburgh, New York.

A BROTHER MISSING IN ACTION:
A REFLECTION

★

Morris Pike

From left to right, Merton, Milton, and Morris Pike

I WAS ONE OF 60 STUDENTS in our high school during World War II. We kept close watch on the war and found things we could do to support the war effort. Most of us worked outside of school as well as helping staff the airplane watch patrol. We didn't drive, we walked or rode our bikes. I lived on the family farm in Stowe, Vermont and was sure our labors continued to provide needed food for the community. A brother eight years older than I remained at home on the farm, having a draft deferment as an essential worker for the war effort. A brother five years older was drafted after spending two years in college; the war experience with the greatest impact on my life centers around this brother, Milton.

Milton was the "golden boy." While that term was never used, it was obvious he was the pride of our parents, neighbors, community, and the high school from which he had only recently graduated. He had multiple talents, charm, and a way of getting just about anything he wanted. Not only was he a hard worker, he also excelled in skiing, so as a member of the ski team he managed to avoid some of the farm chores. He was the one who had the new bicycle, the summer camp scholarships, and enjoyed opportunities our older brother never had.

After he was drafted, he took basic training and then went on to Officer Candidate School. Just a few weeks before he would have finished officer training, he was abruptly sent to fight as an infantryman in Europe. Early during the Battle of the Bulge he was reported Missing in Action. My parents were people who rarely smiled or expressed emotion, but their faces did grow more subdued, and at work they drove themselves harder than ever. The longer we went without word from him, the darker the prospects became of his still being alive. I mourned in my own way, and fortunately, had a much-loved teacher with whom I could share my thoughts.

As more and more people came to believe my brother was probably dead, I began to hear, "If Milton doesn't make it back, you will have to live his life for him." At first, I couldn't believe what was being said. I heard similar words from an aunt, other relatives, and from teachers, as well as the minister at our church. I felt there was no way I could match his academic or social record. I tried to rid myself of that dark cloud, but it became almost impossible. I lost all interest in the progress of the war and looked into all that would be involved in declaring myself a Conscientious Objector if my number came up, and I prayed desperately for my brother's life.

He had been very active in church-related camping and regional church youth groups. I now felt pushed into these, even though my reason was not so much to get out from under the expectations set for me as it was simply to get away from the gloom at home. In doing this I developed some leadership roles that fit me and satisfied those who wanted me to "fill Milt's shoes," but I continued to feel trapped.

Just a few weeks before V-E Day we received a postcard from Milt saying he was a prisoner of war and "not to worry." I worried anyway. The pall of his death was removed, but new worries about his time in prison camp came to the fore. By mid-June, however, he was back in the States, hospitalized for rehabilitation and was promised a brief furlough. One day in July he phoned that he would arrive on the next train. We could meet him in Waterbury. Mother wore her best dress and hat, and Dad put aside his work clothes and dressed up as well. I was invited to go with them to the train, and I went along happily, feeling my "prison" term was also over.

Just as the train pulled into the station, my mother turned to me in the back seat and said, "Now remember, we don't cry!" Milt stepped off the train, and Mother gave him a peck on the cheek. *No hugs or kisses.* Dad simply shook his hand. Following instructions, I hid all the built-up sadness and relief and refrained from the tears I had stored up. Following my father's lead I shook Milt's hand.

On the nine-mile drive home, Milt sat between our parents in the front seat, while I was alone in the back. I don't remember much about the arrival home except that Molly, the farm dog, very cautious at first, suddenly realized it was Milt. She was the one who cried and cried and cried. She wouldn't leave his sight, yet came to announce to each of us that Milt was home, then cried some more.

Obviously, I did not have to live his life for him. My tears fell after I went to bed, and for several weeks after that I had to sort out my relief. Was it more about his safe return or my release? One thing became very clear, however. Hugs and tears are real, and repressing them was devastating for me.

I have since learned our oldest brother learned the same lesson and passed it on to his children and grandchildren. On any special occasion there are always hugs all around, whether just for greetings or goodbye, or for more serious or joyous reasons. Unfortunately, Milt never seemed to get it. He inherited our parents' stolid stance and outlook on life. He went back to college and graduate school and led an undistinguished career as a college professor. I have lived my own life, and it turned out to be freer, more remarkable, and a far more exciting one than that of my "lost brother" Milt.

Morris grew up on a farm still managed by his family. An ordained United Church of Christ minister, he specialized in education and social service ministries. He has traveled extensively on behalf of the Heifer Project International.

HOME AT LAST

★

Louise Ransom

Louise and Robert Ransom

PEARL HARBOR SHOCKED OUR WORLD my senior year in college. Bob, whom I had been dating for several years, was in his first semester of law school. This event electrified most of the male students in my New England educational bailiwick, and they left their schools in droves to enlist in military service. Fortunately, the registrar at Bob's law school persuaded him to finish the semester so that he could automatically be readmitted when the war was over rather than having to compete for admission with students just coming out of college. Happily, the registrar's advice was sound and after the Japanese surrender, he reentered and graduated in 1948.

Meanwhile he tried to enlist in every branch he could think of, but his eyesight was not 20/20 and he was drafted into the Army and inducted at Camp Stewart, Georgia. There were some funny stories connected with basic training. Notable among them was encountering his father's caddy (yes, golfers used caddies in those days) who loaned his poker winnings to finance Bob's trip home for our engagement. He had already been accepted to Office Candidate School (OCS), and we agreed to be married as soon as he received his commission as a Second Lieutenant.

The Philippine Government in Exile

During the engagement period, I graduated from college and went to work for the Philippine Government in Exile in Washington, D.C. President Manuel Quezon and his family, Vice President Sergio Osmena, and the chief officers in their government had to flee the Philippines in the face of capture by the Japanese, and all were in Washington. General Douglas MacArthur had been ordered to leave the Philippines and spoke those three famous words as he left, "I shall return."

I was in the Information Office and had to respond to questions from high school students like, "How is hemp grown in the Philippines?" The poet laureate of the Philippines, Jose Garcia Villa, also in exile, was my comrade in arms, who had to provide answers to similar questions that somehow seemed irrelevant to the Bataan Death March, and the Occupation by Japan. However, it was most interesting to become acquainted with these officials who were very welcoming and cordial to the two Americans working for them — my boss and me. One notable dignitary, Carlos Romulo, later became Secretary General of the United Nations.

Bob graduated from OCS September 1942 and was assigned to be an Anti-Aircraft Instructor in the OCS at Camp Davis in Wilmington, North Carolina. We were married, I, 20, and he, 22, and repaired immediately to Wrightsville Beach just outside of Wilmington. The only housing available was beach houses empty for the winter season. We rented the second floor of a house with an unreliable heater, built on stilts at water's edge. The proximity of the Atlantic Ocean and a wide sandy beach were more than compensatory. A nice summer resort had become a community of Army wives, since the men only came home from the post Wednesdays and weekends. Incidentally, there had been several enemy submarine scares just off that very beach.

We spent a year at Camp Davis, until Bob was transferred to Fort Bliss in El Paso, Texas. It was a long drive in our $150 used Renault, and we chose a route close to the railroad lines just in case it didn't make it. A bonus was a three-day stopover in New Orleans where the dining, drinking, and Dixieland music were so inviting that we slept all day in our hotel room, emerging in the late afternoon to spend all night in the French Quarter.

Fort Bliss, Texas

The great attraction for Fort Bliss in West Texas was the presence of Ciudad Juarez just across the Mexican border. Again, the wining and dining with Juarez nearby were fabulous. We feasted on wild duck with the birdshot still in the meat, and superb steaks probably from bulls slain in the bull ring. The soldiers from Fort Bliss used to go to the bull fights to cheer for the bulls.

I had to confess that up to this point our war had been a ball. I was a Nurse's Aide in the Maternity Section of the Hotel Dieu Hospital and sold gloves at the Popular Dry Goods Company to make a little change. We lived near the post in a West Texas bungalow complete with giant cockroaches. However, as the year was drawing to a close, the U.S. had gained air superiority in Europe, so teaching anti-aircraft tactics to future officers became superfluous, and Bob thought irrelevant to the war effort. By then, he was a First Lieutenant. When the recruiter arrived seeking officers who spoke French, Bob, who was fluent in French, jumped at the opportunity to go overseas. When he came home that night, he climbed into a cold water bathtub (the only way to keep cool in the stifling Texas heat) and contemplated what he had just done. "I have volunteered and been accepted," he told me, "to parachute behind enemy lines and do Intelligence work! We have to leave for Washington right away." Filled with trepidation, we abandoned the old Renault and bought a shiny new Chevrolet for the trip back east. I was in the earliest stages of pregnancy. While on the trip, the big excitement was that D-Day took place.

Office of Strategic Services

I went to my parent's home in Pelham, New York, while Bob reported for training in Washington. The army agency was the Office of Strategic Services (OSS). The OSS, which later became the CIA, was a derring-do intelligence operation under the leadership of General "Wild Bill" Donovan. The training was "Oh So Secret" with all the trainees using code names and never revealing their true identities. When parachute jumping practice was offered, Bob refused it. "I will jump into France when I have to, but I don't feel drawn to practicing it."

In August 1944 he was scheduled to leave for England, so I journeyed to Washington to see him off. He left from our hotel room, and he was a sorry sight. He had to carry all his gear with him for an unknown period of time so he was dressed in a woolen uniform under a full length army overcoat and carrying a heavy duffle bag, and this in Washington's cruelly hot midsummer without air conditioning.

Bob underwent further training in England, followed by landing on Utah Beach in Normandy. He and a colleague drove north through France to their final destination in Maastricht, Holland. En route they happened to be the first Americans into a small French town just liberated from the Germans. The celebrations with the "brave Americans" went on and on, defying description. Bob was assigned to G-2 (Intelligence) of the Ninth Army under Gen. Omar Bradley. His job was to recruit members of the Resistance, mostly prostitutes, and ferry them across the Rhine to mingle with the people there and report on the positions of the German Army units. The code name for that operation was "Mattress." He was not supposed to talk about what he was actually doing, and I prayed that he was safe.

He served in Europe for 13 months. One morning in December 1944, he was the Officer on Duty for the Ninth Army and had the shocking experience of being the first person in the Ninth Army to receive news of the German's last ditch offensive when it made a breakthrough of the American lines near Bastogne, the beginning of the Battle of the Bulge, very costly to both sides. Fortunately, he never had to parachute jump.

Volunteering for the Pacific Campaign

Bob learned that if he would volunteer to go the Pacific Theater, he would get a month at home. Since he had an eight-month old son whom he had never seen, he was quick to volunteer. Consequently, he showed up, completely unexpected, at six AM in my bedroom, having climbed through an open kitchen window. My father put bourbon in the breakfast orange juice to celebrate. For part of that precious month, we went with our baby son to my family's unheated summer home on Long Island. It was a cold damp May 1945, and I took to my bed with flu. Bob spent a great deal of time washing diapers and trying to dry them in the oven. The big news was that we learned of V-E Day (Victory in Europe) that week while on Long Island.

When he left with orders to finally show up in Burma, leaving me, as the saying goes "barefoot and pregnant," he took a circuitous route by hopping various army planes going in the general direction. He took several days off in Cairo to visit the sphinx. As an example of the adventurous nature of OSS operations, one of his close friends was assigned to Ceylon, and rode his horse up the steps and into the main government building there.

In Burma, Bob was assigned to an Army Veterinary Unit in charge of a herd of donkeys. This was one of the more cockamamie projects of the OSS. The donkeys were supposed to be dropped by parachute over the hump of the Himalayas into China. Chinese peasants were to be recruited to ride the donkeys and search out and report on where the Japanese soldiers were located. While awaiting this rather unusual assignment, members of the Veterinary unit became adept at slaughtering the occasional wandering sacred cow (probably someone's grandmother), carving off the edible portions and burying the remainder all within five minutes — a happy change from army rations. Fortunately — I guess — the assignment never took place. During the long boring waiting period for Bob in Burma, the U.S. dropped the two atomic bombs on Hiroshima and Nagasaki, and the war in the Pacific was over. At the time, I rejoiced at the dropping of the bombs for the saving of hundreds, perhaps thousands of American lives, but there were many of us who thought that the dropping of the second bomb on Nagasaki was superfluous and should never have been done. Now, in retrospect, I am sad to realize that we are the only country in the world ever to have employed such a horrendous weapon. I have been to Hiroshima and witnessed its dreadful aftermath.

Home at Last

Bob sailed from Karachi on the army troopship *Tasker H. Bliss*, bound for New York. I received word that on a certain day and time it would arrive at Pier 56 or 57 on the Hudson River. Of course, I was there, jumping up and down with excitement. As the *Tasker H. Bliss* pulled into sight, the men on board were all equally excited, lining the railings and waving their caps wildly. The odd thing — their faces appeared to be yellow, almost matching the color of their khaki uniforms. They had been taking Atabrine, which turns the skin yellow, to prevent malaria.

The troopship arrived accompanied by a loud cacophony of boat horns, whistles, bands playing, people shouting. What a welcome, we on the pier thought, for our guys coming home. It turned out that the battleship, *USS Missouri* on which the Japanese surrender was signed, was arriving up the river just behind the *Tasker H. Bliss*. Of course, the welcome was in recognition of the battleship, but that was all right. The welcome for all of us on the pier and on board the ship was the best thing that ever happened, and I will never forget it.

Louise and her husband Bob were founding members of the Wake Robin community. Upon their move to Vermont from the New York City area, she worked for the Department of Corrections in Waterbury, was co-owner and editor of the Williston Whistle newspaper, and President of the Mount Independence Coalition, a "Friends" support group. Bob was corporate counsel for IBM.

BAD MOMENT FOR A FIGHTER PILOT'S WIFE

★

Janet Rood

Janet and Gilman Rood

WHEN MY HUSBAND WAS STATIONED at the air base near Del Mar, California, I answered his urgent call, left college in my senior year, and went to be with him at the Hotel del Mar, where the Turf meets the Surf. It was not easy to do, as he was at the base three nights out of four.

My Worst Nightmare

One late afternoon while I awaited his arrival on the usual fourth night — his night off and our night together — there was a rapid knock on the door of our room. Cute, I thought, he's knocking. So I opened the door with a grand gesture, bowing low, and there stood a Marine in dress greens. But not my Marine; he was a Major and visibly very nervous. He was accompanied by an enlisted man, also in formal dress.

"Mrs. Rudd?" the Major asked.

"Mrs. Rood," I said.

"Mrs. Rude?"

"Yes, Mrs. Rood."

"I am very sorry to be the bearer of this news, but there has been an accident at the base. I am afraid that I must tell you that your husband has been killed." My heart!

"No, no, not Gil Rood!"

"Are you not Mrs. Searle Rudd?"

"My husband's name is Gilman Rood."

"Oh, now I *am* sorry. I am so sorry. I have the wrong room. I am looking for Mrs. Searle Rudd. Please sit down, my dear woman. May I help you?"

"Thank you, no. I don't need help. But you go along now. Mrs. Searle Rudd will need all the help you can give her."

Life after My Husband Ships Out for the Pacific

When my Marine fighter pilot husband shipped out from San Diego on January 7, 1943, I boarded a train for my home in the East, with one stop to visit my Uncle Fuller in Texas. After he told me to come again and bring the baby, I understood that my misery was not due just to my husband's shipping out but also to my never suspected condition. I headed on to my mother's home in Connecticut, and began to adjust to my situation while waiting for my first mail from the South Pacific.

In late February, a cable arrived from the Mississippi wife of one of the pilots of the VMF-124 squadron, saying: "Major Gise killed in action on first mission. Hal Stewart and my husband lost. Hope Gilman is all right." Since I had heard nothing from the War Department, I had to hope so too.

In May, after a lengthy stop to visit my college sorority sisters at UVM, I headed for the sanctuary of those who brought me up — my grandparents, at their summer camp in West Swanton. It was there that I received the first word from my husband in the form of 76 letters over a period of a week. At the time of his writing, he had received no word from me, although I had mailed something to him of our expected papoose almost every day. When we were finally on the same page, the naming of this expected one started.

My letters went west with lists of names for boys and girls, his came east (or did they go around the world in the opposite direction?) with the entire squadron's vote of "no" to all of my suggestions, but no suggestions coming my way. This went on until September 13, 1943 when I named my daughter after my grandfather, Sherrill Martin Rood. I don't know just how the War Department handled the news of such things, but she received a cable addressed to "Dear Bo Peep." I also received a phone call from a young Marine who had come home to New Hampshire, telling me that my husband would be coming home after his next mission. When Sherrill was five weeks old, he came home, and we all hit the front page with a picture entitled, "So Nice to Come Home To." Only then, did I learn that VMF-124 had been the first warplanes to land on Guadalcanal, and that the next mission was to be Munda in the Solomon Islands.

Heading Back West

Three weeks later with our babe in a basket on the back seat of our new used car, we departed for the west coast, Laguna Beach for our home, and Miramar his airbase. In March 1944 we headed east once again: Morehead City, North Carolina, to be our next home and Cherry Point, his base. Two months later, we were in Columbia, South Carolina, where his new squadron, VMF-133 was forming, and where we made lifelong friends. But, on Sherrill's first birthday as we put a candle in a cup cake in a diner, I started my tradition of singing "Happy Birthday" to my progeny, and we started for the west coast again, this time with a stop at my Uncle Fuller's in Texas. Bedded down finally in a La Jolla motel, my husband went on to the base only to learn that he would be gone in three days! On the third day, the departure of the gathered troops at North Island was a real story. The great bay was so solid with ships that one could barely catch a glimpse of the water. All family members were crowded into a giant Quonset hut for several hours with their departing ones. Then, the signal came for a last goodbye, and all of us were ushered out.

Heading Back East Once Again

Where to now? Back to the east coast again, of course this time my babe and I in my car, along with my new friend Pat in her racy pale blue convertible — going tandem as far as her home in Detroit. Then that last leg for me when I arrived at my mother's in Stamford once again, at two AM, unexpected of course, but this time it was with my babe, now 14 months, and just 20 cents to my name. After Thanksgiving, we headed north, Sherrill and I, to an apartment in Burlington, Vermont. In June, up to West Swanton, for where better to spend a little time before taking my third and last apartment on Pearl Street in Burlington to await my husband's expected homecoming?

In August — what was that date? Bells ringing and sirens blaring, a cacophony while all church bells clamored just past my two year old's bedtime. There was a loud knocking on my door and shouts of, "THE WAR IS OVER! THE WAR IS OVER! COME HAVE A DRINK," but I thanked him and said no. I would stay with my babe. Then I went to her room where she stood in her crib, wondering at the clamor everywhere. I knelt down to tell her the war was over, tears streaming down my face, and that it meant that her daddy would be coming home to us. As if she knew what it was all about!

Several days passed before any word came, and then there was a call. It was from San Francisco! Then, he came and we greeted him in our matching blue dresses that I had made for the occasion. It would be a very long time before I would learn he had been in San Francisco for five days before his call. He had been battling with himself over the fact that he did not want to come.

Born in Wakefield, Massachusetts and raised in Vermont, Janet left UVM during her senior year to join her husband, a Marine fighter pilot. After the war, she and her husband founded G.B. Rood Office Equipment Co. in Burlington. The mother of five children, she is the recipient of the Vermont Arts Council Award of Merit for her distinguished service to the arts in Vermont. She married Fred Herbolzheimer, Jr. in August, 2000.

Draft Exempt

★

Paul Rosenthal

M Y EMPLOYER FROM 1937 TO 1946, Central Scientific Co., had
been a major producer of equipment for science laboratories in
schools. Typical products were vacuum pumps made in small quan-
tities by highly skilled mechanics. Following Pearl Harbor, unskilled
workers began turning these pumps out by the hundreds. My task was
to develop and supervise an in-process quality control and inspection
department for these pumps.

I also became responsible for the production of a fuse, essentially
a precision clock that could actuate an electrical circuit at a set time. I
knew then that the fuse was for the "Manhattan Project," secret code
for the atomic bomb project. In keeping with the secrecy of that project, I did not possess any information about its goal, nor the function
of the fuse within the project.

This wallet card was issued to me towards the end of World War II,
at a time when the appearance of a healthy young civilian who was not
in uniform was apt to raise eyebrows.

Essential Manpower Card

Born in Germany, Paul moved to Chicago, Illinois in 1937 as a skilled instrument maker. Following graduation as a mechanical engineer, he moved to Buffalo in 1948 where he worked in the optical industry and a research laboratory.

Travails of an Air Force Dependent

★

Lillian Sheldon

Lillian and Don Sheldon

World War II changed the lives of everyone in the United States. My husband and I were college sweethearts for two years, due to graduate from the University of Vermont in the Class of 1942. Graduation was moved up to May that year to allow the men to enter military service early. Since UVM is a land grant college, all male students were required to take Basic Reserve Officers Training (ROTC) during their first two years. They had the option of continuing on to Advanced ROTC their final two years, leading to an Army commission on graduation.

Civilian Pilot Training

In his senior year Don took Civilian Pilot Training at Fort Ethan Allen, earning his pilot's license. Proudly, he took me up for a bird's eye view of Burlington and Lake Champlain. Little did we imagine that 56 years later I'd be living in the very area over which we flew

336 ★ OUR GREAT WAR

that day. The shortage of male graduates caused many large companies to recruit women on college campuses for their work force. I signed up with General Electric in Schenectady, New York to work in the payroll department, as math had always been a favorite subject. Later, they notified me of a pay increase before I even started work — a nice surprise.

In the midst of final exams, Don presented me with an engagement ring, and we made plans to marry "after the war." At graduation, Don received his diploma in Mechanical Engineering in one hand, his Commission in the Army Air Force in the other, and orders to report in 10 days to San Francisco, the takeoff point for the Pacific Theater. Because of his civilian license, he hoped to become an Air Force pilot. However, tests revealed a slight dental malocclusion defect that made this impossible. On the train heading west he received new orders to report to the Materiel Command in Detroit, near the huge Willow Run facility.

Detroit was bursting at the seams with defense workers and servicemen, and there was a huge housing shortage. Don found a room in a private home and took meals at a nearby crowded boarding house. He was very lonesome. I was very busy at GE, working long hours and even some evenings. Rules limited us to 50 hours a week. One time I reached that total on a Wednesday of the workweek and decided to visit Don in Detroit. I stayed with an aunt and uncle living there at the time. Don persuaded me that we should get married so I could join him. I phoned my folks in Vermont that we wanted to get married the following month and to please make all the arrangements.

A Hasty Wedding

Don and I arrived in Vermont the evening before the wedding. All I did was buy a long white dress and a going away suit. My folks did a superb job with the planning, even managing to get invitations printed and sent out in time. Mom provided a fine meal for family and close friends, and a neighbor took wedding pictures. Everything went well despite the hasty planning, and Don and I enjoyed a very happy 51-

year marriage. Don died in 1994. How different life has been for our children and grandchildren, who could plan their weddings months or years ahead.

I found a job as secretary to the Superintendent of the big General Motors building in downtown Detroit and joined Don in his rented room. We "ate out" and had our main meal at the boarding house. I was the only gal there. Before long, a UVM classmate arrived at the same Air Force facility. His wife became a plane spotter for the Civilian Air Raid Warning program. She met another spotter who was the manager of an apartment building, and she arranged for apartments for us two UVM couples and two other air force couples.

The apartment was a third-floor walk-up, flat roof building — no elevator, no air-conditioning, in downtown Detroit. I walked six blocks to my job at GM. Don rode the cross town trolley to and from the Air Force facility located in a former auto plant. We had only one room, a tiny bathroom with shower and a very narrow kitchen with a little door opening into the corridor where you could smell what was cooking in other apartments. The Murphy bed folded up into the one closet, which also held the single bureau and hangers for clothes. In hot weather we often had to leave the bed down until late afternoon to let the sheets dry out. The back alley was a favorite spot for howling and prowling cats, something I'd only read about before; a horrible sound.

Married Life in Detroit

Rationing was a real challenge for a new cook. Meat and canned fruit took a big bite out of the food ration coupons. It was hard to make those coupons last out the full month. Air Force pay also came monthly, so sometimes the last week was pretty slim pickings. We four Air Force couples became like family. There was a great shortage of many ordinary needs during the war. Kleenex was one of them. If a truck was spied delivering some goods in short supply, people lined up for a block or more, hoping to get some before the supply was gone. We had one wonderful experience. At that time many large movie theaters often presented a stage show along with the movie. Once we lucked out and saw "This is the Army" with Irving Berlin in person, singing the title song. That was a big thrill.

When our first baby was due, I had my checkups at the large Henry Ford Hospital across town, taking the trolley there and back. I did so the day before our daughter was born — thank goodness I didn't start labor that day. For the last couple of months, I had gone down three flights of stairs only if I knew Don would be home to give me a boost to climb back up. Our helpful apartment manager offered Don her car so he could take me to the hospital.

Daughter Nancy was born a few hours later. My hospital roommate, Schmedlin, had a boy that day. When the nurses brought the babies to us at feeding time, they would mutter, "Schmedlin, Sheldon, Schmedlin, Sheldon," so I always did a double check to be sure I had the right baby.

At the apartment we had to put the crib at one end of the little kitchen; the length of the crib matched the width of the kitchen. One Sunday afternoon, Don's superior officer called to invite us to the airfield where he and Don might have a chance to go up in a large glider being tested there. Because of cold and high wind, the flight was cancelled. The following day that glider crashed, killing all on board; the bad weather may have saved Don's life.

Several times Don was sent to Wright Field in Ohio on business. He would take the night boat to get there for a morning meeting. One time while he was there, a race riot erupted in Detroit, and several servicemen were killed. When Don returned, he hopped a bus for home. Seeing trucks filled with soldiers with guns drawn, he asked the driver if there was a parade nearby. Answer: "Where have you been, soldier? There's a race riot and soldiers have been killed. You'd better hurry home, and be very careful." It was a relief when he walked safely in the door.

In May, 1945 we finally found a two-bedroom apartment in a private home in a pleasant neighborhood. Wouldn't you know — a month later Don received orders to Wright Field in Ohio. Having a two-year-old and expecting a new baby in a few months, we decided it would be nice for me to spend my confinement with my folks back in Vermont.

Don went to Ohio. A month before my due date, everything went wrong. I underwent an emergency Caesarian and delivered a stillborn baby with complications that kept me in the hospital for five weeks. Thank goodness I wasn't alone in a new city. Don did get a short emergency leave.

The war was winding down and Don was scheduled to leave for the Pacific during the end stages of the War with Japan. He completed the many required immunizations and other preparations and came to Vermont for a final short leave. Surprise! The war suddenly ended, and his orders to proceed to the Pacific Theater were cancelled. Seven months later, he was discharged and we resumed a normal existence, settling in his home town of West Springfield, Massachusetts, where we raised our three children.

Lil Sheldon was born in Vermont, graduated from the University of Vermont, and returned to the Green Mountain State to live in Wake Robin after 50 years in Massachusetts as a homemaker, mother, and long time volunteer in community service.

Three Long Years

★

Gwen Steele

Gwen and John Steele

WE WERE FORTUNATE THAT FOR THE MOST PART my husband's service in World War II did not put him in many life-threatening situations. Difficult as it seemed at the time, I know now that my ordeal was as nothing compared with what many others endured. What the war's onset did do was, quite suddenly and unexpectedly, leave me alone for three long years, with all the frustrations of raising our two-and-a-half-year old Mary and seven-month old Jack. When orders did come for John to report to Camp Edwards on Cape Cod, we were not too upset. Usually, officers from ROTC programs called to active duty could expect to be at a training post somewhere in the United States for several months, with their families accompanying them. There was always hope that the war would end before the men went overseas. Camp Edwards! Why not spend the summer of '42 basking on the beaches of Cape Cod?

Commissioned as an infantry lieutenant, John was surprised to find himself assigned to be the personnel officer for the First Amphibian Brigade. He may have hoped to be more in the thick of activity but I, at least, was happy that he would have a desk job in the headquarters group and would not be in the line of fire. My optimism was short-lived. Before I could visit him at Camp Edwards and hunt for a place to stay for the summer, he learned the brigade would not train there, but would ship out within two weeks to an undisclosed location overseas.

The ensuing months were anxious ones. Military operations, of course, had to be held in strictest confidence, so the men were not allowed to tell families where they were going. Often, they didn't know. Typically, they were transported on overcrowded troopships that were slow and often had to take circuitous routes to avoid German submarines. Newspapers hinted that the allied invasion of North Africa was imminent. Then we learned that the Amphibian Brigade had been training in north Ireland and would be in the forefront of the invasion.

Anxiety rose a few more notches. But after his unit got to Africa, this feeling was replaced by envy, as he was transferred out of the amphibian brigade to the newly-organized North African Economic Board headed by Col. Theodore Roosevelt, Jr. Having majored in Economics in college, he proved to be a likely candidate for this spot, where the staff included dignitaries from France, Britain, and the U.S. He wrote of being entertained by a French Count and having dinner with a Caliph — a sumptuous affair at a palace where the grand staircase was lighted by torches held aloft by richly-dressed, 11-year-old boys who stood at rigid attention throughout the whole long evening.

Life on the home front had all the glamour that goes with stoking a coal-burning furnace (I burned coke because it was lighter to shovel); lining up to get bananas and other items in short supply; cajoling the ration board to give me a little extra gasoline so I could take the children to visit my parents at Christmas; taking produce from the "Victory Garden" to the canning center where it was processed for later use in the wintertime; squeezing open those little packets of yellow artificial coloring in order to make the repulsive white margarine look a little more palatable and pretend it is butter; and playing endless bridge games with all the other war widows as we awaited news.

All the time there were poignant reminders of John's absence. Hearing his twin brother's voice so much like my husband's coming from another room could upset me, as did the time when Mary ran eagerly toward her uncle, and then stopping abruptly when she realized that wasn't really her daddy. Jack couldn't remember his dad, but Mary worried about him. Too young to understand metaphors, she was concerned when she heard someone say he was "tied up in red tape."

After a year with the Economic Board, John, now with the rank of Major, joined the staff of the Disciplinary Training Center, the military prison in Algiers where American soldiers whose crimes included everything from murder and rape to desertion to being AWOL were incarcerated. The prison was a tent city of 6,000 inmates, and its program was designed to rehabilitate the prisoners and get the men back to combat. When the commanding officer was rotated back to the states, John became the CO. He was in charge when the whole operation was moved to Pisa, Italy in the fall of 1944. In spring 1945, when his father was dying, he was granted leave to come home.

When he was due to go back, the war in Europe ended, and we hoped he would remain home, but the Army had other plans. They pressured him to return to the DTC in Algiers. After another tearful goodbye, off he went. In his absence a new prisoner, Ezra Pound, had been incarcerated in the detainment center, where he remained until he could be sent to the U.S. and charged with treason. The DTC had to take care of this very unconventional prisoner who could not in any way conform to the prison routine set up for the youthful offenders. Japan surrendered in August 1945 while John was in Algiers. By Thanksgiving, John was back at home in the real world, where, after issuing orders to others, he was taken aback when such duties as hauling out the trash fell to him; or when he told the children to do something, and they looked at me to see whether they really had to. All told, though, he adjusted well and we had many happy years together. We were indeed fortunate.

Gwen grew up in Upton, Massachusetts, graduated from Boston University, and became an English teacher. Her husband served as an officer in World War II and the Korean War. Gwen raised the family largely by herself, while contending with the hardships of the home front. After the war, John had a career in educational administration and the family resided nine years in Germany where he was Director of U.S. Army Dependent Schools.

The Birthday Cake

★

Ann Weathers

Ann and Eliot (Bay) Weathers

PEARL HARBOR! WE WERE ATTACKED ON OUR OWN SOIL. All older Americans remember where they were on that "Day of Infamy." I was a college student, at the time enjoying a house party in a friend's home. To us all, it seemed inconceivable. Slowly, our huge ship of state began its turnaround from isolationism towards a full wartime mobilization: the United States had formally declared war against both Germany and Japan.

Every citizen became involved in one way or another. Men, and later women, signed up or were drafted into military service. "Rosie the Riveter" started to work in factories, filling jobs vacated by men who left for the military; others manned the home front in their own different ways. Shortages of needed materials developed, and this led to rationing for which we were allotted coupons needed for scarce items, such as gas, rubber, silk, shoes, meat, butter, and — sadly for me — sugar.

The following summer, some members of my family gathered for a vacation in the log cabin our parents had built from the spruce trees on our property in Underhill, Vermont on the hillside of Mt. Mansfield. The time span happened to cover my birthday, and my sister-in-law Ruth was determined to celebrate the occasion with a birthday cake. So we all pooled our coupons to buy the sugar to put into the cake batter, which was duly prepared by Ruth and put into the oven. Without our knowledge, the power went out while the cake was supposed to be baking. The cake of course failed to rise. Nevertheless, Ruth carried on in the kitchen and soon emerged in triumph with what appeared to be a frosted pancake covered with birthday candles. When she sliced it, we were astonished to discover this was a two-layer pancake! Mindful of coupons and sugar, we ate it all anyway.

Farmers lost their workers to the war effort, so we students would be trucked out to pull weeds in the onion fields, pick apples in the orchards, or help with whatever other needs might arise. We thought it was great fun. Soon so-called "Victory Gardens" sprang up all over the country, a patriotic effort to increase food supplies. On campus, we had a large vegetable garden right behind the library.

One of the more ridiculous memories I have of those college days was of doing guard duty on the bridge leading over to Amherst, Massachusetts, where I stood with a friend, notebooks in hand, to compare the silhouettes on the pages with any planes flying overhead. We were prepared to call headquarters if something alarming were to show up, but as it happened, much to our disappointment, no enemy planes ever appeared. Many colleges offered an accelerated curriculum for students who wished to speed up their studies in order to finish college sooner and get to work for the war effort. Choosing to stay in college one summer, I found the small student body and fewer class participants a welcome change. We were even allowed to smoke in class! After completing a secretarial course, I went to work as a "gal Friday" for the organization War Prisoners Aid.

Several months later, my fiancé and I were able to make plans for our wedding to take place when he received a leave of absence from the Naval Air Corps. Eliot B. Weathers, known to all by his nick-name

"Bay," had trained as a cadet first in Williamstown, Massachusetts, then in Chapel Hill, North Carolina, and later in Florida at the Pensacola Air Base. For six frustrating months we were forced to cancel wedding plans each month, until finally Bay was able to graduate from cadet to ensign, obtain a leave of absence, and return for our wedding on February 11, 1945.

After a brief honeymoon skiing in Canada, we set off in a used Ford from my home in New York City to Melbourne, Florida, the next training station. During my turn driving we found ourselves cruising along at wartime speed of 35 mph when suddenly the car started to shake and bump violently as it pulled over to the side of the road. It was a blowout. This could have been a serious situation, considering the difficulty of finding tires in a period of war-time rubber shortages. We changed to our spare and proceeded carefully through Georgia to Jacksonville, Florida, to stay overnight with Bay's Uncle Ben. Ben Weathers was a genial banker renowned around the State of Florida. "You need a spare tire?" he asked. "Well, let's go up to the attic to see what we can find." In a large space crammed with a multitude of relics, including a silver saddle presented to him by the local Rotary, he magically managed to dig out a tire of the right size and send us on our way.

After some four months at the Cape Canaveral Naval Air Station, we drove to our next base in the Chicago area. We stayed with a friend of my mother's while Bay trained on a so-called "airplane carrier" in the Lake Michigan waters. As I remember, this was a converted cruiser. I worried about my new young husband's life in such dangerous business, especially if he was late in returning home. He was unfazed and enjoyed the challenge.

Finally, we landed with a pool of ensigns in Grosse Ile, Michigan and awaited Bay's assignment either to the Pacific or Atlantic theater. It was there, while we were living in our room with kitchen privileges, that we heard other boarders talking about a strange new kind of explosion that had taken place in a city called Hiroshima in Japan. It had been caused by dropping an "atomic bomb." Days later another bomb landed on the city of Nagasaki. Before we knew it, the war was over.

We returned home, and Bay was discharged from the military. We moved to New Haven, Connecticut where he would begin law school at Yale University. During the ensuing housing shortage we were lucky to live in one of the Quonset huts set up in the Yale bowl for married veterans such as ourselves. It was there that we started our family, and baby girl Nancy was born.

Many years later, when Bay and I were celebrating our 50th wedding anniversary at our golf club, we set up a table with our wedding album at the entrance to the reception room. My good friend Pat arrived with her husband, and as they opened to the photos, Pat said, "Turn the page, Myron, I want to see Bay in his Navy uniform." As they viewed the pictures a voice behind them said, "Of course, *I* wore a different uniform." Turning, they saw the smiling face of our good friend Koji "Ed" Hiroshima. Once Ed had told us, "You know, you people saved my life. At the time the war ended, I was destined to become a kamikaze pilot."

After graduating from Smith College, Ann married a Navy pilot. When World War II ended, like most wives of servicemen, she became a "suburban housewife," with all the volunteer good works that title implies.

Post-War
Service

POSTWAR
RECONCILIATION AND REHABILITATION
★
Ruth Barrett

MY COLLEGE YEARS AT BARNARD occurred during World War II.
Just across the street at Columbia University, new recruits were
arriving to enter a three-month Navy midshipman program. We held
many dances where we met a lot of young servicemen, but then had to
bid them farewell. The day of my graduation ceremony, June 6, 1944,
turned out to be a sad and prayerful occasion as news of the Normandy
landings flashed and continued throughout the day. Two of my childhood friends died in that horrendous battle. Other friends of mine
were lost in air strikes over Europe and the Pacific,

When the war finally ended, vast reconstruction efforts were initi-
ated. It was to this maelstrom of enlightened postwar aid and assistance
that I came after graduation, totally unaware of what it was about. The
occupying Allied forces were providing food, clothing, and medical
help to the European populace. The United Nations had been recently
formed, and the dormant elements of the League of Nations came to
life in the long-silent halls behind its Geneva edifice.

350 ★ OUR GREAT WAR

Post War Reconstruction Programs

First and foremost were the United Nations Relief and Rehabilitation Administration, the International Refugee Administration, the World Health Organization, and the International Labour Cooperation.

One of the agencies, the Institute for International Cooperation in Paris, had recently been revived at a London conference as the United Nations Educational, Scientific and Cultural Organization (UNESCO). The American poet laureate and U.S. representative to the conference in London, Archibald MacLeish, declared, "If wars begin in the minds of men, it is in the minds of men that the defenses of peace must be constructed." — which became part of the credo in UNESCO's Constitution.

I had been given a three-month contract to join these efforts. We were located in the venerable but careworn Hotel Majestic in Paris, previously a center of operations for the Nazis and the American Army. The hotel staff worked there throughout all the changes of regimes. Now, educators, scientists, social scientists, and cultural specialists of multinational and multi-linguist origins were working together, crammed into all the nooks and crannies of the building, including the restrooms. The Director-General was the scientist, Julian Huxley, and the establishment was jokingly called "Huxley's Zoo."

I was assigned to work with a Czech statistician to conduct a cost-of-living study of Paris to determine how much our staff should be paid. At UNESCO I made lifelong friends of people coming from all parts of the globe who like me were not cognizant of what to do but just wanted to help. When my contract ended, the budget was strained, so temporary contracts like mine could not be renewed. My helpful colleagues urged me to go to another part of Paris where a recruitment office was hiring for some new activity.

The Marshall Plan

The U.S. Secretary of State, General George Marshall, had delivered a speech at Harvard that electrified the world. Gen. Marshall proposed a sweeping plan for European economic recovery. In London, Ernest Bevin described it as one of the greatest speeches in world history. Between 1947 and 1952, the plan provided $13 billion worth of technical and economic aid. America's best and most capable men administered the program in partnership with European governments, at their invitation.

Once again, I was venturing into unknown territory. The day of my initial interview, I was asked to consider an assignment in Ankara, Turkey. Somewhat stunned, I requested a few days to consider, and spent hours in libraries trying to inform myself and reach a decision. When I returned to accept the offered position, I was told that there was another assignment for me, this time in Rome. This was a closer and more familiar world, so I accepted immediately and was given a railway ticket plus a few Italian lire. Within just a few days, I was in a Rome railway station at midnight, surrounded by porters, not knowing any Italian, trying to communicate in rusty Latin, French, and Spanish. I was finally rescued by the person who had come to meet me but had been delayed by an automobile breakdown.

My new home was once again to be another venerable hotel that had been occupied by the Nazis, followed by the American Army. Instead of UNESCO, I was now placed on the payroll of the U.S. State Department, which meant the "Marshall Plan." My major tasks involved managing the continuous flow of cables between Washington and Rome, and guiding numerous U.S. agricultural specialists who were flocking to Italy to direct a massive revitalization of the battle-worn country. Beginning with studying Italian and exploring Rome, I soon had the opportunity to visit every part of the country and to participate in inspecting and assessing the devastation. My job was to coordinate the diverse contributions of the various deeply-committed agencies (mentioned above). As an adjunct to my position, I had the opportunity to view many of the art treasures that had been in protective hiding during the war. Museums were "ghost towns" then, unlike the days to follow when thousands of tourists would begin flocking to Italy. While England and France received the largest amount of financial aid, it has been estimated that the relative impact of Marshall Plan funds on Italy was probably greater still. From this effort to improve food production evolved the UN Food and Agricultural Organization.

My Career with UNESCO

As the UNESCO organization in Paris was continuing to grow and expand, I was encouraged to reapply to that organization, which led to my rehiring. One of my early assignments there was to prepare a staff manual on protocol that provided a measure of conformity for how to communicate with member states, e.g., to whom to write, and in what language. What started as a bilingual activity involving English and French would eventually grow to a manual that included many more working languages. The program-coordinating activities I had been assigned led to my being given broader responsibilities as UNESCO representative to the United Nations in New York, and later in Paris. Ultimately, relations with 20 inter-government agencies and some 300 non-governmental agencies were part of my responsibilities. I remained with UNESCO for 20 years until my retirement.

Epilogue

It was tremendously invigorating and inspiring to have played a small part in what may have been one of America's finest hours. Reconciliation and reconstruction on a global scale? Yes. The war to end all wars? Alas, it was not to be.

A graduate of Barnard College with advanced degrees from New York University, Ruth was involved after World War II in coordination of programs and activities of several international agencies, including the United Nations, UNESCO, and the Marshall Plan. During her career, she lived in Paris and Rome and gained a working knowledge of French, Spanish, and Russian.

Japanese War Crimes Trials

★

Kenneth Severson
U.S. Army

T HOUGH THE SHOOTING WAR WITH JAPAN ended on August 14, 1945, World War II did not end officially until December 31, 1946. As a young man just graduated from high school, I enlisted in the army. I went to occupied Japan in 1946 as a member of the 43rd Army Engineers who were building the Yokota Air Force Base north of Tokyo so that the giant B-29 U.S. bombers would be able to land there. I remained in Japan until 1948.

Japanese War Crimes Trials

Of my many experiences in Japan, one of the highlights was for one day attending the Japanese War Crimes Trials in Tokyo on August 27, 1947 while the trial was in progress. Hundreds of Japanese had been arrested after the conflict for committing war crimes; trials were being held in several Far East countries. Eleven hundred prisoners accused of war crimes were housed at Sugamo Prison in Tokyo, including the

25 prisoners whose trial I was to witness that day. Depending on the severity of the alleged war crime, Japanese prisoners were classified as Class A, Class B, or Class C prisoners. The Class A prisoner group was accused of the most heinous crimes, e.g., ordering the bombing of Pearl Harbor on December 7, 1941. Let us look at the 25 most important war criminals that I observed on that day, August 27, 1947.

General Douglas MacArthur, the Supreme Commander for the Allied Powers, had the responsibility of forming the International Military Tribunal for the Far East (IMTFE). Eleven judges from 11 different countries presided at the trial. Each country involved also provided a chief prosecutor. Sir William Webb, Chief Justice in Queensland, Australia, was the chief judge, with the other judges coming from Canada, China, France, India, Netherlands, New Zealand, Philippines, Soviet Union, United Kingdom, and the United States.

For admittance to the courtroom building, each person had to show a special pass to a Military Policeman (MP) who then handed to each observer a folded card. The card listed the names of the judges, the countries they represented, the chief prosecutors from those countries, the names of the prisoners and where they would be sitting, the layout of the courtroom, and the eight rules of conduct that would be strictly enforced for all spectators by the MPs. Armed military policemen were everywhere — outside the building, throughout the corridors, and especially in the courtroom. We were verbally admonished to be perfectly quiet. The proceedings in the courtroom were translated into a number of languages. I put on the headphones at my seat and dialed for a translation in English.

The trial was conducted in a hastily constructed 100 foot by 80 foot room; it was built by the occupation forces in the former auditorium of the Japanese War College in the center of Tokyo. The 11 judges sat on an elevated platform at the front of the room and peered down at the 25 prisoners facing them. We spectators sat on the side of the room, a bit higher than the judges so we were able to observe all aspects of the proceedings.

Before the prisoners were brought in, MPs thoroughly searched the seats where each would sit. This trial did not want a repetition of what occurred at the German War Crimes Trial of General Hermann Göring, Adolph Hitler's Air Marshal and chosen successor at the start of the World War II. On October 14, 1946, the evening before his execution, he took his own life with poison smuggled in by a henchman.

Everyone except the judges was to be seated before the prisoners entered the room. As I watched, an MP opened a door and led the prisoners in single file to their seats directly in front of me. In the front row sat Doihara, Hata, Hirota, Minami, the notorious Tojo, Oka, Umezu, Araki, Muto, Hoshino, Kaya, Kido and Kimura. Directly behind them sat Hashimoto, Koiso, Oshima, Matsui, Hiranuma, Togo, Sato, Shigemitsu, Shimada, Shiratori, Suzuki and Itagaki. It was a bit awesome for me, an enlisted man, to be sitting so close to a group of Class A war crimes prisoners composed of 19 generals and admirals and six senior Japanese officials. There sat General Hideki Tojo (1884-1948), who was the Japanese Minister of War and served as Premier of the country during wartime. He was Japan's Head of government, just as were Roosevelt, Churchill, Stalin, and Hitler. It was he who ordered the attack on Pearl Harbor, starting the war that would claim hundreds of thousands of lives. Once the prisoners were seated, the 11 judges were announced and entered in single file, taking seats at the front of the room with Chief Judge Sir William Webb presiding in the center.

Final Sentencing

On the opening day of the War Crimes Trial, all the prisoners pleaded "not guilty." As the trial ended on November 4, 1948, Sir William Webb read the verdict. It took him eight days to read the more than 1200-page verdict to the court. The trial provided a transcript of almost 50,000 pages; 414 witnesses testified during the trial; 779 affidavits and depositions were provided by others; and 4,336 exhibits were put into evidence.

On November 12, 1948 Judge Webb, who up to this point had not sentenced any individual to death, announced the sentences. Seven of the 25 were sentenced to death by hanging in Sugamo Prison. These included Tojo, Itagaki, four ex-generals, and ex-ambassador Koki

Hirota. Togo was sentenced to 20 years, and Shigemitsu to seven years — the lightest of the sentences handed down to a Class A war criminal. The remaining prisoners were sentenced to life imprisonment in Sugamo prison. The executions of the condemned prisoners took place at Sugamo Prison on December 23, 1948. The bodies were cremated, then the ashes taken aboard a plane and scattered over the ocean offshore of Japan.

Many other Japanese war criminals were executed at Sugamo prison following subsequent trials. None of the Class A war criminals sentenced to life served a full life sentence unless the individual died in prison of natural causes. The rest had been paroled or pardoned by 1958. Many other accused prisoners being held at the prison were freed for reason of lack of evidence. Sugamo prison, which had been built in the 1920s, was torn down in 1971.

I am indebted to author John Ginn for his book *Sugamo Prison, Tokyo*[1] for details related to the trial and its outcome. The entire proceedings of this trial extended over a period of two years and 98 days. I can only pass on my own reflections as someone who sat on the sidelines for a day and observed one of the historic events of our lifetime. I still possess my admittance pass to the trial and the card outlining the setup of the courtroom, the names of the judges, prosecutors and defendants, and the rules of conduct for trial spectators — an unforgettable day.

Born in Forest City, Iowa, Ken attended the University of Northern Iowa, and did graduate studies at Columbia University, University of Vermont, Nova Southeastern University, and Harvard University. He was a teacher for 41 years, including stints as principal and superintendent of schools. He has lived in Iowa, Japan, New Hampshire, California, and Vermont.

---

[1] Sugamo Prison, Tokyo. John L. Ginn. Jefferson, North Carolina, McFarland & Company, 1992.

List of Contributors

Winooski Memorial Library
1 Main St Champlain Mill Level 2
Winooski, VT 05404
802-655-6424

DATE DUE

NOV 1 8 2011			
12-8-11			
1/31/12			

Demco